A Respectable
Minority

THE NORTON ESSAYS IN AMERICAN HISTORY

Under the general editorship of

HAROLD M. HYMAN

William P. Hobby Professor of American History
Rice University

A Respectable Minority

The Democratic Party in the Civil War Era, 1860–1868

Joel H. Silbey

W · W · NORTON & COMPANY · INC · New York

First Edition

Library of Congress Cataloging in Publication Data
Silbey, Joel H
   A respectable minority.
   (The Norton essays in American history)
   Bibliography: p.
   Includes index.
   1. Democratic Party–History.   2. United States–Politics and
government–Civil War, 1861–1865.
3. United States–Politics and government–1865–1869.   I. Title.
JK2317 1860.S57 .   1977   329.3′009′034   77–24048
ISBN 0–393–05648–1
ISBN 0–393–09087–6 pbk.

1 2 3 4 5 6 7 8 9 0

Contents

v

To
Allan G. Bogue

To begin with, parties are inevitable
—Lord Bryce

The Democratic party is not a thing of shreds and patches, organized for a transient purpose, and thrown hap-hazard together in undistinguishable mass without form, consistency or proportion, by some sudden and temporary pressure, and passing away with the occasion which gave it being; or catching, for a renewed, but yet more ephemeral existence, at each flitting exigency as it arises . . . molding itself to the form of every popular humor, and seeking to fill its sails with every new wind of doctrine, as it passes . . . over the waves of public caprice—born and dying with the breath that made it. No, sir. The Democratic party is founded on PRINCIPLES which never die: hence it is itself immortal.
—Clement L. Vallandigham, 1855

Preface

THE CIVIL WAR DEMOCRACY had to find a new political role for itself and react to strange conditions in the country at large. It was, after 1860, the opposition party in a situation of national danger, a badly divided minority party trying to regain its place and dominance, the party out of power in the midst of a war in which the government did its best to propagandize Northerners into an inflexible consensus against disunion and the South. All of this was new, strange, and very difficult. Party members, therefore, had to find their way through the complexities of wartime politics and election battles conscious of their own chaotic condition, of their recent rejection by the electorate, and of the fact that the usual stock in trade of an opposition—to challenge government policies and pose alternative courses of action—was a dangerous course to pursue, even in free elections, when the governing party vigorously argued that the opposition was committing treason against the Union.

Party members accommodated themselves to the post-1860 situation by reverting to the traditional role of a political opposition. After a short period of confusion and adjustment, they forcefully challenged the government's policies, particularly the administration's determination to use whatever means necessary to destroy the South and inflict blows against its social system in the name of winning the war. They carped, nagged, and viewed with alarm, all in the most provocative and bitter style. They did not readily acquiesce in or celebrate the government's efforts even to win the war.

For their efforts, they learned quickly that it was not a good time to be a Democrat. They were roundly condemned by their opponents and painted far and wide as members of a party that ''had sunk so low'' in their behavior and opposition ''that it seemed impossible to sink lower.''[1] The Republican charges of disloyalty and Copperheadism rang throughout the rest of the nineteenth century, placing the Democracy perpetually on the defensive as the party of four years and more of treason. Most devastating of all, as the Republicans delighted in pointing out, the voters turned on them. The party emerged from the war, according to Horace Greeley, badly beaten, on the edge of final oblivion, as nothing more significant than ''a myth, a reminiscence, a voice from the tomb, an ancient and fishlike smell.''[2] Even August Belmont, chairman of the Democratic National Committee during the Civil War, was moved to call the 1860s ''the most disastrous epoch in the annals of the . . . party.''[3] Badly divided and scarred as it was, shorn of leadership and unity by the unhappy events of 1860–1861, beset by violent factional disagreements, weak in Congress throughout the war and Reconstruction periods, unable to win the presidency again until 1884, and then only with a minority of the popular vote, the party seemed to reflect for the period as a whole one historian's description of it as ''the reeling Democracy.''[4] Not until 1874 were the Democrats to regain control of Congress, and not until well into the twentieth century were they again to be the majority party in the nation.

On the other hand, despite such apparent political weakness, ineptitude, and infidelity, there are reasons to look closer at the character and quality of the Democratic opposition. An argument can be made that, in contrast to the standard picture of lukewarm patriotism, weakness, chaos, and fragmentation, the Democrats were acceptable enough to enough voters to offer competitive opposition to the dominant Republicans and posed, therefore, significant strategic problems for the majority party. Despite their internal squabblings and their identification with the cause of peace without victory,

1. The comment is attributed to James Russell Lowell by Milton Lomask, *Andrew Johnson: President on Trial* (New York, 1960), p. 186.

2. *New York Tribune,* April 3, 1868.

3. Quoted in Irving Katz, *August Belmont* (New York, 1968), p. 91.

4. Allan G. Bogue, ''Bloc and Party in the United States Senate, 1861–1863,'' *Civil War History* 13 (September 1976): 241. It should be noted that Professor Bogue was referring here to only Democratic patterns in the Thirty-seventh Congress, but the description fits the standard characterization of the party in the whole period.

appeasement of the South, inability to believe in the restoration of the Union, and uncertainty about the chances of Northern victory, the Democrats effectively performed many of the functions of a major, competitive party within a closely divided two-party political culture. Although it lost its popular national majority in the 1850s, the party never surrendered its beliefs or gave up the fight to recapture enough votes from the Republicans to enable it to regain the dominance it had enjoyed in American politics in the period before the realignment of 1854–1860. The Democracy had more electoral success than superficial glances indicate. They party was the heir to a great deal of traditional voting strength in the North which continued to support it throughout the 1860s. Democrats won many elections, threatened effectively in scores more, and worried the Republicans incessantly, despite being marked with the brush of treason by their political enemies. Their efforts, and their success, carried the American political system a long way back toward the fairly evenly balanced two-party system that had dominated American politicis in the antebellum era. They were able during the 1860s to establish the foundations and set loose the forces that were to bring victory in 1874.

But there were clear limits to their achievements. The Democracy survived as a strong, major party during the Civil War years. But the party was unable to restore the natural order of politics: Democratic control of the federal government, so fondly remembered as the hallmark of Jackson's and Polk's America. In short, the Democracy demonstrated its strength in the electoral arena but not enough to control the legislative and executive policies of the nation. Why were these things as they were? Why could the Democracy survive its internal collapse in 1860 and the onslaughts that were subsequently directed against all of them but not overcome electoral deficits and restore itself to command of the political system?

The answers to these questions lie, first, in the internal dynamics of the party: the Democrats' view of their situation and role, and their consequent behavior. Second, the answer rests in the external environment in which they acted: the structure of popular voting behavior, the images they projected to the electorate, and the way the voters perceived and reacted to them. The state of the Civil War Democracy involved, on one level, its voting strength; on another, the plans and actions of the party's leadership. Obviously, however, these elements were closely and directly related because they interacted constantly, and determined each's situation. Over all lay the potent impact of political tradition on Democratic fortunes, the continuing power, even in wartime, of the imperatives of nineteenth-century partisanship.

All of these things did not flow together naturally or easily. Rather, they produced continuing tensions that party leaders had to cope with, not always successfully. Like all parties, the Democratic party was an electoral coalition. Decisions about strategy and tactics, advocacy and behavior, flowed from its puruit of victory at the polls. But the party was more than that as well. As an organization embodying a tradition, representing an ideology, and encompassing an intricate web of relationships among factions and between leaders and led, it did not simply react to external stimuli. The winning ethic was not always the party's only goal. The Democracy's operations were often not rational in terms of specific electoral needs. The party often needed more than victory: it also needed to retain its soul. That dichotomy reflected the influence of forces from the past on its behavior, as well as the complexities posed by internal configurations of power within the party and by specific relationships and assumptions among party members. The Democratic party was an old organization with established traditions and deeply rooted beliefs about proper behavior and argument sometimes at variance with the winning ethic. A tension therefore developed between the desire to win and the internal commitments and partisan imperatives still strong within the organization even after its defeat in 1860. The presence of the forces creating that tension during the war and immediately thereafter explain why the Democrats survived after 1860 and why they did not do better than they did in their bid to regain power.

The Democratic party of the Civil War has not been well served by historical scholarship. To quote David Donald, in research in the politics of the period, the historian has been "a camp follower of the successful army."[5] American historians have agreed, more often than not, with the negative assessments of contemporaries. They have

5. David Donald, "Died of Democracy," in *Why the North Won the Civil War*, ed. David Donald (Baton Rouge, 1960), p. 77. In regard to Civil War historiography,

pictured the party as divided into two main groups, the War Democrats, who basically suspended partisanship, and the peace-at-any-
price men, the Copperheads, who ran the party organization during
the war. The latter group, an irresponsible set of party politicians, did
little but harass the administration, interfere with the war effort, and
make the job of defeating the South much more difficult than it would
otherwise have been. The wartime party was, therefore, an "im-
pediment, not an asset to the nation," held together "by nothing
but hope for office" and unable to perform "even the function of a
responsible opposition party."[6] Although recently modified somewhat by a number of shrewd reassessments, this picture still remains
the major theme of Civil War political studies.[7]

More critically, until very recently, most historians have ignored
the wartime Democracy. We have few studies of party operations in
different localities, party personalities, or party structure and strategy
in this period, especially in contrast with the spate of materials
available about the majority Republicans. There have been a few
first-class books and articles published on various aspects of Democratic politics and performance during crucial situations in the
period.[8] We know something about what kind of people the Demo-

---

the English historian Marcus Cunliffe has written that "the easy appeal of biography
and of military history of a romantic or antiquarian nature has had insidious consequences. More important but less obviously attractive topics have been neglected.
There is for example still no full study of the Northern Democrats. . . ." Marcus
Cunliffe, "Recent Writings on the American Civil War," *History* 50 (February 1965):
32.

6. In order, the quotes are from Allan Nevins, *The War For the Union* (New
York, 1960), 2: 191; Herbert Agar, *The Price of Union* (Boston, 1942), p. 431; Frank
Evans, *Pennsylvania Politics, 1872–1877* (Harrisburg, 1966), p. 18.

7. See Richard O. Curry, "The Union As It Was: A Critique of Recent Interpreta-
tions of the Copperheads," *Civil War History* 13 (March 1967): 25–39; idem, "The
Civil War and Reconstruction, 1861–1877: A Critical Overview of Recent Trends and
Interpretations," *Civil War History* 20 (September 1974): 215–38.

8. David Lindsey, *"Sunset" Cox, Irrepressible Democrat* (Detroit, 1959); Eric
L. McKitrick, *Andrew Johnson and Reconstruction* (Chicago, 1960); Frank L. Kle-
ment, *The Copperheads in the Middle West* (Chicago, 1960); LaWanda Cox and John
H. Cox, *Politics, Principles and Prejudice, 1865–1866* (New York, 1963); Leonard P.
Curry, "Congressional Democrats: 1861–1863; *Civil War History* 12 (September
1966): 213–29; Katz, *Belmont;* Frank L. Klement, *The Limits of Dissent: Clement L.
Vallandigham and the Civil War* (Lexington, Ky., 1970); George McJimsey, *Genteel
Partisan: Manton Marble, 1834–1917* (Ames, Iowa, 1971); Martin Mantell,
Johnson, Grant and the Politics of Reconstruction (New York, 1973).

crats were at the mass level, a little about the behavior of individual leaders, and a certain amount about the political environment in which they lived and worked.

But what knowledge we have remains fragmentary and episodic. Most work focuses primarily on the Reconstruction period, particularly the "critical year" or so from Andrew Johnson's accession to the passage of the Reconstruction acts. Much less has been done on the Civil War years. We have no systematic overview of the party's structure, aura, behavior, and situation comparable, even in a limited way, to Roy Nichols's masterly study of the disintegration of the party's organization and leadership group in the decade before the Civil War.[9] Nor do we have any analysis of the electoral structure within which the party operated comparable to a number of recent studies of voter behavior and mass partisan commitment in the 1850s and 1890s. Finally, much of the interpretation of the Democrats has been affected by perusing them from unfriendly Republican sources, the perspectives of the Johnsonian Unionists, or from only one bloc of the Democrats themselves. In none of these do the Democrats appear quite respectable. From none do we get a picture of the political world as the Democrats themselves saw it.

The picture usually painted is a badly distorted one. Not that there were not "good" Democrats and "bad" Democrats, although those are value judgments, but because it oversimplifies a very complex situation and fails to understand what the Democratic party was all about in this crucial period of its operations. It was not simply a matter of a pro-war versus peace division within the party. It was also a matter that went to the root of how people perceived politics, how they believed their party should act to further its conservative outlook, and how it should endeavor to win elections. Until there is a close examination of the unsuccessful army, a significant gap will remain in our scholarship concerning the American political system in the Civil War era.

In the pages that follow, I hope to illuminate the interplay and nature of these forces as they affected the behavior and fortunes of a

9. Roy F. Nichols, *The Disruption of the American Democracy* (New York, 1947).

major political party caught in civil war, as well as reveal something about how the American political system functioned in the middle of the nineteenth century. This is both an institutional and a behavioral study. The methods employed here combine the quantitative approach to electoral analysis informed by the findings of social scientists about politics, with the more traditional and complementary methods of the historian, that is, burrowing into the manuscripts, newspapers, and other surviving materials from the 1860s. The first provides the necessary structure for understanding the process of politics being examined; the second provides the details and insight into the structured operation. The emphasis is on context, situation, and strategy, not directly on personalities and dramatic events. This is not a detailed study of day-to-day party activities, a focused study of party leaders, a detailed history of the party's organizational network, nor a description of the nature and sources of mass voting behavior. It is, rather, an anatomy of party history, an attempt to provide a framework for understanding by sketching the landscape over which the Democrats had to travel, the nature of the partisan network of leaders and voters, and their perceptions and ideas, and the interaction among them, probing the boundaries and nature of the complex relationships that shaped the actions and determined the route the Democrats followed on the political landscape.

Surveying the wreckage of the party he had so assiduously followed to its disaster in 1860, Roy Nichols wrote that

the Democratic party seemed in desperate straits. The war which it had striven to avoid had apparently destroyed the last shreds of its power as a national party. Driven back to the states, it must begin a long, uphill struggle for survival. In them, however, there was much to work with. While the party controlled but few of the local governments, it had vigorous organizations and effective machines in a number of states, particularly in pivotal areas, and in them there was but slight cessation of activity. Here they were to gain strength in retirement and emerge quickly to take advantage of opportunities soon to come to them. The Democracy was not to remain long in total eclipse.[10]

This is the story of their opportunities and resurgence, as well as their limitations and problems.

10. Ibid., pp. 511–12.

Acknowledgments

MANY FRIENDS, STRANGERS, AND INSTITUTIONS have been most generous with their aid and support while I was working on this book. The Cornell University Library is a magnificent home base for research in American history. Hendrik Edelman, assistant director of the Library for the Development of the Collections; Marie Gast, head of the Maps, Microtexts, and Newspapers Department; and Carolyn Spicer, head of the Reference Department, have been most forthcoming in meeting my needs. Among the many other libraries visited, I am particularly grateful to the staffs of the Library of Congress, the New York Public Library, and the Henry E. Huntington Library and Art Gallery, San Marino, California. The Institute of Historical Research of the University of London provided me with facilities in which to compose the first draft of the manuscript. The Social Science Research Council, the Penrose Fund of the American Philosophical Society, the Humanities Research Fund of Cornell University, and the research fund established by the estate of Colonel Return Jonathan Meigs administered by the History Department at Cornell all supplied necessary financial resources. I thank them all.

Carol Cole, David Hughes, Gerard Bradley, and Tom Disare served as willing and enthusiastic research assistants, as did Marc Kruman who was also a most intelligent counselor as my ideas developed. Madelyn Rhenisch and Connie Ingraham typed various drafts of the manuscript with finesse and good humor. Pat Guilford skillfully typed the final version, and her quick eye saved me from many mistakes. At one time or another, Richard O. Curry, Seymour Drescher, Samuel P. Hays, Michael Holt, Richard L. McCormick, Andrew Milnor, John L. Shover, Irwin Unger, Allen Weinstein, and Frank Young provided me with much encouragement and needed insight. Two generous, patient, and perceptive editors, Harold

Hyman of Rice University and James L. Mairs of W. W. Norton, improved the manuscript markedly by their intelligent critiques. Four good friends must be especially singled out. Richard Polenberg, Walter LaFeber, Phyllis Field, and Lee Benson all read and commented on the completed manuscript and went far beyond the usual calls of duty with their assistance and advice. Samuel McSeveney also read the manuscript in draft form. Besides being perceptive, he was always encouraging and helpful, and in every way proved the quality of his friendship.

Once again, my wife, Rosemary, has cheerfully performed research, editorial, and clerical tasks efficiently. Most of all, she has given the kind of moral encouragement needed to continue with an often intractable project. She knows how much her help has meant to me.

My other great debt is expressed, however inadequately, in the dedication to this book. At the practical level, Allan Bogue read and criticized the manuscript, and genially placed his own knowledge of Civil War politics at my disposal. On a different plane, he has been for twenty years a good friend, a wise counselor, and a magnificent teacher. Whether he likes it or not, this book is as much his as it is mine.

A Respectable
Minority

1

"A Party of Habits, Prejudices and Traditions"

"The election of Mr. Lincoln will be a national calamity," the editor of the Democratic organ, the *Illinois State Register*, lamented on November 7, 1860, the morning after election day, succinctly summing up the arguments of Democrats throughout the country over the preceding months of intense political conflict.[1] When the editor wrote, he did not yet know who had won. By later in the morning, however, it became clear that the Republicans had, despite the vigorous opposition of the other parties and the threats of the Southern secessionists. Within a few days of the election, the Democrats' worst fears were borne out as political leaders in the deep South successfully set in motion the machinery of state secession. Despite the fact that they remained in power for four months after the election, the Democrats were unable to do anything about the disaster that had overtaken the Union. After their recent campaign experience it was not even clear that they could still function effectively as a political party.

Persistent factionalism, a voter revolution, and a catastrophic national split had eroded the party's popular support in the 1850s, especially in the Northern states, compromised its internal integrity, sapped its vigor, and rendered ineffective its stand against the onrushing Republicans. By May 1860, a former Democrat, Senator Preston King of New York, viewing the shambles of the party's national convention at Charleston, could assert that "The power and prestige of the democratic party is broken and gone forever." The confronta-

1. Springfield *Illinois State Register*, November 7, 1860.

tion between the two Democratic candidates that followed in that year, "as hostile against each other as against the common enemy," confirmed King's bleak outlook.[2] The wounds incurred were deep and searing, and the remaining sores continued to fester. Now, the secession of the Southern states, with their desperately needed bastions of Democratic strength, immeasurably intensified the party's crippled state. Nor did the crisis of the Union provide an encouraging climate for a political party trying to work out its own partisan concerns and seeking a means of regaining power.

Many in the party appeared shattered by the outcome. The Democrats had proven to be weak and ineffective at the moment of the nation's greatest danger. They had had neither the will nor the resources to prevent Republican victory. Nothing could have been more condemning of a party organization. "Lincoln and Hamlin, the sectional candidates of the Black Republican party," one editor wrote, "have been elected President and Vice-President of the United States by a decided majority. It is useless to speculate upon the result, but it is . . . humiliating to every conservative and union-loving man in the country."[3]

Nevertheless, even as the results of the election came into Democratic newspaper offices and party headquarters throughout the nation, the mood of party members was not limited to gloom and foreboding. The party would come back and then save the Union. The editor of the Albany (N.Y.) *Atlas and Argus* reassured the party faithful that they need not despair entirely, for "with such a body of indomitable men" as still remained Democrats, "the defeat of today is but the postponement of victory."[4]

There was, in fact, a major ground for optimism. As hopelessly divided as their party was, individual Democratic candidates in the Northern states had made a respectable showing at the polls. They had won but three electoral votes there, but there had been few landslide victories for the Republicans and, in fact, a number of very close races in the critical large states. Despite the tribulations of the Democratic party in the fifties, thousands of voters still remained loyal. Their

2. Preston King to John Bigelow, May 10, 1860, in John Bigelow, *Retrospections of an Active Life* (New York, 1909), 1: 289; *New York Herald,* November 6, 1860 (see also November 20, 1860).

3. *York* (Pa.) *Democratic Press,* November 13, 1860.

4. *Atlas and Argus,* November 7, 1860.

continued support offered hope for the future despite the party's present difficulties.

"The Strongest on Earth"

The widespread popular commitment to the Democracy, with its promise of continued vitality, grew out of a political milieu that has pervaded much of our history. Electoral analysts have been deeply impressed by "the stubborn *historical continuities*" of American voting behavior: the continued relevance of social and political cleavages rooted in the mists of history to the voting habits of affected individuals long after the immediate events associated with the cleavages' formation have disappeared.[5] At the core of the resulting historical inertia of American voting behavior lies the tenacity with which most Americans relied on party identification as the basis of their voting choices. "The sheer descriptive and predictive power of party identification can be scarcely be overstated," a political scientist has remarked. "Knowing that one fact about a group of people tells us more about their political perceptions and political activities than will any other fact about them."[6]

Out of a network of primary-group relationships—family, racial, religious, nationality, class, and residential—individuals develop a set of values, beliefs, and interests that they often seek to advance or protect in the political arena. Individual parties come to be identified as favorable or not to these commitments. They are seen as standing for certain things in the voters' minds, general positions about the nature of the society, its direction, and what government should and should not do. In a political world of great complexity and confusion, parties are the major instruments ordering events and articulating particular individual and group desires. They establish for the average citizen "a point of reference" for political guidance.[7] Parties thus

5. Stein Rokkan, *Citizens, Elections, Parties* (New York, 1970), p. 175. See also Philip Converse, "Change in the American Electorate," in *The Human Meaning of Social Change* ed. Angus Campbell and Philip Converse (New York, 1972), p. 308.
    6. Frank Sorauf, *Party Politics in America* (Boston, 1968), p. 160.
    7. As the foremost modern interpreters of American voting habits have written, "having the party symbol stamped on certain candidates, certain issue positions, certain interpretations of political reality is of great psychological convenience" to the individual voter. Angus Campbell et al., *Elections and the Political Order* (New York, 1966), pp. 248–49.

become aggregations of persons sharing certain attitudes, assumptions, and commitments, evoked by the party label and to which they continually react.

This is not a static condition. The deeply rooted and persistently reinforced phenomenon of party loyalty develops into something else. Over time, parties acquire a status in the mind of individuals which transcends considerations of utility and survives pressures to change. They become social-psychological institutions that have meaning and command loyalty regardless of issues and changes in the political milieu. This status deepens and intensifies throughout the life of most Americans. The activities and excitement associated with the frequent election campaigns, as well as the exhortive activities of the party organizations between elections, reawaken and reinforce these commitments. Occasionally, such loyalties may slacken somewhat, but throughout our history usually they have been passed on within comunities, in all of their intensity, to succeeding generations. Donald Stokes has suggested that these kinds of strong party attachments "may simply pass into the content of a given subculture and be maintained in much the same way as differences of dress, speech or childrearing are maintained between classes, regions and social groups."[8]

The individual enters the electorate, therefore, as a "biased coin," preconditioned to favor particular positions and candidates. Party membership and loyalties also shape the way people view each new situation that comes up in a political campaign or during the political process.[9] Before a candidate is nominated, an issue developed, a campaign speech made in any given election, each party can count on an enormous residue of strong support that will always be there regardless of the vagaries of the political climate. Such a situation means that no party, no matter how much in disarray, internally

8. Donald Stokes, "Voting," in *International Encyclopedia of the Social Sciences* (New York, 1968), 16: 392.

9. This "capacity of party identification to color perceptions holds the key," Stokes has summed up, "to understanding why the unfolding of new events, the emergence of new issues, the appearance of new political figures fails to produce wider swings of party fortune. To a remarkable extent these swings are damped by processes of selective perception." Donald Stokes, "Party Loyalty and the Likelihood of Deviating Elections," *Journal of Politics* 24 (November 1962); 691.

divided, and fumbling it seems to be, would be without a certain and quite often significant portion of the popular vote.[10]

All of this provides strong clues to understanding the American electorate and the Democratic party in the Civil War era. If anything, political parties played a much more dominant role then than they do now.[11] Potent antiparty strains existed in the thinking of reformers, intellectuals, and some social groups, but such sentiments were foreign to most Americans. The American political culture in the pre–Civil War years was dominated by a strong national-party system, clung to tenaciously and with an intense loyalty for ideological, social, and symbolic reasons, with a vigor and devotion revealed on every election day.

Political parties, Representative Howell Cobb of Georgia noted in 1848, are associations of men "acting in concert with each other, to carry out great fundamental principles in the administration of government. . . . [A party] carries the beautiful theory of our system into practical operation." Or, as another observer wrote in 1852, "what thinking and acting are to the individual, party is to society. Party is the great engine of human progress. It is a combination of men of similar views, and kindred sympathies, for moral or political supremacy. It leads to the war of knowledge upon ignorance, the conflict of holiness against sin, the struggles of freedom against tyranny. . . . A world without party would be incapable of progress."[12] Even Charles Sumner, for so much of his career at war with the leadership and direction of his own party, articulated similar sentiments. "Parties are unknown in despotic countries," he noted in 1860, "they belong to the machinery of free governments. Through parties, principles are maintained above men. And through parties

10. "Each election," Professor Campbell and his colleagues have written, "is not merely tossing the coin again; like all strong prejudices the electorate's basic dispositions have a tremendous capacity to keep people behaving in accustomed ways." Campbell et al., *Elections and Political Order*, p. 126. There is much evidence that this traditional partisan force is in decline in the last half of the twentieth century. See, for example, Norman H. Nie, Sidney Verba, and John R. Petrocik, *The Changing American Voter* (Cambridge, Mass., 1976).

11. "Party zeal ran higher than it has since," one politician who grew up in that era later recalled. Cornelius Cole, *Memoirs of Cornelius Cole* (New York, 1908), p. 109.

12. *Congressionsl Globe*, 30th Cong., 1st sess., *Appendix*, 775; Nahum Capen, *The History of Democracy in the United States* (Boston, 1852), 1: 1.

men in power are held to a just responsibility."[13] Thus, as the editor of the *Nation* summed up in 1866, his generation believed that "parties are essential instruments in the conduct of public affairs."[14]

These were never random sentiments of a few prominent leaders. The influence, and particularly the "discipline of party," was felt everywhere and by most Americans. Representatives in Congress and in the state legislatures, as well as many outside of government, expressed a strong sense of loyalty to shared ideas and a steadfast devotion to a common cause as organized and articulated by their party.[15] The parties' influence on the lives of others was as persistent and intense. Looking back to their nineteenth-century boyhoods, a number of prominent Americans, Democrats and Republicans alike, recalled the fervor of partisan attachments in their surroundings. "My father was obsessed by a sense of party loyalty," Woodrow Wilson's vice-president Thomas Marshall recalled of his Civil War boyhood in Indiana, "and I have never been able to divest myself of it." During the war, he recalled, "my grandfather and my father were notified by the Methodist preacher whose church they attended that he would have to strike their names off the roll if they continued to vote the Democratic ticket. My grandfather . . . announced he was willing to take his chance on Hell but never on the Republican party."[16] The future Progressive editor, Brand Whitlock, also recalled that, in the atmosphere of his Ohio boyhood in the 1860s, "it was natural to be a Republican; it was more than that, it was inevitable that one should be a Republican; it was not a matter of intellectual choice, it was a process of biological selection. The Republican party was not a faction, not a group, not a wing, it was an institution. . . . It was a

13. Quoted in Richard Hofstadter, *The Idea of a Party System* (Berkeley and Los Angeles, 1969), p. 269.

14. *Nation*, May 29, 1866.

15. Gideon Welles, quoted in *Diary of Gideon Welles*, ed. Harold Beale (New York, 1960), 2: 429. For the impact of party on legislative behavior, see Joel H. Silbey, *The Shrine of Party: Congressional Voting Behavior, 1841–1852* (Pittsburgh, 1967); and Herbert Ershkowitz and William Shade, "Consensus of Conflict? Political Behavior in the State Legislatures During the Jackson Era," *Journal of American History* 58 (December 1971), 591–621.

16. Thomas R. Marshall, *Recollections of Thomas R. Marshall* (Indianapolis, 1925), pp. 89, 70–71.

fundamental and self-evident thing, like life, and liberty, and the pursuit of happiness, or like the flag or the federal judiciary. It was elemental like gravity, the sun, the stars, the ocean. It were merely a synonym for patriotism, another name for the nation. One became, in Urbana and in Ohio for many years, a Republican just as the Eskimo dons his clothes. It was inconceivable that any self-respecting person should be a Democrat." And when Whitlock announced some years later that he had become a Democrat, the reaction was intense. "It could hardly have been worse," he recalled, "had I announced that I had been visiting Ingersoll, and was an atheist."[17]

Nor was this ever seen as an issueless politics of "tweedledum and tweedledee." To the people caught up in politics, their parties reflected their deepest values, creeds, and outlooks. Morton Keller, in describing the political world of the nineteenth-century cartoonist Thomas Nast, argued that to Nast "and his audience politics was a deeply meaningful form of expression, a receptacle for their profoundest fears, beliefs, expectations."[18] At the center of those politics were the parties. The latter were more than just names or organizations. In fact, neither major party in the 1860s possessed sophisticated organizational components. They were not without structure. Patronage activities and campaign techniques required a level of organization at the state and local levels. National committees coordinated activities as much as they could. Still, internal discipline, certainly among the rank and file, did not come from a set of legal rules or an all-powerful central organization. Discipline emerged, instead, from a sense of individual commitment almost impossible to shake. Parties enshrined hereditary animosities between different groups in the country. An individual's party identification, therefore, explained political virtue and truth to him, and indicated the best means of fulfilling his perceived goals. This is why the rank and file did not lightly change allegiance. Their party was something more to them than a simple, logical, dollars-and-cents matter, an electoral organization to which

17. Brand Whitlock, *Forty Years of It* (New York, 1914), pp. 27, 32.
18. Morton Keller, *The Art and Politics of Thomas Nast* (New York, 1968), p. viii.

one happened to adhere. Their values and ideals were involved in their party and parties were an integral part of their community ideals.[19]

Such commitments kept men operating within their parties even when they disagreed with some aspect of its affairs and direction. At the Democratic National Convention that nominated Stephen A. Douglas in 1860, a delegate from Missouri noted that he had opposed the nomination of Douglas. Nevertheless, "he went with this Convention for weal or for woe, intending to live and die in the Democratic party." It was the sort of attitude that led the antislavery William Henry Seward to write in 1848 that he would support the slaveholder Zachary Taylor for president against the antislavery Free Soil party "on precisely the same grounds on which I have hitherto voted for Whig candidates, because they are commended to me by the Whig party. . . ." Or caused the wife of a Democratic politician to write in 1866 that during the war "we felt political bonds to be the strongest on earth, for friendship and religion were trampled in the dust."[20]

This spirit of party loyalty, this "faith and love" for one's party, often expressed in powerful and metaphoric style, was angrily condemned by those trying to break partisan shackles. "A loco would 'vote the Ticket,' " one unhappy observer complained, "if Gabriel's drum was sounding." Horace Greeley, continually hamstrung in his efforts to wean Democratic voters away from their leaders, was as unhappy. Democrats, he wrote, "may have roast baby for breakfast every morning, with missionary steaks for dinner, and yet rule the country forever." In short, the "spirit of party operates unconsciously on the minds of even moderate and reflecting men, and warps and

19. As one Whig wrote in 1850, he would not have a Whig *"vote for the best man in the world if he was a democrat."* To do so would be *"to vote against his own blood."* John E. Stuart to Mary E. Stuart, 12 December 1850, in *Stuart Letters of Robert and Elizabeth Sullivan Stuart, 1819–1864,* ed. Helen S. M. Marlatt (Washington, D.C., 1961), 1: 166.

20. *Official Proceedings, Democratic National Convention, 1860* (Baltimore, 1860), p. 234; William Seward, "Letter from Governor Seward to the Whigs of Orleans County, August 21, 1848" (printed pamphlet in New York Historical Society Collections), p. 13; Rebekah B. Shunk to Mrs. Howell Cobb, November 6, 1866, in "Howell Cobb Papers," ed. Robert P. Brooks *Georgia Historical Quarterly* 6 (December 1922): 385–86. For a contrary assertion, see "The Issues Involved in the Presidential Contest, Speech of the Hon. William L. Yancey . . . Delivered at Memphis, Tenn., August 14, 1860" (Frankfort, Ky., 1860), p. 3.

perverts their judgment. With the mass of partisans its sway is overwhelming and reason and justice perish under its malign influence."[21] But to most Americans party and party loyalty were not
malign. Their party remained communities of sentiment, and symbols
of unusual intensity.

This power of party attachments had an important impact on
nineteenth-century elections. Never in American history was voting
turnout higher. There was widespread participation at every electoral
level. Contests were bitterly fought. They were dominated by what a
contemporary observer called the primary "princple of action" of the
parties, "opposition to each other right or wrong."[22] Richard Jensen
has used the metaphor of two crusading armies to describe elections
fought in this atmosphere. Each contest, he has argued, was conceived
as a great battle between two opposing, highly disciplined, and united
armies. All but a few voters were loyal soldiers in one or another of the
armies: election campaigns centered around the ability of each military organization to mobilize its full strength on election day. Most
voters proved to be, in V. O. Key's apt term, "standpatters," not
switchers. They perceived reality in partisan terms, considered new
conditions through the lenses of party identification, and followed
their party's direction and candidates in every election regardless of
the comparative virtues of other courses of action and other
candidates.[23]

As a result, in the quarter-century after 1828, voting behavior had
settled down into a fairly persistent stability, only occasionally and
briefly disrupted by flashes of electoral volatility. In election after
election, what one observer has called the "tenacity" of "older lines
of cleavage and conflict" held among those who went to the polls,

21. Chauncey M. Depew, *My Memories of Eighty Years* (New York, 1922), p.
16; E. C. Stedman to Charles Stedman, October 18, 1862, in *Life and Letters of
Edmund C. Stedman,* ed. Laura Stedman and George M. Gould (New York, 1910);
Horace Greeley to J. S. Pike, April 28, 1850, quoted in Jeter Isely, *Horace Greeley and
the Republican Party* (Princeton, 1947), p. 34; Senator James A. Bayard, in
Congressional Globe, 37 Cong., 2 sess., p. 651.

22. Julius Lemoyne to Charles F. Adams, Jr., July 22, 1845, Adams Family
Papers, Massachusetts Historical Society, Boston, Mass.

23. Richard Jensen, "Armies, Admen and Crusaders: Types of Interparty Election Campaigns," *The History Teacher* 2 (January 1969): 33–50; V. O. Key, *The
Responsible Electorate 1936–1960* (Cambridge, Mass., 1966).

regardless of candidates, immediate issues, or the pressures of changing circumstances.[24] A party's popular vote was not built from different segments of the population in successive elections but primarily from the same groups of people as in the election before. The very high statistical correlations between the Democratic vote in successive elections pinpoints this voter stability. Gerald Pomper found, for example, that the national Democratic vote was highly correlated between each succeeding pair of elections in the 1836–1860 period. The 1852 vote, for example, correlated with that of both 1844 and 1848 at about .80.[25] The pattern within individual states and for local and state elections reveals the same kind of stable voter support from election to election. In one period between 1838 and 1844 in New York State, for example, correlations of the Democratic vote averaged .90 over six different elections.[26] Patterns in other states were similar.

Of course, despite the intensity and persistence of this partisan commitment, elections were never completely replays of previous contests. There was always a certain amount of volatility, occasional shifts of voters, and surges to one party or the other as short-term electoral forces temporarily shook party adherents enough so they sat out an election or voted for the opposition. Factionalism and intraparty bitterness momentarily depressed or enhanced a party's totals. Some party voters stayed home on election day, sometimes because they were consciously rebuffing their party or because the issues and forces at work in a particular campaign failed to lure them to the polls.

24. Samuel Barnes, "Ideology and the Organization of Conflict: On the Relationship Between Political Thought and Behavior," *Journal of Politics* 28 (August 1966): 529.

25. Gerald Pomper, *Elections in America* (New York, 1968), p. 268.

26. The New York State figures are taken from Lee Benson, Joel H. Silbey, and Phyllis F. Field, "Toward a Theory of American Voting Patterns: New York State, 1792–1970," in Joel H. Silbey et al., *The History of American Electoral Behavior: Quantitative Studies* (Princeton, 1978). This psychological attachment to parties and tenacious voting habits is also empirically demonstrated for a number of Midwestern states in Ray Myle Shortridge, "Voting Patterns in the American Midwest, 1840–1872" (Ph.D. diss. University of Michigan, 1974); and in the research of Professor Peyton McCrary and his colleagues. See Peyton McCrary, Clark Miller, and Dale Baum, "Class and Party in the Secession Crisis: Voting Behavior in the Deep South, 1856–1861," *Journal of Interdisciplinary History,* forthcoming; and Peyton McCrary, "The Civil War Party System, 1854–1876: Toward a New Behavioral Synthesis?" (Paper delivered at the Annual Meeting of the Southern Historical Association, 1976).

Occasionally, the number of stay-at-homes was disproportionately high among members of one party for these reasons, and therefore favored the other.[27] In every election enough of these short-term forces existed to create excitement and potential turnovers despite preexisting commitments. This potential was particularly enhanced by the very close margins between the parties at most elections, making each very vulnerable to any indifference or defection by its faithful.

From the late twenties into the midfifties, there had been few landslide elections. The Democrats had controlled the presidency and Congress for most of the time since the intoxicating days of Andrew Jackson's first election. But the Whigs had usually been able to wage a very competitive campaign against them, both nationally and in most states. Thus, although the Democrats won three of the five presidential elections between 1836 and 1852, the Whigs had averaged 48.3 percent of the national vote in those five elections to the Democrats' 48.2 percent. Even in the apparent Democratic landslide in the presidential election of 1852, both parties maintained a fairly stable percentage of the popular vote both nationally and in some of the key Northern areas compared with their vote in the very tight national contest of 1844. In 1852, for example, the Democrats took 50.7 percent of the national vote compared to 49 percent in 1844. Similarly, in the three Middle Atlantic states of New York, Pennsylvania, and New Jersey, they won 50.9 percent of the vote in 1852 as against 49.5 percent in 1844. Other regional and state changes were similarly slight.[28]

27. Again the work of Peyton McCrary is useful here. See his computations of tunout and nonvoters in successive presidential elections in "The Civil War Party System," especially Tables I, II, IV, and V.

28. The figures for some key states and other regions were:

	1844	1852
New England	45.6	44.0
Midwest	50.5	50.8
New York	48.9	50.2
Pennsylvania	50.5	51.2
Connecticut	46.2	49.8
Indiana	50.1	52.1
New Hampshire	55.2	56.8
Illinois	54.4	51.8

But most short-term factors in any election, while important in determining victory or defeat in a closely divided electorate, did not alter fundamentally the underlying stability of the popular vote. The spasms of discontent were usually temporary, affected only a few people, and had no lasting impact on the basic components of each party's support. Most people continued to vote as they always had. People chose, in the first instance, to vote for one of the two national parties since they believed it fulfilled their self-interest in a way that the other party did not. Their children continued to support the same party into the 1850s because they continued to believe that it still reflected their interests and the other party still did not.

The State of the Democracy, 1860

Beginning in the early 1850s, however, a series of political shocks signalled the onset of a critical period of voter realignment and a new national political pattern. Voter realignments, a rare phenomenon in American political history, involve a powerful reaction against normal political processes and a basic shift in the partisan loyalties of certain voters.[29] This is what happened from 1854 onward, most critically in the Northern states. The normal continuities in popular voting behavior, so characteristic of the nineteenth century, were replaced first by a period of extraordinary voter volatility and then by the hardening of a new pattern of electoral stability in which many voters wound up in party homes new to them.

The shocks that caused these changes centered around a series of ethnocultural, regional, and economic issues of particularly threatening quality. They began when the fears and prejudices of certain ethnocultural groups against others, particularly against Catholics and foreigners, grew powerful enough to trigger a profound voter revolution. A massive Irish and German immigration, stimulated by economic disaster and political discontent in their homelands, filled up many American seaboard and inland river cities in unprecedented numbers. In 1853 alone, for example, over 300,000 immigrants

29. See V. O. Key, "A Theory of Critical Elections," *Journal of Politics* 17 (February 1955): 3–4. The fullest development of this theory has been in Walter Dean Burnham, *Critical Elections and the Mainsprings of American Politics* (New York, 1970).

entered the United States. Their poverty was as appalling to many Americans as their numbers and their strangeness. The changes they wrought in the character of some Eastern cities were frightening. At the fringes of poverty, unable to find steady employment easily, discriminated against repeatedly, they clustered uneasily in increasingly crowded and degenerating slum areas. The fact that so many of these immigrants were Catholics reinforced a massive and growing social fear on the part of many Americans who believed that the United States was in profound danger. Not only the nation's physical landscape but its values and beliefs, its control over its own destiny as an Anglo-Saxon–Protestant nation, were in danger of being overwhelmed or forced into channels repellant to millions of citizens.[30]

This fear and the resulting backlash hit both existing parties hard. Local Democratic leaders in many parts of the North reported a massive rejection of the party by some of its stronger adherents in favor of nativist parties and similar groupings. The Democracy, with America in the greatest danger, the rejectionists charged, was unable or unwilling to confront the threat. In fact, the rejectionists continued, Democratic leaders more often than not seemed indifferent to the danger, and even welcomed the immigrants as potential Democratic voters. The danger was too great for indifference and for the continuation of normal politics and traditional political associations. As a result of these fears and anger, the *New York Tribune* reported in 1855, "a large mass of the Democratic party is afloat."[31]

Nor was this the only reason for discontent in the 1850s. The accusation by antislavery groups that renewed Southern aggression in the territories was supported by the Democratic high command, in deference to its Southern masters, further fueled a backlash against the party in the North. While most Democrats in the North supported the Kansas-Nebraska bill, Douglas's strong arguments in favor of opening Kansas to settlement by slaveholders fell upon many deaf ears

30. See Ray Billington, *The Protestant Crusade, 1800–1860* (New York, 1938); Ronald P. Formisano, *The Birth of Mass Political Parties, Michigan, 1827–1861* (Princeton, 1971); Joel H. Silbey, *The Transformation of American Politics, 1840–1860* (Englewood Cliffs, N.J., 1967).

31. *New York Tribune,* September 5, 1855. See also (in addition to Formisano, *Birth of Mass Political Parties*), Michael Holt, *Forging a Majority, The Birth of the Republican Party in Pittsburgh, 1848–1860* (New Haven, 1969).

among the party faithful. Some of these Northern Democrats were concerned enough about the issue to revolt against their normal loyalties from 1854 on. They indicated the state of their disaffection by joining, in the first stage, anti-Nebraska meetings, calling themselves anti-Nebraska Democrats, and constantly opposing the territorial policies of the national Democratic administration.[32] But their revolt did not stop there.

Before very long, both of these issues, along with a number of other irritations, proved devastating to the Democratic party as disaffected party members actively sought more accommodating political alternatives to their traditional party home. Bitter factionalism erupted within the Democracy and multipartyism flourished as unhappy party members broke away from the organization. Other Democrats apparently dropped out of the political system, no longer willing to support Democrat policies or candidates but unwilling to join an anti-Democratic movement. The reaction of all these voters against the Democracy produced an era of electoral instability that lasted through the presidential election of 1860. In contrast to the usual glacial movement in each party's share of the vote between successive elections, vote totals swung wildly from election to election in most Northern states. In New York State, as one example, the number of counties in the largest state in the Union that shifted more than 5 percent from each party's previous total in successive elections between 1854 and 1860 averaged thirty-five, compared with only four annually between 1850 and 1853. Some of the swings were enormous. In Allegany County, New York, for example the Democrats lost 20.7 percent in their total vote between 1853 and 1854, a pattern repeated in many other counties as well. In other large Northern states—Pennsylvania, Ohio, Indiana, and Illinois—similar large swings and electoral volatility at the county level was also the rule from 1854 onward.[33]

32. Formisano and Holt deal with the territorial issue. See also, among many others, Robert Johannsen, *Stephen A. Douglas* (New York, 1973), and Roy F. Nichols, *The Disruption of the American Democracy* (New York, 1947).

33. The election returns used throughout this chapter were either supplied by the Inter-University Consortium for Political Research at Ann Arbor, Michigan, or were compiled from the *New York Tribune Almanac*. See also *Congressional Quarterly's Guide to U.S. Elections* (Washington, D.C., 1975).

Unfortunately for the Democratic party, the changes were not transient. A permanent voter revolution was occurring. It was noticeable at first because the actual sources of voting support for each party changed dramatically between successive elections as many voters altered their party commitments and rearranged their loyalties. Such defections did not occur uniformly across the North. They were particularly heavy in areas of New England settlement and vigorous evangelical Protestant activity along the shores of the Erie Canal and the Great Lakes and in the surrounding areas of New York, Pennsylvania, Ohio, and Michigan. There, many traditional Democratic voters left the party of their fathers.[34]

Elsewhere in the North, however, the amount of change was less. Among Protestant groups not as sensitive to the social pressures of Catholic migration, and among the Southern-born or -descended citizens of the lower Ohio Valley, pockets of this strength remained firm in their partisan commitment to the Democracy. Their loyalties remained strongly rooted in their past associations. Furthermore, after the first wave of disaffection from the Democracy, their fortunes also improved somewhat as a few defectors returned and some non-Democrats joined the party. In urban-Catholic areas and in places of German settlement in the Middle West, Democratic loyalties began to develop among large numbers of new voters as well.[35]

As a result of the voter backlash, the geography of Democratic support changed somewhat. More critically, however, by the time disaffected and floating voters came to rest, support for the Democratic party leveled off at a point lower than it had been before the realignment. In Connecticut, for example, the Democrats averaged about 46 percent of the vote in presidential elections between 1840 and 1852 but only 43 percent in the two elections immediately thereafter. In Illinois, Democratic vote totals went from 50.6 percent to 46 percent of the statewide vote in the same two periods. And, most

34. This is dealt with very effectively in Holt, *Forging a Majority,* and Formisano, *Birth of Mass Political Parties.* Benson, Silbey, and Field, "Toward a Theory of American Voting Patterns," traces and measures the shift in New York State.

35. I have not dealt with the social bases of party competition more extensively since my main interest here is not the nature of political cleavages but, rather, the size of the party vote.

striking, in New Hampshire they fell from an average vote of 55.6 percent to 44.1 percent in the same elections.[36]

This was not the end of the Democrats' troubles. Throughout the period of voter instability, a vigorous anti-Democratic political leadership worked intensively to combine anti-Catholic, Free Soil, and other discontented voters into a united and potent anti-Democratic coalition. They were very successful. By the end of the decade, the new voter alignments produced by the turmoil were hardening into permanence.[37] By 1860, the Republicans held fourteen of the eighteen governorships in the states north of Mason and Dixon's line, controlled all but three Northern state legislatures, occupied 102 of the 146 Northern seats in the House of Representatives (six others were held by anti-Democratic Unionists), and had won twenty-nine of the thirty-six United States Senate seats in the Northern states. A voter alignment, as potent as it was rare, had reversed the fortunes of the parties in the North. A new voter stability seemed to promise the Republicans enough normal support to solidify their political control for a generation.

The Competitiveness of the Democracy

The electoral situation in 1860 looked worse for the Democrats than it was. Despite the profound trauma of the electoral realignment, the Democrats continued to enjoy substantial popular support. Many Democratic partisans in the Northern states, as we have seen, had been relatively unaffected by the conflicts of the period and had not left their political home. Elections in many places continued to be decided, therefore, by narrow margins. As a result of the realignment, these closely divided state totals were based on one-sided votes in different counties of each state. The Democrats actually controlled few counties in several of the largest Northern states, but the ones that they did, in terms of total population and potential for future growth,

36. Between the presidential elections of 1852 and 1856, the mean Democratic loss in the nonslaveholding states was 7.3 per cent.

37. The Republicans in the 1850s united Protestantism with Northernism and Americanism. "Party, religion and national character all intertwined." Formisano, *Birth of Mass Political Parties,* p. 328. See also Eric Foner, *Free Soil, Free Labor and Free Men* (New York, 1970), for a pertinent analysis of the rise of the Republicans.

easily matched the more numerous but less densely populated Republican counties. In New York State for example, the Democratic vote was overwhelmingly concentrated in New York City, certain upstate cities, and a few counties in southeastern New York near the city, while the Republicans controlled thirty-six to forty counties regularly, encompassing the major part of the land area of the state. But the few counties controlled by the Democrats balanced, in terms of total population, the Republican counties. Nor was this phenomenon confined to New York. Surveys of similar counties in a number of other key Northern states reflect the same phenomenon. As a result, the Democrats, while no longer the majority party in the Northern states, remained a powerful organization with enough potential support to continue to challenge the dominant Republicans.

The party's fortunes in the last elections before the outbreak of the Civil War attested to its continued strength. In the presidential race of 1860, the combined Democratic vote was 47.6 percent of the national total. In the states that did not later secede, the Democrats averaged 44.7 percent in the presidential contest. Both figures compared favorably with earlier Democratic vote totals. The party's candidates actually gained support over 1856 and were also very close to their average national and Northern strength in all of the presidential elections between 1840 and 1856, an era of sustained Democratic strength. Then they had averaged 48.7 percent of the national vote (1.1 percent more than in 1860), and 45.7 percent in the nonseceding states (1.0 percent more than in 1860).

There was another dimension to their vote. In the presidential election of 1860 the Democrats won only twelve states with eighty-four electoral votes and only twenty-three electors in states that did not later secede. But in seven Northern and Border states with forty-six electoral votes they won at least 50 percent of the popular vote. (They lost some of these because of their organizational split.) They won at least 45 percent of the popular vote in three more states with fifty-nine electoral votes. Thus at the presidential level they remained at least superficially competitive in ten of twenty-one loyal states, with 91 electoral votes of 203.

The Democrats' high totals were not confined to the presidential

Table 1.1

Combined Democratic Percentage of the Popular Vote for President, 1860, Nonseceding States

55% OR BETTER		50–54.9%		45.0–49.9%		BELOW 45%	
California	61.3	Missouri	54.5	Illinois	47.9	Ohio	44.9
Oregon	54.9	Kentucky	53.9	Indiana	47.0	Iowa	43.8
		Delaware	52.2	New York	46.3	Wisconsin	43.3
		Maryland	52.0			Michigan	42.6
		New Jersey	51.9			New Hampshire	42.4
						Connecticut	42.0
						Pennsylvania	41.1
						Rhode Island	38.8
						Minnesota	36.4
						Maine	33.8
						Massachusetts	24.0
						Vermont	23.3

race. In fifteen of twenty-two Northern and Border states' state-office contests in 1859–1860 the Democrats won over 45 percent of the popular vote. Furthermore, they also did well in many congressional races in the states that did not later secede. The Democrats held only forty-four seats in the House of Representatives from the Northern states in the Thirty-seventh Congress. But, more to the point, even where they had not won seats they made strong showings in individual races in such populous states as New Jersey, Ohio, Wisconsin, Illinois, and Indiana, and only a little less so in New York, New Hampshire, and Pennsylvania.

This residual strength and consequent competitiveness can be measured with some precision. An index of competition for each state based on all of the electoral results in the presidential, congressional, and state-office contests in 1859–1860 pinpoints how much support the Democrats continued to enjoy in elections on the eve of the Civil War. They had a "safe" margin in only one state (California), compared to the Republicans' three, but three other states can be classified as intensely competitive and eight as moderately competitive, including such crucial large states as New York, Ohio, Illinois, and Indiana.[38]

38. The index is based on how much the loser needs to gain to become the majority party in a given race. It is computed on the basis of 100 by dividing the percentage of the

Similarly, despite their congressional setbacks, the Democrats remained in a very good position in races for the House of Representatives. They held seven "safe" seats and were dominant in nine more. There were thirty-eight intensely competitive seats and thirty-two moderately competitive seats, many of which the Democrats already held. In sum, eighty-six of the seats were up for grabs or Democratic controlled in the House, a majority of the seats remaining in the Union. The Democrats were not as well off as the Republicans, however, with the latter's forty-eight safe seats and twelve in which they were the dominant party. The Republicans were clearly in the ascendant in the Northern states. But the margins were very close and the Democrats did retain imposing residual support among Northern voters.

Unfortunately for the Democracy, this strength remained potential at best. Events in 1860 underscored the problem of the party when that potential was not effectively mobilized. The party had split bitterly. Three conventions, two candidates for president, two rival national headquarters, two campaigns, and much virulent sniping characterized the party in 1860. There were attempts at reconcilation, of course. Samuel L. M. Barlow, an important behind-the-scenes New York financier who was close to many Southern leaders in the Breckinridge camp, as well as to August Belmont, Stephen Douglas, and others among their rivals, worked assiduously for cooperation and reunion. In many states the rival factions managed to paper over their differences and fuse together against the hated Republicans. Nevertheless, the fissures were real, the belligerence between the

---

vote of the runner-up party by one-half of the total percentage of the winning and runner-up parties. The index was developed and applied in Paul David, *Party Strength in the United States, 1872–1970* (Charlottesville, Va., 1972). A composite index was used here averaging together each party's percentage in the races for president, Congress, and highest state office. Finally, I have defined a state as intensely competitive electorally if its index is more than 95, moderately competitive if its index is between 90 and 94.9, dominated by one party if the index is between 85 and 89.9, and a safe situation if the index is less than 85.

Obviously, in all of these computations I am ignoring the fact that the Democratic party was actually split in 1860. However, my interest here is in measuring the number of Democratic voters available, ignoring, for the moment, the crucial problem of how to bring them all under one electoral roof. I have not included in this analysis the Border states whose wartime history generally left them outside of Democratic hopes and calculations.

Table 1.2
Democratic Electoral Percentages and Index of Competition
Nonseceding States
1859–1860

STATE	PRESIDENT 1860	STATE OFFICE	TOTAL CONG. VOTE	INDEX OF COMPETITION (3 ELECTIONS)
Maine	33.8	42.5	43.3	79.6
New Hampshire	42.4	46.9	47.9	91.5
Vermont	23.7	29.1	23.0	50.5
Rhode Island	38.8	53.2	26.1	74.5
Massachusetts	24.0	22.9	37.3[a]	57.4[a]
Connecticut	42.0	49.7	49.0	93.7
New York	46.3	46.8	45.9	92.6
New Jersey	51.9	49.2	50.6	96.3
Pennsylvania	41.1	46.7	44.2	88.4
Ohio	44.9	48.4	45.8	91.1
Indiana	47.0	48.1	47.4	93.8
Illinois	47.9	48.2	48.3	96.3
Michigan	42.6	43.4	42.9	85.9
Wisconsin	43.4	48.4	43.1	89.9
Iowa	43.8	44.6	44.8	88.7
Minnesota	36.4	45.2	45.3	84.6
California	61.3	90.0	57.4	60.9
Oregon	59.4	—[b]	50.04	90.5

[a]This is artificially inflated since the Democrats combined with dissident Republicans and Unionists in congressional races in Massachusetts. But since the state was one of the most one-sided in the country, nothing is changed in the analysis.

[b]There were no statewide races in either 1859 or 1860 in Oregon.

Douglas and Breckinridge men was deep. "The Democratic party upon which [rest] all my hopes of good to the world through human government," former Representative George W. Jones of Tennessee wrote to Andrew Johnson in August 1860, "has been distracted, disrupted, broken up, destroyed."[39] Not quite. But there was a basic organizational split, a feeble campaign presence, and an inability to

39. George W. Jones to Andrew Johnson, August 15, 1860, in *The Letters of Andrew Johnson*, ed. Leroy Graf (Knoxville, 1972), 3: 656.

mobilize the party's full potential, let alone find the means to crack the hardened electoral structure now favoring their opponents. Despite all of their hopes and the potential available, the Democrats had not been at their best in 1860 and their future remained problematical.[40]

Still, the party remained a community of strong supporters who frantically wished to vote Democratic come what may. Indeed, if anything, the bitter confrontations of the period since the rise of the Republican party served not only to remind the mass of Democrats, if not their leaders, of their loyalties, but to reinforce them as well. An unfriendly critic of the party once noted that Democratic voters "have been taught to look with suspicion upon everything that was not labelled "Democracy.""[41] Events in the mid- and late 1850s and in the presidential election of 1860 confirmed and deepened that suspicion.

"The Evils of Political Meddling"

In the first place, Republican vituperation against the Democratic party and Democratic voters was persistent, intense, and unyielding. Republicans blamed the Democracy for all of the country's ills, past and present. Its legitimacy itself was often called into question. Throughout the Civl War era the Repubicans made it clear that "two out of every three of the more uninformed, the intemperate and vicious portion of most communities" were Democrats. Or more directly, "the ragged infantines of steeves and brothels, the spawn and shipwreck of taverns and dicing houses" formed the core of the Democratic support aided only by some "weak-minded men of respectability."[42]

Such bitter rhetoric only caused Democrats to burrow deeper into their common associations for defense and hope. They were in a war for the nation. Democrats were forcefully reminded how parties

40. The final chapters of Nichols, *Disruption of the American Democracy*, contain the best description of the party in 1860. See also Johannsen, *Stephen A. Douglas.*

41. William D. Jones, *Mirror of Modern Democracy: A History of the Democratic Party from Its Organization in 1825, to Its Last Great Achievement* (New York, 1864), p. 260.

42. Ibid., p. 240; George Templeton Strong, *The Diary of George Templeton Strong, 1835–1875*, ed. Allan Nevins and Milton H. Thomas (New York, 1952), 3: 491.

continued to institutionalize into opposite camps the complexes of sentiment and opinion that divided the nation. They were convinced that they were ideologically different from their opponents. They also believed that these ideological differences were rooted in a long-standing, basic confrontation in the country between two views of government power, the nature of personal rights and individual liberty, and the proper mode and policies for promoting the general welfare.

During the 1830s and 1840s, the Democrats had matured a series of proposals in the economic realm which they strongly advocated to the nation. These had run the gamut from specifics such as support for a low tariff and a stand against federal aid for internal improvements, to a generalized call for a limitation on the role and responsibilities of the federal government in the economic realm—all of which contrasted quite sharply with positions taken by the Whigs during the same period. Democrats contested vigorously against the Whigs over proper banking policy, the level of tariff rates, and the rest of the economic policies that differentiated them from their opponents. In election campaigns, newspaper and pamphlet rhetoric, in state legislatures and in Congress, Democratic (as well as Whig) spokesmen had demonstrated both a very high degree of unity behind the economic policy imperatives of their party, and an intransigent stance against the proposals of their adversaries.[43]

There had been other strings to the Democratic bow as well. They were strong expansionists and supported aggressive action in foreign affairs, again quite contrary to what the Whigs advocated at the same time. Angry partisan disputes over territorial expansion and foreign policy had marked the 1840s and 1850s. Finally, the Democrats also favored unrestricted immigration, freedom of religious practice, and from interference in matters of religious and social values generally, clear signals of their friendship with and support of many alien groups in the country. All stood in stark contrast to what the Whigs advocated on these matters. Thus, the Democrats of Wayne County, Michigan, attacked, as early as 1835, Whig attempts "to create a spirit of

43. See Silbey, *Shrine of Party;* Ershkowitz and Shade, "Consensus or Conflict?"

jealousy and distrust between native born citizens and foreigners . . ." and the attempts of the Whigs "to connect religion
and politics" which was "subversive of a fundamental principle of
Republican institutions . . . and tending to engender a spirit dangerous to the peace of society and to liberty."[44]

Events in the 1850s had honed the Democrats' traditional
ideological commitments into an oft-repeated litany of the woes that
would afflict the country in the event of a Republican triumph. During
the fifties and into the campaign of 1860, in response first to the rise of
virulent nativism directed against the new waves of immigrants, and
then to the Republican onslaught against them, the Democrats, while
continuing to speak about economic issues, foreign affairs, and expansion, increasingly focused their attention on what they saw as
Republican attempts to regenerate a virulent Whig tradition of federal
intervention in every aspect of American life, adding to it a nativist
commitment to limit immigration and restrict alien individual and
group conduct they found uncongenial. At heart, Republicans, as
the Whigs before them, were centralizing, overbearing, Federalist-
Tories, intent on destroying the liberties of the American people
through the extensive intrusion of government power into the personal
lives, conduct, and beliefs of individuals and groups within the Union.
The essential "principle of Republicanism," as seen through the
Democratic filter, was "to meddle with everything . . . to force their
harsh and uncongenial puritanical creed down the throats of other
men, and compel them to digest it under pains and penalties." Behind
laws regulating or prohibiting the sale and consumption of alcoholic
beverages, vigorously debated throughout the fifties, or other legislation governing the language of school instruction, which textbooks to
use, who could teach, or the sources of financial support for schools,
Democrats saw a Republican determination to foster a particular code
of behavior and belief on all Americans.[45] This cultural interven-

44. Quoted in Paul A. Randall, "Gubernatorial Platforms for the Political Parties
of Michigan, 1834–1864" (M. A. thesis, Wayne University, 1937). The differing
stances of the parties on these issues in one state is well treated in Formisano, *Birth of
Mass Political Parties.*

45. See Formisano, *Birth of Mass Political Parties;* Holt, *Forging a Majority;*
Paul Kleppner, *The Cross of Culture: A Social Analysis of Midwestern Politics,
1850–1900* (New York, 1970).

tionism posed grave threats, in the Democrats' view, to individual freedom in America. Party spokesmen, therefore, railed against "the evils of political meddling with morals, religion and the rights of distinct communities," of allowing the government to "invade the territory of the Church" on behalf of only one particular point of view within a highly pluralist nation.[46]

This commitment to political interference in matters of social behavior was not the only fearsome thing Democrats perceived in the rise of the Republicans. They continually blasted the Republican party as a sectional conspiracy guilty of intensifying, for its own nefarious purposes, sectional tensions within the Union. A long time before, Martin Van Buren had argued that the best counter to potential sectional divisiveness and tensions was the party system with its cross-sectional relationships and nonsectional attitudes.[47] The Democrats had fought for this idea since. Now, they argued, the Republicans had established a parochial party which cared nothing for Southern support and which was frankly playing on sectional antagonisms to further its own interests. The result could be nothing but ultimate disaster for the American nation. Since there now was only one union party left in the country, they argued during the presidential campaign of 1860, the only way of preserving the Union from disruption and disaster was by supporting the national Democracy against the particularist forces working to destroy it.[48] In its national platform in 1860, the Douglas wing of the party repeated the planks on the slavery issue that had appeared in every Democratic platform since 1852,

46. *New York Herald,* September 21, 1860; Horatio Seymour, *Public Record of Horatio Seymour,* Comp. Thomas M. Cook and Thomas W. Knox (New York, 1868), p. 21; C. L. Vallandigham, *The Record of Hon. C. L. Vallandigham on Abolition, the Union and the Civil War* (Columbus, Ohio, 1863), p. 13.

Their view hardly squared necessarily with constitutional and political reality. But the point remains that the Democrats saw things this way and reacted in terms of their belief and fears. See also Joel H. Silbey, "Social Conflict and the Coming of the American Civil War: The Perspective of the New Political History" (paper presented before the Annual Meeting of the American Historical Association, 1976).

47. Martin Van Buren to Thomas Ritchie, January 13, 1827, Martin Van Buren Papers, Library of Congress.

48. See, as one example of this stance, Samuel J. Tilden to William Kent, October 26, 1860, in *The Writings and Speeches of Samuel J. Tilden,* ed. John Bigelow (New York, 1885), 1: 291ff. Democratic newspapers throughout the North played on this theme constantly. See the editorials reprinted in Howard Perkins, *Northern Editorials on Secession* (New York, 1942), Vol. 1.

notably arguing against antislavery agitation and pining for a return to the Compromise of 1850 as the final solution of slavery matters. It urged obedience to the fugitive slave law and condemned those who would circumvent the latter. The Democrats also argued once more that only the people of the territories should be competent to determine if they wanted slavery there or not. The contrast with the Republican perspective could not have been sharper, something the Democrats continually hammered home.[49]

The third charge against the Republicans that the Democrats developed in this period involved a theme that was to grow stronger as the years passed, that concerning race. The Republican party was dedicated, Democrats argued, to promoting the interests of the Negro in the United States even at the expense of the white. In New York, among other states, the Republicans were supporting the extension of Negro suffrage as the first and major step toward their plan of Africanizing the United States. The Democrats, opposing this vigorously, sought only to protect the rights and interests of the white men in what had always been and should continue to remain a white man's country.[50]

There was much ideological congruence on these matters among the different Democratic factions. Both party platforms in 1860, for example, adopted the united Cincinnati platform of 1856, reaffirming the economic and federal noninterference planks of earlier Democratic platforms. Each included similar planks favoring the acquisition of Cuba, the protection of Americans at home and abroad against the actions of foreign governments, and the improvement of communications with the Pacific Coast by means of the construction of a transcontinental railroad. Each faction adopted similar platform planks on abiding by the fugitive slave act and condemning those Northern states

49. The essential point that the Democrats reiterated in all of their planks was their commitment against anything more than limited federal intervention in most economic and social matters as a prelude to dangerous and unnecessary destruction of the liberty of the people. The platform is conveniently reprinted in Kirk H. Porter and Donald Bruce Johnson, *National Party Platforms 1840–1972*, 5th ed. (Champagne, Ill., 1973), pp. 30–31.

50. See, for one example, the *Illinois State Register*, September 14, 1860; Phyllis F. Field, "The Struggle for Black Suffrage in New York State, 1846–1869," (Ph.D. diss., Cornell University, 1974); Eugene Berwanger, *The Frontier Against Slavery: Western Anti-Negro Prejudice and the Slavery Extension Controversy* (Urbana, Ill., 1967).

that did not do so. Both saw the Republicans as radical destructionaries of all that had made the country great, prosperous, and free. Both saw themselves as part of a conservative tradition that fought to preserve the inherent liberties of most Americans within a white man's country. They differed, of course, over the role of slavery in the territories and the responsibility of the federal government to protect it there. Although this was the crucial plank that led to the division of the Democracy, the extent of their ideological similarities underscored their very large areas of agreement as old Democrats.[51]

To most Democrats, these ideology and policy positions were powerful stuff. There is no question that they sincerely believed what they were arguing as the logical growth of their creed since the days of Andrew Jackson. But they also believed it was good campaign material as well, that would win votes by holding good Democrats in their place and winning other voters away from the Republicans. They believed that their very pointed rhetoric would reinvigorate the fears and past memories of loyal Democrats because it contained the kinds of emotive symbols and code words that touched a deep chord throughout the Democratic community, from Irish dockworkers in Boston, New York, or Cincinnati, to Southern-born or -descended farmers in the Ohio Valley, to respectable newspaper editors, lawyers, merchants, and bankers in large and small cities throughout the North. At the same time, they thought that the specifics of their conservative appeal could also win over enough anti-radical voters from both former Whigs and former Democrats to be able to reconstitute a conservative-Unionist electoral majority behind their party's candidates.

Intensifying the recognition of common attitudes and needs, then, the campaign of 1860 only contributed further to the impressive Democratic potential. There were, in other words, a number of positive forces working on behalf of the Democracy that, if properly handled, could restore them to a significant national political role, even in a truncated Union. Throughout the tribulations of the fifties, the party had not lost its appeal and meaning to thousands of Northerners.[52] To the Republican *New York Tribune*, the Democratic

51. The Breckinridge Democrats' platform is conveniently reprinted in Porter and Johnson, *National Party Platforms*, p. 31.
52. Michael Holt has argued that one of the major characteristics of the realign-

party in the 1860s was "a myth, a reminiscence, a voice from the tomb, an ancient and fishlike smell." But to many the party remained a powerful magnet, an intense community of like-minded individuals. E. L. Godkin, another Republican, remarked once that whatever the Democracy "may once have been," it remained "a party of habits, prejudices, and traditions."[53] These "habits, prejudices, and traditions" continued to be strongly influential in American politics as the 1860s opened.

The Democracy's major problem was to find the means of reuniting all Democrats under the party's banner. Once that was accomplished, it had to attract additional voters—the uncommitted and any lukewarm Republicans—so that Democratic competitive minority totals would become winning majorities. If the prevailing electoral structure of 1860, with its apparent Republican majority, was all that there was to politics, the Democrats would have been in trouble. But temporary dissatisfactions, a series of political setbacks, or a particularly attractive candidate could hopefully cause short-term defections from one party to the other. In the presidential elections between 1840 and 1856, the average swing in the popular vote between succeeding elections had been 5.1 percent nationally (and 4.9 percent in the nonseceding states), figures which indicated that if all went well, there were grounds for Democratic optimism for the years ahead. It would be up to their leadership to harness the forces working for them and to find the way to overturn the domination of the Republicans. The importance that so many Northerners attached to the survival and success of the Democratic party assured that the effort would be made.

---

ment of the 1850s was "the politics of impatience," a reaction against the old parties, a general weakening of party loyalty and a revulsion against parties. This would seem to criticize my argument about the imperative of party loyalty in the era. Needless to say, I think Holt overemphasizes a partially valid point. Some people, no doubt, felt this way for a while, but, as in all realignments, only a comparatively few voters in the total electorate turned away from the Democrats, and when they finally settled in their loyalty to their new party, the Republicans, it was as deep and intense. See Michael Holt, "The Politics of Impatience: The Origins of Know-Nothingism," *Journal of American History* 60 (September 1973): 309–31.

53. *Nation,* July 2, 1868; *New York Tribune,* April 3, 1868. Although Republicans, as members of a very new party, obviously did not have the kind of traditional, persistent, and deep-rooted loyalty that Democrats did, most of them did feel another very important aspect of the same kind of emotions: a long-standing, intense, and vitriolic hostility to the Democratic party and a desire to defeat and keep down the Democracy if they could.

2
"Relight the Old Watch Fires":
The Democracy Finds Itself,
1860–1862

THE DEMOCRATIC COMMUNITY with its symbols and emotive memories still survived as the 1860s opened. And so did the Democracy's corpus of ideas and policies, its shared perspectives and common assumptions. But without unity and direction, forged by the party leadership, the mass of potential voters would remain a mass: imminent but powerless—especially if the divisions of the years 1857 to 1860 persisted into the era of changed and threatening status for the country and the Democracy. The task of the party leaders therefore was grueling, difficult, and confusing. The nominal national leaders of the party, President Buchanan, and the 1860 nominee, Stephen Douglas, were caught up in their own preoccupations, or continued to be objects of bitter antagonism. Although there were prominent Democrats in Congress and in state offices, no one stood out as someone around whom the party could rally. There was among party members, therefore, some flailing around, excessive rhetoric, and even hysteria. Much uncertainty was expressed. Occasionally, there were exclamations that party members seemed "terribly disorganized."[1]

Nevertheless, beyond the immediate organizational weaknesses and leadership problems, there was also a willingness to work together

1. Victor Hickox to Stephen A. Douglas, January 8, 1861, Stephen A. Douglas Papers, University of Chicago Library. Two studies cover Democratic party activities for part of the period discussed in this chapter. See Robert Johannsen, "The Douglas Democracy and the Crisis of Disunion," *Civil War History* 9 (September 1963): 229–47; John T. Hubbell, "The Northern Democracy and the Crisis of Disunion, 1860–1861" (Ph.D. diss., University of Illinois, 1969).

as Democrats always had and to respond to cues and directions as to what they should do. What ultimately triggered a reawakening of communal spirit and the desire to come back together were the fears for the future of the nation engendered by Republican ideals and their determination to put those ideals into practice. Conscious of their common values and common purpose, and the awesome danger to the country from the plans of their opponents, articulate Democrats determined to fall in behind their party to save the Union. "Democrats are waiting to hear the views of their leaders. . . . We are willing to follow them anywhere and back up their opinions and actions," was the way one hopeful party member put it in early January.[2]

In the year and a half after the presidential election, various Democratic leaders moved to confront the problem of their party's role. In all of their actions the Democratic leaders were sometimes forced by events and sometimes they were able to call the tune. Whatever confusion existed in their behavior came because this was a party defining its mission in the aftermath of a number of destructive trauma. But it quickly became clear that there was no extensive weakness here or grounds for thinking they would not come back. The Democrats were successful almost from the very beginning in finding their feet and reestablishing a role within the Union—or what was left of it. Their quick return to the political wars, even in the face of their stunning defeat in 1860 and all of their problems since the mid-1850s, underscores the strength of the partisan forces working for continuity in this era. The Democrats' fears of the policies of their opponents and the force of their own beliefs propelled them into almost automatic opposition to the Republicans. They knew no other way. As bent as their organization had been, their instinct was to engage in political conflict.

The Democrats' period of redefinition moved through three stages, although their actions and attitudes often crisscrossed the different periods, particularly after war broke out. In the first period, between the election and the outbreak of the war, they moved firmly to forestall the horrors of sectional politics. At the onset of war the Democrats confronted new uncertainty as to what should be their

2. George Converse to Samuel S. Cox, January 2, 1861, Samuel S. Cox Papers, Brown University Library, Providence, R.I.

policy toward the government. This confusion finally resolved itself in the third period in favor of fervent, persistent opposition to the Republican administration.

"Defeated But Not Conquered"

In the public arenas of politics in the winter of 1860–1861, extending to the firing on Fort Sumter, the actions of party spokesmen were generally clear and crisp, determined and well articulated. In these months the factionalism that had plagued the party since 1857 was played down as the party leaders sought desperately to bar the consequences of the Republicans' ideological commitments and behavior. They had four months to act resolutely before the Republicans ascended to office. "Defeated but not conquered," in Congressman Clement Vallandigham's words, they acted vigorously in that period to shape events.[3]

Democratic rhetoric in the secession crisis was a continuation of the common themes of party politics during the 1850s. They repeatedly asserted their unionism against the twin threats from abolitionists and secessionists. "The integrity of the country is the first great, absorbing issue," the editor of the *Detroit Free Press* summed up for all of them in December. "We are ready," he continued, "to act with any and every man of whatever party, faith or section, who is for the perpetuity of the Constitution and the Union." Their assault on the Republicans, "whose fanaticism" on the slavery question, they argued, "has precipitated the [present] misery upon us," was violent. Democrats believed, as Congressman Samuel Cox recalled five years later, that "there was a hope" that the South could be kept in the Union by appropriate congressional policies.[4] But they doubted if the Republicans were capable of preserving the Union. "The Republican leaders are utterly blind to all dangers," August Belmont complained at the end of 1860. "I do not believe that the party intends making any concessions."[5]

The real key to the problem, as the Democrats saw it, was the

3. *Congressional Globe*, 36 Cong., 2 sess., p. 38.
4. *Detroit Daily Free Press*, December 11, 1860. Cox's remark is in his *Eight Years in Congress, 1857–1865* (New York, 1865), p. 18.
5. August Belmont to Stephen A. Douglas, December 26, 1860, Douglas Papers. See also August Belmont to William Sprague, December 13, 1860, in August Belmont,

Republicans' extremist ideology and the party's resulting intransigence. The Republican party, they vigorously asserted, was bent on an ideological crusade, pressing "the conservative masses beyond endurance" in their determination to free the slaves and hurt the South. Republicans were willing to allow the Union to be dissolved into "an internecine war" for sordid partisan purposes. They wished to impose their own permanent rule on the truncated Union in order to inaugurate "old federalism, with more than [a] federalistic tendency to strong central government" and particularly to engraft antislavery policies on the new administration and the country. "Will the people stand this much longer? Will they consent to a dissolution of the Union to please the crazy fanatics who have managed this antislavery agitation? Will they make the negro their god, and give up their national greatness, their prosperity . . . everything . . . for the sake of worshipping according to the creed of Wendell Phillips?"[6]

To Democratic eyes, the Republicans seemed to think so. They had to be disabused. "This was not the time for the exhibition of party spirit." No political party "deserves the confidence of the American people whose leaders and members, preferring party to country, and the unity of their party organization to the Union of the States, will rush madly into civil war, fraternal strife and disunion, in preference to a fair and honorable compromise, founded upon such mutual concessions as are consistent with the rights of all the states and may be essential to the existence of the Federal Union." If only they "will forget their party schemes . . . for a day and imitate the patriotic example of the Democracy," the Union would be saved.[7]

Letters, Speeches and Addresses of August Belmont (New York, 1890), p. 32; W. B. Woods to S. S. Cox, January 12, 1861, Cox Papers; Henry D. Bacon to Samuel L. M. Barlow, January 17, 1861, Samuel L. M. Barlow Letters, Henry E. Huntington Library, San Marino, Ca.; *Detroit Free Press,* December 11, 1860; Concord *New Hampshire Patriot,* January 16, 1861.

6. Cox, *Eight Years in Congress,* p. 188; W. Neil to S. S. Cox, January 10, 1861, Cox Papers; Henry D. Bacon to S. L. M. Barlow, January 17, 1861, Barlow Papers, J. B. Colt to Thomas Hart Seymour, February 14, 1861, Thomas Hart Seymour Papers, Connecticut Historical Society, Hartford, Conn.; William B. Reed, "A Paper Containing a Statement and Vindication of Certain Political Opinion" (Philadelphia, 1862); *Illinois State Register,* February 15, 1861; *Daily Chicago Times,* in Howard C. Perkins, *Northern Editorials on Secession* (New York, 1942), 1: 429; *Providence Daily Post,* February 2, 1861, in ibid., p. 443; *New York Herald,* January 21, 1861.

7. *Illinois State Register,* January 17, 1861; *New Hampshire Patriot,* February 20, 1861, December 12, 1860.

Unfortunately, the Republicans met any attempts at a compromise or a settlement with nothing "but sneers and scepticism," Congressman Cox afterward recalled. The Republicans were not yet in power in the winter of 1860–1861, but their imminence gave them great influence on events. Unfortunately, as Cox saw it (not quite accurately), their actions drained "the cup of reconciliation dry" and left no alternative but disunion and war.[8] It was up to the Democrats, therefore, to take the initiative in this crisis and find a way to save the Union. Their aim was to act as a powerful pressure group by maintaining a position of critical opposition to the ideas they expected the Republicans to espouse in the Union's crisis. They did not believe that the Republicans, even though triumphant at the moment, could or would last long as a powerful force or even as a party. As one Democratic party newspaper had said during the campaign, such an idea was "simply absurd."[9]

Their point was to reassert the basic conservative unionism that party leaders had articulated throughout 1860, reaffirming their old principles, in an effort to find a means of compromise with the South. They believed that secession was unacceptable: they would not let any state depart from the Union. They attacked the Southern secessionists for their intransigence and failure to accept the possibility of compromise. At times, a few Democrats were even in favor of strong antisecession measures by the federal government. But, most of all, the Democrats worked to reassure the South. They circulated petitions, called state conventions to apply pressure, and began to prepare for forthcoming local and state elections to drive the Republicans from office. At the New York state convention in January 1861, the delegates declared their sole aim was "to assure the conservative men of the South that they have at least the sympathy of 312,000 electors of New York in the contest in which they are engaged, and to keep the border states in the Union, and thus ultimately to restore its integrity." Finally, the bulk of the Democracy came closer and closer to a clear policy of no-coercion.[10]

They particularly feared that the incoming administration would

8. Cox, *Eight Years in Congress,* pp. 29, 206.
9. Albany (N.Y.) *Atlas and Argus,* September 13, 1860; August Belmont to John W. Forsyth, December 19, 1860, in Belmont, *Letters,* p. 39.
10. *New Hampshire Patriot,* December 26, 1860; Thomas M. Cook and Thomas

use force against the seceding states, an action that would not restore the Union but would make matters far worse then they were. Obviously the government had "the right to use all the force it can command to prevent the disruption of the Union, to put down revolution and rebellion . . . but it is apparent to every intelligent mind that to attempt coercion in the present condition of affairs would be certain to make a bad matter worse; instead of preventing the secession of one or more states it would drive the whole South into open rebellion." In short, Douglas cried, "war is disunion, war is final, eternal separation." Therefore, if disunion becomes inevitable the Southern states would be allowed to go in peace. "Never," Cox said on the floor of the House, will Democrats "thrust Republican wrongs down the throats of the South at the point of a bayonet." There is no need to. "Let the cry of the democracy be, COMPROMISE OR PEACEABLE SEPARATION."[11]

Northern leaders should, therefore, not provoke the South by inflammatory actions or legislation. Rather they should demonstrate that the North was becoming moderate and conservative. Democratic state legislators introduced stronger fugitive slave bills, measures against armed expeditions into other states, and bills to give up slave stealers for trial—legislation, in other words, guaranteeing security for slave property. Isaac Toucey's suggested program for the Connecticut state Democratic convention was typical. "I think you will concur with me," he wrote, "in seconding every effort to elect a State ticket and legislature favourable to a repeal of our 'personal liberty law' so called, & a guarantee to the South of their rights by constitutional amendment securing to them the full benefit of the Dred Scott decision . . . & the Crittenden amendment."[12]

W. Knox, comps., *The Public Record of Horatio Seymour* (New York, 1868), p. 31 (hereafter, *Record of Seymour*). See also *Detroit Free Press*, January 30, 1861; August Belmont to Stephen A. Douglas, February 11, 1861, Douglas Papers.

11. "So far as I know, I believe all Democrats say peaceable secession rather than civil war." A. E. Rogers to S. S. Cox, February 26, 1861, Cox Papers. The quoted material is from *New Hampshire Patriot*, December 12, 1860; Frank L. Klement, *The Limits of Dissent: Clement L. Vallandigham and the Civil War* (Lexington, Ky., 1970), p. 66; Cox, *Eight Years in Congress*, pp. 206–7; *Congressional Globe*, 36 Cong., 2 sess., p. 1461; *Detroit Free Press*, January 30, 1861.

12. Isaac Toucey to Thomas H. Seymour, January 23, 1861, Seymour Papers; *New Hampshire Patriot*, December 12, 1860; William Dusinberre, *Civil War Issues in*

When the second session of the Thirty-sixth Congress met in December 1860, the floors of the House and the Senate became important public forums for the Northern and Border State Democrats. Throughout the winter they maintained their strong stance against the twin threats of secession and the incoming administration. Their rhetorical warfare was intense and continuous, along the lines already laid down in their campaign pamphlets, newspaper editorials, and public speeches. They were very active behind the scenes as well. Douglas worked to hammer out compromise proposals; others offered their own ideas in committee and on the floor. Ultimately, most Democrats threw their support behind Senator John J. Crittenden's series of constitutional amendments as the most effective means of restoring the Union. Crittenden designed his amendments to reassure the South by guaranteeing that no one could ever interfere with slavery in the states where it existed constitutionally, nor prevent its future expansion into the territories of the United States.[13]

As the Democratic editors wrote and Democratic legislators spoke their fears, party leaders were preparing for an unprecedented number of state party conventions to be held in early 1861 in most of the Northern states. They were unprecedented because they were being held out of season, even in states where no elections were coming up, and were actually serving as grand party rallies to maintain and further the Democratic offensive. The tenor of most of these meetings was the same as already had been expressed by the other Democratic spokesmen: their fear at the course of public events, the threats that the Republicans posed to the Union, and the need for a conservative policy in Washington.[14] Most critically for the Democrats as a party, the meetings also involved attempts to mold all factions of the party back together in the face of the crisis of the Union.

As one editor wrote, "in the face of this danger to the country" is

---

Philadelphia, 1856–1865 (Philadelphia, 1965), p. 104; *Illinois State Register,* December 21, 1860.

13. The activities of Douglas and other Democrats when Congress met are well recounted in Robert Johannsen, *Stephen A. Douglas* (New York, 1973), pp. 808–74.

14. The resolutions of the various state Democratic conventions are conveniently printed in *The American Annual Cyclopaedia and Register of Important Events of the Year 1861* (New York, 1862) (hereafter, *Appleton's Cyclopaedia*), under the various state headings.

there any Democrat "who will not exclaim, let all personal bickering cease, let all personal aspirations be merged in patriotism?" The New York and Ohio Democratic state conventions made a special point to note that all Democrats were invited and urged to attend irrespective of previous factional roles or positions. At the New York convention it was clear that those assembled wanted to keep all questions of previous internal party divisions off the floor in the interests of a united Democratic voice on the crisis of the Union because "our national difficulties are too great—and our obligation to apply to them a Democratic cure too binding to permit our disturbing ourselves about trifles." Contrary to all past Democratic experience in that most factious of states, all delegates present were admitted "without entering into or determining any question of regularity of organization or prejudicing thereby the decisions of any previous Democratic conventions as to questions of organization." Their attempts at unity succeeded and allowed them to complete their second purpose. The attack on the Republicans was continued, broadened, and intensified.[15]

Finally, the Democrats sought to make a series of spring elections referenda on the policies and positions of their opponents. The issue was "Peace or War, Union or Disunion. To vote the Democratic ticket is to vote for Peace and the Union; to vote the Republican ticket is to vote for Civil War and disunion." The results were encouraging. The party took four of the six congressional seats contested in Connecticut and Rhode Island away from the Republicans and made substantial gains in Pennsylvania's local elections as well. Everywhere they reduced Republican majorities.[16] In this first stage of the crisis of the Union, between their party's debacle in November 1860 and the early part of the new year before Lincoln's inauguration, the Democrats seemed well on their way to establishing the foundations for a vigorous political survival. The Democratic leadership had worked very hard to mark out a clear conservative position of strong and determined opposition to secession and the Republican party and in favor of

15. *New Hampshire Patriot*, December 12, 1860; *Proceedings of the Democratic State Convention Held in Albany, January 31, and February 1, 1861* (Albany, 1861), p. 5. See also *Congressional Globe*, 36 Cong., 2 sess., p. 821.

16. *New Hampshire Patriot*, March 6, 1861. The election results are in *New York Herald*, April 6, 1861.

peace and Union. Coupled with the enthusiasm of their followers, this well-orchestrated drive to push policies before the country had helped them to cover over many of the splits that had so confounded them during the events leading to the presidential election. One good may come from all these troubles, one Democrat wrote in January, "that some way may lead from them to the reconciliation of our divided democracy for the common cause for which we should all fight." And so they had. The unity and self-assurance of the Democratic party grew as the crisis deepened. As the situation developed, the party leaders were told that all elements in the party were in agreement to prevent disunion or coercion, and in favor of compromise. By May the newspapers were celebrating the party's unity in its great mission. "It was not only united, but all classes are looking up to it as the only party that can make successful war or secure honorable peace." Whatever organizational problems and leadership failings Northern Democrats had suffered in the late 1850s, there seemed to be few signs of them now as all party factions joined together in opposing the misdirections of the Republican leadership.[17]

Whether anyone consciously hammered out proposals for compromise among the warring factions, and then their reunion under the party banner, is doubtful. There is little evidence of it. More to the point, as the Democrats in the North faced the consequences of the rise of the Republicans, they began acting together in traditional fashion. They established themselves as a loud and articulate opposition to the looming threat even before the Republicans came to power. Of course, what made this possible was that, rhetorically and ideologically, they were continuing directions already well set out in their arguments and campaigns through the 1850s. Their attitude at this time was well expressed by Congressman William A. Richardson of Illinois, writing to Stephen A. Douglas at the end of November. "We are beaten but not conquered. . . . The great point now is to keep our ranks closed up and stand firmly by our guns . . . and we can do it since we are united upon the old issues dividing us from the

17. W. Neil to S. S. Cox, January 10, 1861, Cox Papers; *Atlas and Argus,* May 29, 1861. This is not to argue that the anger of the past was not still felt and often expressed. Many letters from this period in such collections as that of Thomas Hart Seymour attest that they still were.

Republicans."[18] In short, underneath the fragmentation of the late 1850s still remained a strong and cohesive hard core of shared values, attitudes, and memories. And all of that helped to reinvigorate the party. Between November 1860 and March 1861, the Democrats moved back together in the face of a common enemy and danger. The irony was that they then faced new challenges to their renewed unity.

"Sink the Partison in the Patriot"

Despite the violence of their dissent during the postelection period, when war broke out in April initial Democratic reaction was similar to that of other Northerners: profound shock, and an intense determination to put down the rebellion. They had not changed their minds about the Republican responsibility for the war, but all that now had to be put aside. "I am with you in this contest," Fernando Wood said, "I know no party now." It was "our country right or wrong." War had come, and "the government under which our lot is cast must be maintained and vindicated. . . . It is the position of patriotism and the ground of reason." After the war was over we can "settle the account with the sectionalist fanatics and demogogues [i.e., Republicans] who have put the country in peril."[19]

Stephen A. Douglas expressed this unreserved policy and attitude clearly and strongly. As early as December 1860, he made it quite plain that he was ready "to make any reasonable sacrifice of party tenets to save the country." He worked assiduously in the following months to promote harmony between his defeated party and the new government. After war erupted, he was quoted as favoring the immediate hanging of Southern sympathizers in the District of Columbia unless they repented their treason; and he pled to his party in his last speech to help rescue the country first and think about partisan differences later.[20]

18. William A. Richardson to Stephen A. Douglas, November 27, 1860, Douglas Papers.

19. Wood's comment is quoted in DeAlva S. Alexander, *A Political History of the State of New York* (New York, 1909), 3:6. See also *New Hampshire Patriot*, April 24, 1861; *Atlas and Argus*, April 19, 1861.

20. Stephen A. Douglas to August Belmont, December 25, 1860, in *The Letters of Stephen A. Douglas*, ed. Robert Johannsen (Champaign, Ill., 1961), p. 505 (hereafter, *Douglas Letters*).

Other Democrats responded similarly in the first flush of the war and for some time afterward. Signs of acquiescence came from Democratic editors and party leaders ranging from Caleb Cushing and the *Boston Post,* whose editor cried "DROP POLITICS," to Andrew Johnson, Daniel Dickinson, James Buchanan, and George Pendleton. "Many [Democrats] fear," the *Detroit Free Press* noted in October 1861, "that in sustaining the administration in carrying on the war they are thereby sustaining republican principles and abandoning their democratic platform. On this point they should be disabused." We are fighting, the editor continued, "to uphold the Union first." There will be plenty of time for the return of partisan politics once the war is over. Democratic congressmen made it clear that to further such ends they would vote for all troops and supplies needed "to enable the Government to maintain its honor and dignity." Although occasional disclaimers were sometimes heard, indicative of later developments, the general thrust of Democratic reaction was willingness to forgo partisanship at this moment in order to allow the war to be won by a united country.[21]

The pro-Union, pro-war, reactions of the Democrats surprised Republicans. But they quickly seized the opportunity to push the Democrats into a most troublesome political period. Republican spokesmen began calling for what they called no-partyism—the suspension of all partisan activities in the face of the danger to the Union, in order, they said, to present a united Northern front against the threat facing all of them. All Northerners had to "sink the partisan in the patriot." For "the purposes of the war the Administration party . . . really becomes the nation."[22] There can only be two parties, that of the union and one that supports the rebels: "in the

21. This acquiescence by the Democrats runs through their correspondence, newspapers and in the *Congressional Globe.* See, for example, ibid., 37 Cong., 1 sess. pp. 94, 95; Daniel S. Dickinson to J. C. Spencer, May 7, 1861, in *Speeches, Correspondence, Etc. of the Late Daniel S. Dickinson of New York,* ed. John R. Dickinson (New York, 1867), 2: 550–51. The "drop politics" remark is in the *Boston Post,* August 6, 1862. The *Free Press*'s comment is in issue of October 15, 1861. See also *Cincinnati Daily Enquirer,* April 18, June 10, 1861; *Indiana State Sentinel,* May 10, 1861.

22. Albert G. Riddle, *Recollections of Wartime, 1860–1865* (New York, 1895), p. 164; William Claflin to Joseph Holt, October 20, 1862, Joseph Holt Papers, Library of Congress.

presence of this tremendous issue [of preserving the Union] all the paltry divisions, distinctions, quibbles, claptrap and moonshine of our political parties sink into insignificance and public contempt.'' In the place of the old and now discredited party organizations stands instead ''a general rally'' in support of the administration and of fighting the war.[23]

The Lincoln administration did its part to further nonpartisan cooperation with the Democrats. Lincoln appointed a number of prominent Democrats to office, including, in early 1862, Buchanan's last attorney general, Edwin M. Stanton. Despite some fears that Stanton would not get along with his new colleagues, the appointment of ''a consistent Democrat'' to this major agency of war direction was a great triumph for a policy of nonpartisan cooperation.[24] There were other signs of cooperation as well. In Pennsylvania's Twelfth Congressional District in 1861, in a race to fill a vacancy, the Republicans supported the Democratic candidate on a platform advocating the Constitution and the enforcement of the laws. In many places, Democratic local and state conventions, the supreme policy-articulating and electoral-organizing units of the party, stopped meeting throughout 1861 and into early 1862, even on such sacred party days as the eighth of January, the anniversary of Andrew Jackson's victory at New Orleans. When conventions did meet, some of them refused to make any nominations.[25]

A second phase of the no-party movement opened when the Republicans began to promote the organization of a Union party to channel all men, regardless of previous party membership, into a single political movement. By early 1862 the idea was well advanced in some states and was earnestly supported by many individual Demo-

23. *New York Tribune,* September 11, 1861; *Albany* (N.Y.) *Evening Journal,* August 10, 1861; *New York Herald,* October 9, March 27, 1862. In New York and Vermont, among other states, the Republican state Committees asked their Democratic counterparts to lay aside designations and unite in common electoral tickets. See *New York Tribune,* August 10, 1861.

24. *Boston Post,* January 18, 1862. The Democrats' happy reactions to Stanton's appointment can be seen in Samuel Medary and J. H. Smith to E. M. Stanton, January 14, 1862 and H. H. Leavitt to Stanton, January 16, 1862, Edwin McMaster Stanton Papers, Library of Congress.

25. The organizational inactivity of the Democrats during the first year of the war was well covered in the many party newspapers so far cited.

crats. Daniel Dickinson, for many of the antebellum years the epitome of the regular organization Democrat and, after Douglas's death, perhaps the most outspokenly nonpartisan of all Democratic Unionists, told a ratification meeting that "this Union movement is popular and not partisan. It commends itself to every loyal citizen, and all loyal men should enter it heart and soul." No single party, he pointed out, could vindicate the Constitution and nation—only a union of all parties could undertake the job. Until the rebellion ended the Democrats and Republicans together had "to suspend all party action" except through the Union organization.[26] Traditional partisanship indeed seemed dead.

The Republican tactic, whatever its other virtues and purposes, was a shrewd political move. It created critical problems for the Democratic party. Obviously, if its leaders accepted the no-party stance they were paralyzed as an electoral organization. They could not undertake actions designed to regain power until the end of the war. A few Democrats, therefore, from the first, were hesitant about the push for nonpartisanship and there was internal party sniping over the question. "The support of many so-called democrats" for the Republican administration, Senator James Bayard charged, was "the folly of petty men" and "a false position." How can we, another asked, form a union with "these Northern traitors," or allow ourselves "to be swallowed up by the Republicans"? It is clear enough that while many Democrats had accepted the need for no-partyism, others held back. After a visit to downstate Illinois in April 1861, Douglas wrote to Lincoln, "I found the state of feeling here [among Democrats] and in some parts of our state much less satisfactory than I could have desired."[27] This remained true among pockets of Democrats everywhere in the North throughout 1861 and early 1862. Obvi-

26. Reprinted in Dickinson, *Speeches*, 2: 200, 215. See also *Proceedings of the Convention of Loyal Leagues Held at Mechanics Hall, Utica, Tuesday, 26 May, 1863* (New York, 1863); B. F. Hallett to C. G. Greene, September 11, 1861, in *New York Tribune*, September 15, 1861.

27. James A. Bayard to Thomas F. Bayard, July 7, 1861, Thomas F. Bayard Papers, Library of Congress; Columbus (Ohio) *Crisis*, July 18, 1861; W. L. Dewart to Hedrick B. Wright, September 26, 1861, quoted in Stanton L. Davis, *Pennsylvania Politics, 1860–1863* (Cleveland, 1935), p. 202n; Stephen A. Douglas to Abraham Lincoln, April 29, 1861, in Johannsen, *Douglas Letters*, p. 511.

ously, the power of traditional partisanship remained very much in evidence.

There were also conditions to the Democratic acceptance of bipartisanship that did not seem important at first. A number of Democrats made it clear that no-partyism in no way meant that they supported the Republican party and its policies. Further, there could be no change in the purpose of the war, i.e., solely to restore the Union. Nor would they abandon their party organization for the Union party, even as they supported the government. We can best promote our country's interests, Horatio Seymour argued, "by preserving our time-honored organization. It has been so closely identified with the history and progress of our country, that its dissolution would seem like the severance of the last bond which holds our country together." Our own opponents would look upon the "dispersion of this ancient party, identified as it is with the growth, greatness and glory of our land" as a calamity. "Did not a shadow fall upon our country when it was torn apart at Charleston; and do not men of all parties point to its disruption as one of the causes of this unnatural war?"[28] Furthermore, the success of the Democracy will encourage Southern unionists, "the dissolution of the Democratic party would discourage them." Opposition parties were also very necessary as bulwarks of freedom, for without them "they would cease to be protections against abuses of power or the inroads of corruption."[29]

Finally, there was also a strong policy component in Democratic objections to union. To support the Republican attempts to bring Democrats into the Union organizations would be to "commit the Democratic party . . . to measures of policy which . . . are highly objectionable" to them. Nor, while believing in a vigorous prosecu-

28. B. F. Potts to S. S. Cox, June 30, 1861, Cox Papers; *Record of Seymour*, pp. 41, 50.

29. "Parties are essential to the just and economical administration of the Government. . . . Parties exercise a beneficial influence in various ways. They serve to elevate good and able men to office. They curb extravagance and corruption. . . . There was a law at Athens which subjected every citizen to punishment who did not take sides in the parties which divided the Republic. This law was founded in the deepest wisdom." *York* (Pa.) *Democratic Press*, February 21, 1862. The "dissolution of the democratic party" quote is in Seymour's speech at Utica Ratification meeting, October 28, 1861, in *Record of Seymour*, p. 42. The final quote is from his acceptance speech, September 10, 1862, in ibid, p. 50.

tion of the war, could they support the mismanagement of the war effort. They could not "endorse" the "blunders, incompetence and dishonesty of the republican officials." So, then "why disband?" Parties break up "when the objects for which they were organized have been accomplished." This has not yet happened. "The mission of the Democratic party has not been fulfilled. It has still the Constitution to protect and the Union to restore." We are "of the opinion that no alternative remains but to make a bold, inflexible, fight in all quarters. Everywhere to organize and [to] wage the war on the invincible strength and right of our principles. . . . If we do not succeed in this way we are doomed to failure."[30]

This feeling of political militancy on the part of many Democrats can be seen in their reaction to Senator Douglas's course of action in the Union crisis. At first, his response was similar to that of most Democrats, a fear of the excesses and commitments of the Republicans and an attempt to establish clearly the Democratic party as the party of national preservation. His strong commitment to the Union was always tempered by warnings to the Republicans that support for the Union in this crisis was not support for Republican principles. He wrote to one group of Southern citizens early in the crisis that "no man in America regrets the election of Mr. Lincoln more than I do." And he followed this up by drawing a line of opposition as clear as anyone's against Republican extremism. He told Lincoln in a meeting in Washington in late February that he would oppose the administration's political measures even as he defended their pro-Union policies.[31]

But for Douglas, the problem quickly centered on the Republicans' refusal to back down from their position against any further expansion of slavery into the territories. As Robert Johannsen has

---

30. *Detroit Free Press,* August 10, 16, 1861; *New York Herald,* August 7, 1861; *Atlas and Argus,* August 9, December 12, 1861; Isaac Henry to Franklin Pierce, July 20, 1861, Franklin Pierce Papers, Library of Congress. The response of state chairman Dean Richmond in August 1861 to the Republicans' invitation to form a joint ticket sums up this Democratic attitude very well: "We would be false to the party which we represent if we considered any proposition of union with former political opponents, except on the basis of principle." Quoted in the *New York Tribune,* August 9, 1861.

31. Stephen A. Douglas to Ninety-Six New Orleans citizens, November 13, 1860, in Johannsen, *Douglas Letters,* p. 499. The remarks to Lincoln are reported in Johannsen, *Stephen A. Douglas,* p. 842.

perceptively written, Douglas then "quickly recognized that the restoration of the Union could only be achieved at the cost of [his] party principle."[32] With the outbteak of war, he not only fully accepted the need to pursue a policy of no-partyism, but went much further in his postinaugural embracing of the Lincoln administration. From then on he was in trouble with many Democrats "on account of the great love that the Republicans profess now to have for him." Both "Senators Pugh and Douglas have . . . went too far," was the way one intense, if ungrammatical, party member put it in early January.[33] Douglas tried to make his position clear and to warn other Democrats of the dangers they faced if they were not careful. "It seems that some of my friends," he wrote, "are unable to comprehend the difference between arguments used in favor of an equitable compromise, with hope of averting the horrors of war, and those urged in support of the Government and flag of our country, when war is being waged against the United States with the avowed purpose of producing a permanent disruption of the Union. . . . It was not a party question, nor a question involving partisan policy; it was a question of Government or no Government, country or no country. . . . I am neither the supporter of the partisan policy nor the apologist for the errors of the Administration. My previous relations to them remain unchanged; but I trust the time will never come when I shall not be willing to make any needful sacrifice of personal feeling and party policy for the honor and integrity of my country. . . . If we hope to regain and perpetuate the ascendency of our party, we should never forget that a man cannot be a true Democrat unless he is a loyal patriot."[34]

Douglas provided insight into his course when he reported on a conversation he had had with Lincoln. He spoke to the president, he said, "of the present and the future, without reference to the past." But that was exactly where the problem lay. The masses of loyal Democrats could not readily forget that past and therefore found it very difficult throughout the crisis to support the Lincoln administration. Ideologically and emotionally, Lincoln and his supporters were

32. Johannsen, "Douglas Democracy," p. 233.

33. Virgil Hickox to J. Madison Cutts, May 13, 1861, in Johannsen, *Douglas Letters,* p. 514n; Joseph Burns to S. S. Cox, January 8, 1861, Cox Papers.

34. Stephen A. Douglas to Virgil Hickox, May 10, 1861, copy in *Appleton's Cyclopaedia, 1861,* p. 281.

their enemies. As one of Douglas's political friends wrote, "the democrats here have been educated by reading his [Douglas's] speeches to believe that Mr. Lincoln has no constitutional right to pursue his present course."[35] Such Democrats, therefore, were not ready to perceive the Republican administration as anything more than the extremist, fanatical, partisan threat they had said it was. The question is not the correctness of Douglas's unionist policy or the shortsightedness or narrow-mindedness of other Democrats in the face of new or changed conditions, but rather the powerful influence of the ideologies, the traditions, and the perspectives of the political culture into which these people had been born and grew up. Despite the crisis of the Union and the rhetorical obedience to nonpartisanship that followed, the American political culture in the nineteenth century had taught a much different lesson from the one Douglas now articulated. The anger and suspicion between the contending parties left little room for common causes even when reasons for them existed. This partisan imperative was working strongly on the Democrats as well as on the Republicans in 1861 and 1862. After a long history of bitter party strife, it was natural for many in both parties often to think in terms of partisan advantage despite superficial agreement that national needs outweighed such narrowness.

In such an atmosphere, a series of irritations only exacerbated matters. Everything from patronage to particular policies of the administration increased the natural distrust between the two parties. As one observer put it, "anxiety, distrust and revenge still hold universal sway among the politicians on all sides."[36] In Ohio in 1861, the Republicans redistricted the congressional districts of the state —adversely for the Democrats as the latter saw it. In Michigan, Republicans played on alleged conspiracies between local Democrats and Southerners in the interest of winning partisan advantage early in the war. The Republicans' attempts to pass, under the cover of war necessity, financial and tariff legislation which adhered to their own party's position was considered unfair, too. In early 1862 the Republican-controlled United States Senate expelled Democrat Jesse

35. Douglas's comment is in Johannsen, *Douglas Letters*, p. 510; Virgil Hickox to J. Madison Cutts, May 13, 1861, in ibid, p. 514n.
36. *New York Herald*, 13 October 1861.

Bright of Indiana for what appeared to be only sordid political reasons. Delaware's Senator Bayard summed up the Democrats' anger at this, as well as the more general condition of affairs, when he charged that "the spirit of party, always remorseless and unreasoning" had added "but another victim" in Senator Bright "to the many who in past time have been sacrificed at the shrine of party."[37]

All of the actions of the Republican party, one Democratic paper summed up in early 1862, "evince the strong tenacity with which they cling to their party. Their leading journals are as unscrupulous in their attacks upon the Democracy as they have ever been. Where they have the power they exercise it with an iron hand. Have they an important officer to elect they are extremely careful to select him from their own ranks. In our halls of Congress they exhibit a domineering spirit unworthy [of] the dignity of the place. . . . Do these facts manifest a conciliatory, a self-sacrificing spirit, on the part of the Republican party? . . . Their very actions prove the insincerity of their teaching." There has been an "extraordinary outbreak of partisan bitterness and . . . spite." They say that " 'there is no party.' It seems to us there is a party, not representing the people, but unfortunately possessed of power, a party made up of fragments of factions, each having some traditional injury to avert at the hands of the Democracy. . . . They not only hate the Democracy, whom they proscribe and insult; but they make war upon their principles and obliterate . . . every measure with which they were identified."[38]

The trouble was, as E. M. Stanton noted early in the war (and before he entered Lincoln's cabinet), that "no sooner had the appearance of imminent danger passed away, and the [Republican] administration recovered from its panic, than a determination became manifest [among its leaders] to give a strict party direction to the great national movement." Since the "patriotic attempt" of the Democrats

37. *Congressional Globe,* 37 Cong., 2 sess., p. 651; David Lindsey, *"Sunset" Cox, Irrepressible Democrat* (Detroit, 1959), p. 65; Frank L. Klement, "The Hopkins Hoax and Golden Circle Rumors in Michigan, 1861–1862," *Michigan History* 47 (March 1963): 1–14. Other examples of these tensions are in Virgil Hickox to J. M. Cutts, May 13, 1861, in Johannsen, *Douglas Letters,* p. 514n; James A. Bayard to Thomas F. Bayard, July 7, August 31, 1861, Bayard Papers.

38. *York (Pa.) Democratic Press,* February 21, 1862; *Illinois State Register,* February 25, 1862; *Atlas and Argus,* August 3, 1861.

"to mollify the bitterness of party differences had been defeated —spurned"—henceforth, the two parties "must be as distinct as oil and water—as far apart as earth and sun."[39] In consequence, the Democrats retained their party organization and ran separate election tickets in most states, particularly where they remained strongly competitive. Only in one or two places, such as in Massachusetts where the Democrats were pitifully weak, did they join anti-Republican "conservative" or Union parties. There were election contests in all of the states in 1861, albeit in a variety of party combinations. There were Union parties, straight fights between Democrats and Republicans, three-cornered fights among War Democrats, other Democrats, and the Republicans. But, perhaps most important, in every state there was political competition.[40]

Still, despite the rebirth of the partisan imperative, this period was a difficult one for the Democracy. For well over a year after the war's outbreak no-partyism had been thoroughly drummed into the consciousness of all Americans. As a result there continued to be hesitation in Democratic ranks. Not all Democrats perceived the partisan necessity at the same time or with the same intensity. Some, such as Senator Bayard or Congressman Clement L. Vallandigham of Ohio, were ready almost from the beginning to adopt an opposition stance. Others entirely ignored all of the irritations, anger, and working of traditional influences in their commitment to the Union and resolution not to be drawn into politics. A number of others were irritated by the administration's policies and felt the tugs of partisan commitment, but held back in fear of the inappropriateness or the consequences of premature political activity. The role of the opposition party in a period of intense, war-induced patriotism was filled with dangerous pitfalls. The Republicans were quick to meet renewed partisan ac-

39. E. M. Stanton to James Buchanan, June 8, 1861, in *The Works of James Buchanan*, ed. John Basset Moore (Philadelphia, 1910), 11: 203. Columbus (Ohio) *Crisis*, in *Chicago Times*, November 21, 1861.

40. The contests and results of the elections of 1861 are reported in *Appleton's Cyclopaedia, 1862*, under each state's entry. Useful introductions to the developing Democratic opposition and its resulting expression are in William G. Carleton, "Civil War Dissidence in the North: The Perspective of a Century," *South Atlantic Quarterly* 66 (Summer 1967); 390–402; and Leonard P. Curry, "Congressional Democrats: 1861–1863," *Civil War History* 12 (September 1966): 213–29.

tivities with ever-stronger suggestions that the Democrats were disloyal and deserting the Union. "Sectionalism is the strongest passion and the controlling power in the Northern states today," ex-President Pierce wrote, and the Democrats could well suffer because of it.[41] After the clarity of their role during the postelection secession crisis, all of those cross currents caused much uncertainty and many unhappy moments among the Democrats.

"The Natural and Only Government"

If there was anything that was needed to clear their minds and enable them to proceed along the road to opposition, the actions of the government provided it. The Republicans, during the war, made themselves even more obnoxious, in the Democrats' view, than they already were. From the beginning of hostilities, the bulk of the Democratic party had argued that the conflict should be allowed to have only limited impact on American society and that the sole reason for fighting, therefore, was to restore the Union, nothing more. They would support the war with all their means to that point. They would never accept the dismemberment of the Republic.[42] On the other hand, given the nature of war as a revolutionary force, the makeup of the Republican party, and their natural suspicion of the latter, Democratic leaders before too long became convinced that they had to go into opposition—not to the war, but to the way the administration seemed to be broadening its scope and purpose. The trouble with the Republicans, Horatio Seymour charged, is that "one wing . . . is conservative and patriotic, the other is violent and revolutionary." Before very long after March 1861, Democrats saw abolitionists in the ascendency, setting the war policies of the government and successfully perverting the war's aims. They were "getting wild on everything." Whatever Lincoln had started out to do, some Democrats charged, by 1862 the war had become "an abolition

41. Franklin Pierce to John H. Steele, March 21, 1862, Pierce Papers.
42. "The Democratic party will never consent," Congressman Samuel S. Cox said in 1862, "under any set of circumstances to the mutilation or dismemberment of this Republic. That is the gospel." *Congressional Globe*, 37 Cong., 2 sess., p. 78. See also, *Illinois State Register*, September 10, 1861, among many other assertions of this point of view.

war—a war for general emancipation." Some of the intelligence the Democratic leaders were getting from within the government only confirmed the fears and suspicions of all but the most hardened nonpartisan. "No one here talks conservatism any longer," Samuel Barlow was told, "or speaks of the old Constitution or of anything but a renewed and desperate raid for subjection of the rebels."[43]

More than assumptions, conjectures, and rumors underlay the Democratic fears, however. They saw in the legislation of the Thirty-seventh Congress a prime example of what the Republicans were up to. Their emancipation laws for the District of Columbia and legislation to confiscate the property of Southerners in rebellion clearly set the tone for what was to follow. The Democrats protested mightily in debate. As Congressman Cox charged, they had to. "This Congress which ought to be engaged in putting down this armed rebellion, has striven to circumvent the plans of the President, by its immature and vindicative bills of confiscation." Its "ill-timed and ill-advised legislation on slavery" only "throws the apple of discord among us."[44]

Unfortunately for their view of propriety, Democrats in the Thirty-seventh Congress could exercise little more than rhetorical muscle. They stood together against the usurpations on behalf of their traditions and conservative commitment. Party unity and divisions between parties in the roll-call voting continued to be, as it had been so often before the war, an important fact of congressional life.[45] But the

43. Seymour's comment was in a speech at a Democratic meeting in Utica, New York, on October 28, 1861. See *Record of Seymour*, p. 41; H. B. Whitney to T. H. Seymour, March 8, 1862, Thomas H. Seymour Papers; *Address of the New Jersey Democratic State Central Committee to the voters of the state, October, 1862* (Trenton, 1862), pp. 4–5; T. J. Barnett to S. L. M. Barlow, October 6, 1862, Barlow Papers. Barnett was a Republican and a member of the government in Washington who kept in touch with Barlow.

44. Cox, *Eight Years in Congress*, p. 258; H. B. Whiting to Thomas H. Seymour, September 29, 1862, Thomas Seymour Papers.

45. There were differences among Democrats on some of the legislation they confronted. But whatever shadings of conservatism they demonstrated in their behavior, Democrats, most of the time, voted in polar-opposite position from their opponents. See Curry, "Congressional Democrats"; and his *Blueprint For Modern America: Nonmilitary Legislation of the First Civil War Congress* (Nashville, 1968). There is additional insight into the behavior of the Democrats in Congress in Allan G. Bogue, "Bloc and Party in the United States Senate, 1861–1863," *Civil War History* 13 (September 1967): 221–41.

Democrats never held enough seats to block their opponents. In the Senate there were fourteen of them and thirty-one Republicans at the opening of Congress in mid-1861. In the House, Democrats held 44 seats to the Republicans' 106.[46] Given such margins, the Republican-dominated House and Senate, while often irritated, could and did ignore Democratic protests. The result was the enactment of the Republican program with all of its dangers, as the Democrats saw the world, to the republic.[47]

Lincoln's issuance of the Emancipation Proclamation in September 1862 continued the process. Its audacity removed "the scales from the eyes of those stupid thick-headed persons who persisted in thinking that the President was a conservative man and that the war was for the restoration of the Union under the Constitution." Nevertheless, to Democrats, the president's action was only the culmination of a process in which the Republicans had changed the rules and broadened the war's scope. They were, by then, pushing through measures "which no one dared to urge eighteen months since." All of this despite the fact that, as one Democratic editor saw it, "the evil in our system was not slavery, but unwarranted meddlesome attacks upon slavery." The only true policy for the American government, another wrote, was "the Constitution as it is, the Union as it was, and the Negroes where they are."[48]

At the same time that the Republican party had entered into a policy of abolition, Democrats believed that it had also begun to destroy the liberties of the Northern people. Throughout the war Democratic spokesmen repeatedly harped on the corruption of the political process and the suppression of individual liberties throughout the Union. The situation in the Border states where, in the name of national security military occupation and restrictions on individual rights had become a persistent fact of life, particularly troubled them.

46. There were three senators and twenty-eight representatives listed as Unionists. Most of these were former Whigs from the Border States. So few were their numbers that House Democrats made no official caucus nomination for speaker.

47. Both Bogue and Curry point out in their research that one result of Democratic impotence in Congress was their high degree of absenteeism in the face of the Republican onslaught.

48. *Record of Seymour*, p. 55; *Detroit Free Press,* January 9, 1863; Charles Ray Wilson, "The *Cincinnati Daily Enquirer* and Civil War Politics: A Study in 'Copperhead Opinion' " (Ph.D. diss., University of Chicago, 1934), p. 8.

But elsewhere, too, there were many oppressive acts designed to erode American liberties. Franklin Pierce discerned federal agents spying on him wherever he went, in furtherance of their "reign of terror." The actions of individual Union generals in suppressing newspapers and Democratic speakers also "put a gag into the mouths of the people." Every action of the government "has been a glaring usurpation of power, and a palpable and dangerous violation of that very Constitution which this Civil War is professedly waged to support." But, again, their opposition was in vain given their numerical weakness. They could only look on in dismay at "the drift of the Republicans," which was, the editor of the Albany (N.Y.) *Atlas and Argus* summed up, to subvert the Constitution by "perpetuating a bloody war, not to sustain, but to overthrow it."[49]

The Republicans had chosen to promote partisan ends by subduing Democrats and uplifting Negroes, all in the interest of revolutionizing society. This could not be allowed. The Democratic party had cooperated with the administration in good spirit to save the country. But the Republicans' behavior and demands "made political unity . . . an utter impossibility." You had, Representative Cox reminded the Republican congressmen in late 1862, "and would yet have, the whole conservative force in a war to overthrow the organization of the Southern confederacy." All of the North was "united on that," Cox continued. "But you were determined to divide the North," and have, by "culpable and treacherous divergence from the plain path marked out by the Crittenden resolution." Republicans were "determined to make this a war against populations, against civilized usage . . . [and thus] to defeat the cause of the nation, by making the old Union impossible." The North, national committee chairman Belmont warned at the same time, "was and still is ready to fight for the union and the Constitution, but it is not ready to initiate a war of extermination."[50]

49. Franklin Pierce to Sidney Webster, April 21, 1861, Pierce-Webster Letters, Library of Congress; *Detroit Free Press,* May 15, 1863; *The Record of Hon. C. L. Vallandigham on Abolition, the Union, and the Civil War* (Columbus, Ohio, 1863), p. 102; *Atlas and Argus,* August 13, 1861.

50. New York *World,* January 20, 28, 1863; *Detroit Free Press,* August 16, 1863; *Boston Post,* September 20, 1862; Cox, *Eight Years in Congress,* p. 274; August Belmont, *A Few Letters and Speeches of the Late Civil War* (New York, 1870), p. 105.

The Democrats had to act, therefore, in a restorative mission. The time had come for the party to enter the lists forthrightly and clearly. You are "spending your blood and substance," the editor of the *Illinois State Register* summed up for its Democratic readers, "to crush one class of vipers, let us be on our guard that in ridding ourselves of these that we do not tamely fall into the hands and be put under the control of another pest, who abhor the Constitution and its guarantees. . . ." It was "as important to subdue the abolition element in Congress to bring about a reconciliation of our unfortunate difficulties" as it was "to conquer the notorious Jeff Davis and his followers." Therefore, Democrats would use "the freeman's legitimate weapon, the ballot" to change "the administration of the government" and return the country "to peace, prosperity and Union."[51]

The commitment to renewed political warfare, never far below the surface of Democrats' thoughts, now flowered as much as the most committed could wish. "We do not claim more virtue or intelligence than we award to our opponents," Seymour argued, "but we now have the sad and bloody proof that we act upon sounder principles of government." The Democratic party, in the words of the old party wheelhorse John L. O'Sullivan, was "the natural and only possible government of our Democratic confederation." A year of Republican rule had proven this. The time had come to move, to reorganize Democratic forces, to "RELIGHT THE OLD WATCH FIRES—NOMINATE STRAIGHT TICKETS—STAND OR FALL BY THE DEMOCRATIC ORGANIZATION."[52]

In late 1861 and early 1862, there had been a number of gingerly attempts to bring Democrats, former Whigs, and Border State Unionists into alignment under some kind of nonpartisan conservative umbrella. In Congress, following the leadership of the former Whig John J. Crittenden, Democrats attended several organizational meetings along with the self-styled Unionists from the Border. But little came of these since at the same time Democratic leaders began

51. *Record of Seymour*, p. 33; *Illinois State Register*, May 3, 20, 1862; *York (Pa.) Democratic Press*, September 19, 1862; Edward G. Ryan, *Address to the People by the Democracy of Wisconsin* . . . (Milwaukee, 1862), p. 8.

52. *Record of Seymour*, p. 58; John L. O'Sullivan to Samuel J. Tilden, May 6, 1861, in *Letters and Literary Memorials of Samuel J. Tilden*, ed. John Bigelow (New York, 1908), 1: 159; Columbus (Ohio) *Crisis*, in *Chicago Times*, November 21, 1861.

themselves moving in a different way to reorganize their party. Bland unionism and conservatism was not good enough for many Democrats in early 1862. The work of a number of congressional Democrats provided a focus and a stimulant to move into clear opposition. The move was led in the first instance by Vallandigham of Ohio, already emerging as a major critic of Republican war policies and one of those who had, since the war began, been hostile to the idea of no-partyism and concerned about where this would leave the Democrats. Vallandigham had tried to call together Democratic congressmen several times since the beginning of the war to consider a partisan stance. Some meetings had taken place. But all were abortive as many of the Democrats continued to hesitate about just what their role should be. As Vallandigham himself wrote, ''the Democratic party was not dead: it only slept. . . . Yet it is amazing that our people . . . should have submitted to usurpation and despotism which would have roused Greece even to resistance after two thousand years of servitude.'' Now this was about to change, the party was ''now stirring itself.''[53] A new move bore fruit.

Vallandigham asked the Democratic congressmen to meet in March 1862 in the Capitol. He sent out preliminary letters to Democrats in the various states urging them to support his call. When the meeting was finally held, agreement was won to issue, in the style of the time, an ''Address to the People,'' particularly the Democratic faithful, urging them to political action. The bulk of the Address was an arraignment, first, of administration policies which were destroying the Union and, second, of the easy assumption that the Democratic party should be disbanded in order for the war to be carried on more effectively. Democrats recognized the need to support the government ''in all constitutional necessity, and proper efforts to maintain its safety, integrity and constitutional authority.'' But that is not what was being asked of Democrats. They were being asked ''to give up your principles, your policy, and your party, and to stand by the

53. Crittenden's activities can be followed in Albert Kirwan, *John J. Crittenden: The Struggle for the Union* (Lexington, Ky., 1962); James Garfield Randall, *Lincoln the President: Springfield to Gettysburg* (New York, 1945), 2: 219; J. F. Robinson to John J. Crittenden, February 6, 1862, John C. Ham to Crittenden, May 12, 1862, John Nollen to Crittenden, May 20, 1862, all in John Jordan Crittenden Papers, Library of Congress; Clement L. Vallandigham to Franklin Pierce, April 11, 1862, Pierce Papers.

Administration in all its acts." This they could never do, particularly for the sake of the country. The Democratic party

is the only party capable of carrying on a war; it is the only party that has ever conducted a war to a successful issue, and the only party which has done it without abuse of power, without molestation to the rights of any class of citizens, and with due regard to economy. . . . If success, then, in a military point of view be required, the Democratic party alone can command it.[54]

A milestone along a path already well marked and increasingly trodden, the Address dramatically signalled the formal revival of partisanship by a major group of national Democratic leaders and intensified interest in building up the tactical plans necessary for party victory and the consequent preservation of cherished principles and values.[55]

"This is Not the Time to Reorganize the Democratic Party"

In the same letter to Stephen A. Douglas quoted earlier, Congressman William Richardson warned that the Democrats should stick to old issues, since on those they were united, but "should present as few new points as possible for fear that our friends will divide upon the new ones."[56] Ironically, the result of the revived partisan feeling among many Democrats was as Richardson had predicted. Some good partisan Democrats with long traditions of party devotion, loyalty, and service, men such as Andrew Johnson, David Tod, John McClernand, John A. Dix, John Cochrane, and Daniel Dickinson, were deeply disturbed by the partisan revival and challenged the wisdom and necessity of it, no matter what the provocation. Longtime fervent nationalists, they were militant in defense of the Union and the war. And, most important for the party, they were equally militant against any vestige of normal politics during the crisis of the Union. The war is "a question too great for party," Dickinson warned, "let no

---

54. "Address of Democratic Members of the House of Representatives of the United States, To the Democracy of the United States," in Vallandigham, *Speeches, Arguments, Addresses and Letters of Clement L. Vallandigham* (New York, 1864), pp. 362–69. The meeting is described in Klement, *Limits of Dissent*, pp. 74–75.

55. See the reactions, among others, of the Albany (N.Y.) *Atlas and Argus,* May 10, 1862; *Boston Post,* May 12, 1862.

56. William A. Richardson to Stephen A. Douglas, November 27, 1860, Douglas Papers.

political organization, as such, be supported or encouraged or tolerated."[57]

A few of these Democrats, such as Benjamin Hallett of Massachusetts, urged simply that the party make no nominations for office during the crisis. But others were determined that the Democracy stop all political activity completely. The real issue, John McClernand wrote, is submission to rebellion or the repression of it." He doubted "the possibility . . . of manufacturing a political movement which can be distinguished from hostility to the government and the war," for there was "no middle ground between loyalty and disloyalty." Democrats who engaged in party politics, therefore, were "antagonistic to the Union and to patriotism." They "create[d] division and aid[ed] and encourage[d] rebellion." Given that, Democrats should not be concerned about alleged abolitionist radicalism, or the policies of the government. That was of no consequence until the end of the war when the Democrats could reassert their party doctrines. Until then, the party should be dead.[58]

The War Democrats who left the party in 1861 and 1862 over its commitment to oppose the Lincoln administration remain an elusive group, difficult to pinpoint in numbers, or in places of concentration, or as to the socioeconomic sources of their behavior, if any. War Democrats existed in every state and in most factional groups alongside committed partisans. But there were no readily apparent geographic, social, or previous factional bases for the splits. Obviously, personalities, old feuds, and individual perceptions played some role in determining which side people were on. But beyond that it is difficult to pinpoint any particular set of influences making one man adopt a partisan stance, another refusing to do so. The question of the role normal politics should play in wartime was answered differently

57. Cochrane summed it up: "party is the bane of our country; it is the poison of our effort." His speech is in the *Proceedings of the Convention of Loyal Leagues;* Dickinson's comment is in his speech to a Union war ratification meeting, October 9, 1862, in Dickinson, *Speeches and Letters*, p. 211.

58. John McClernand to S. S. Cox, December 4, 1861, Cox Papers; Rueben Van Pelt, *Speech Delivered at a Mass Meeting . . . to Ratify the Nomination of Edward Haight . . .* (New York, 1862), pp. 6, 7; Dickinson, "Speech at Union War Ratification Meeting," in Dickinson, *Speeches and Letters*, p. 211; John A. Dix to John Van Buren, September 21, 1862, John A. Dix Papers, Columbia University Library, New York, N.Y.

by individual Democrats without, it seems, any overriding social condition or previous experience determining the side one took.[59]

But, regardless of these elusive elements, the War Democrats' position was clear. They believed they had to take the course they did, leaving, as they said, their party for the war. Lyman Tremaine, an old party wheelhorse, whom New York Democrats nominated for state attorney general in 1861, refused the nomination and left the Democratic state convention with a number of associates to go over to the new People's Union party, joined to the Republicans through the naming of the same candidates.[60] Others followed suit in different states. Some were nominated for office and shared place and power with the Republicans, particularly early in the war. But in most instances they were absorbed into the Republican apparatus and used by the Republicans for their own purposes. Whether the War Democrats ever looked back or not is questionable. Like so many others in this era of intense political rhetoric and belief, they were convinced that what they were doing was the only right thing to do.

Regular party leaders tried, at first, to bring their dissenting colleagues back into the fold. As Wisconsin Democratic leader Edward G. Ryan reminded them in 1862, in a frequently repeated party appeal, "blind submission to the Administration of the government is not devotion to the country or the Constitution. The administration is not the government." Rather, "fidelity to the Constitution is loyalty to the Union."[61] But the War Democrats remained unyielding. Their fulminations against their former party were persistent and bitter throughout the war. Their condemnation of the allegedly treasonous activities of their former colleagues was taken up gleefully by the Republicans with great effect. By 1863 and 1864 their acquiescence in the more extreme actions of the administration became increasingly intense. T. G. Alvord demanded that the government not apologize

59. There is no good analysis of the War Democrats. For insights on a number of them, see Martin Lichterman, "John Adams Dix, 1798–1879" (Ph.D. diss., Columbia University, 1952); Dickinson, *Speeches and Letters*. A recent survey, Christopher Dell, *Lincoln and the War Democrats* (Madison, N.J., 1975), leaves many problems unresolved.

60. *New York Herald*, September 10, 1861. See also Alexander, *Political History of the State of New York*, 3: 24.

61. Ryan, *Address*, p. 1.

for any wartime excesses alleged by the Democrats and argued that the Northern people "wanted this war carried onto the knife—with bitter uncompromising hate." John Cochrane wound up on John Frémont's radical anti-Lincoln ticket in 1864.[62] By the very nature of such stances the regular Democrats had to wash their hands of them.

The impact of these divisions on the party was not profound in a power sense. The War Democrats were occasionally troublesome and always an embarrassment to the regular organization. There were occasional complaints against this "meanest combination of bastard Dems" uniting with the Republicans against their former colleagues.[63] But their actions were the revolt of some party elites, not of a mass of party loyalists. The War Democrats were never numerous enough to affect the fortunes of the party to any significant extent. Clearly, the large mass of party members remained loyal to Democratic ideas and organization, even in opposition. In the state elections of 1861, for example, War Democrats ran separate gubernatorial tickets in Maine, Vermont, and California. They successfully split away a large minority of Democratic voters from the regular ticket in that year of party confusion over the course it should take. In both of the first two states, however, the Democratic vote, even if combined, did not pose a serious threat to the Republicans. The latter made up the normal majority party in both states by substantial majorities. In 1862, there were still separate War Democratic tickets for governor in Maine and California as well as in New Hampshire (but not in Vermont). Their proportion of the party vote declined from the previous year and again their presence did not affect the normal distribution of power in those states. In 1862, also, in the Tenth Congressional District of New York State, the War Democratic incumbent Edwin Haight ran (with Republican support) against the regular party nominee in one of the rare moments when offices other than the most prominent statewide ones were contested. Haight lost to the regular Democratic nominee.[64]

---

62. *Proceedings of Loyal Leagues*, 34–35.

63. S. S. Cox to William English, October 23, 1861, quoted in Lindsey, *Cox*, p. 57.

64. The election results are listed in the *New York Tribune Almanac for 1862* (and 1863).

In short, War Democrats did poorly among Democratic voters. The bulk of the Democratic vote remained loyal to the regular party nominees. More significantly so far as the course of party operations was concerned, by 1862 such activities had largely passed away as the War Democrats more and more worked within the Union coalitions that the Republican leadership developed to counter the regular Democratic threat. By then, in most competitive states there had been a return to two-partyism between the Union party and the Democrats. And the Democratic popular vote changed little as a result. The War Democrats stand out, therefore, as a group striking for their position contrary to the stance of most partisans in the crisis of the Union, celebrated perhaps for their ability to equate the Lincoln administration with the needs of the hour, useful on Republican speakers' platforms as examples of true commitment against petty partisanship and for the Union, and quite ineffective in mass political terms, a small group who embarrassed their former party compatriots for a time but who had little impact on the fortunes of the Democratic party during the war.

"Never . . . So Imperative a Necessity"

The angry lashing of the War Democrats confronted Democratic regulars with a number of political problems. But too much attention to the group can distort understanding of the party's behavior in the Civil War period. True, many Democratic congressmen, among them New York's large bloc, refused to sign Vallandigham's congressional Address in 1862.[65] But the differences over the Address were more ones of timing, tone, and auspices than over whether or not there should be opposition as such. It was clear enough that as time passed more and more of the party faithful accepted the need for an organized and vigorous opposition.[66] The mood of most Democratic spokesmen by mid-1862 was extraordinarily harsh, combative, and partisan.

Between May and October, Democratic state conventions met in many places. Their tone, resolutions, and behavior clashed with those

65. The signatories are listed in *Speeches, Arguments . . . of Vallandigham*, p. 362n.

66. See, as one example, John Danforth to ?, December 26, 1861, Thomas H. Seymour Papers.

taken as recently as the past spring. Then, some of the conventions that had met had not made nominations and, while condemning certain Republican actions, all concentrated on the need to win the war. Now, militant partisanship was the common tone. They were having no further truck with bland measures or insipid nonpartisanship. In July, there were conventions in Pennsylvania, Indiana, and Ohio; in September, in New York. Neither Pennsylvania nor Indiana Democrats had met in 1861. But now they vigorously asserted the need to defeat the rebellion and the need for the Democratic party to maintain its "distinctive organization" in order to put down "and render harmless the assaults of Northern sectionalists upon constitutional liberty." To their previous and continuing condemnation of the Republicans for their inflexible sectionalism and agitation against the South, they added a list of current and continuing assaults by the Republicans on the liberties of the American people and the Constitution of the United States. "Never in the history of the country," the resolutions of the New York Democratic convention summed up, "was there so imperative a necessity for the thorough organization of the Democratic party," and union of "all the conservative elements of the nation. . . . For the mere purpose of maintaining their power and their hold upon the spoils of office [the Republicans] have contributed to the success of the rebellion, by pertinaciously pressing their party issues, by dividing the sentiments of the North, by attempting to make this a mere partisan war. . . . To their gross mismanagement and malignant interference we must attribute the present disastrous condition of the country."[67]

The Democratic party had been through a very difficult time since the national conventions of 1860 and never more so than in the period

67. The first quotes are from the platform of the Rhode Island Democratic convention in *Appleton's Cyclopaedia, 1862*, p. 745; New York's resolution is in ibid. See also, *Illinois State Register*, September 9, 1862. Institutionally, the final act of the Democratic reunion, already accomplished in fact, occurred a year after the congressional and state elections of 1862, when the executive committees of both the Douglas and Breckinridge factions of the national Democracy met in great geniality at the St. Nicholas Hotel in New York City to plan a joint call for the next national convention.

after the presidential election as they digested their stunning loss and its even more stunning implications. They had moved through several stages in their journey back to political confrontation. There had been some searing divisions and internal fighting. There had occasionally been confusion and uncertainty and clashing perspectives as to what should be done. No one man saved the Democrats at this juncture or redirected their energies toward politics once more. Rather, the imperatives of the political culture and structure were at work. Obviously, the raw materials for outright opposition were there. A heritage of intransigence and adversary relations between parties had long existed. Ingrained political distrust, clashing ideological viewpoints, the strong force of traditional institutions and perspectives forced the factions of the party, rent by old wounds, back together and ultimately led them into a position of political partisanship which all but a small minority of Democrats accepted—because this was their accustomed stance and they were comfortable in it and understood it.

By the middle of 1862, the Democracy, through its few congressmen, many newspapers, and increasing amount of electoral activity, had reasserted its critical role in the political system, albeit in the unaccustomed role of the minority party. Democrats still faced problems: their minority position, the defections, remnants of former bitterness, as well as anxieties over their position in opposition to a war increasingly claimed by their opponents to be one of patriotism and nationhood. Further, their prewar leadership was gone. But partisan politics was reborn, that was clear. The Democrats' problem was now to find the means to mobilize sufficient numbers of voters to turn the country from its revolutionary course.

Their speeches recognized that they had returned together and were already actively working together and the existence of two separate national executive committees was an artifact of other times. (There is a report of this meeting in the *New York Herald*, September 8, 1863.)

3

"Nothing But Convulsion Can Come of This Despotism": The Democratic Response to Republican Policies, 1861–1865

THE DEMOCRATS WHO took up the burden of party leadership in 1861–1862 were an untried group. Whatever logical order of succession and hierarchical pattern of leadership the party had developed in the 1850s had been damaged by the electoral realignment, the party split in 1860, and the trauma of secession. For years party leadership had rested in Congress and the state capitals. But a significant part of the rising leadership, those slated to take over the party from its old men still active in 1860, were the departing Southerners. Jefferson Davis, Howell Cobb, and Robert M. T. Hunter, all contenders for the Democratic nomination in 1860, John D. Breckinridge of Kentucky, and Alexander Stephens of Georgia; in short, the party's Southern command had all gone. In the North, Douglas died in April 1861; and he left behind him a badly mauled party holding few statewide offices and a congressional group not only weak in numbers but also short on experience. Three-quarters of the Democrats in the House of Representatives at the opening of the Thirty-seventh Congress in mid-1861 were serving their first term. Seven others were in only their second. John Phelps of Missouri, serving his ninth and final term, was the senior Democrat in the House. The senior Northerners were William Richardson of Illinois, and George Pendleton, Samuel S. Cox, and Clement Vallandigham of Ohio. The last three were only in their third terms in Washington. Furthermore, twelve of these men served but this single term in the House.[1]

In the Senate the situation was similar. Three Border State Democrats—James Bayard, Willard Saulsbury, and James Pearce —plus Jesse Bright of Indiana and John R. Thomson of New Jersey were the only ones of the eleven Democratic senators not serving their first term. Only Bayard and Bright had played much of a leadership role before the war. Nor were most of the serving Democratic senators destined to stay around for very long. During 1862, Thomson died, Andrew Johnson left to become war governor of Tennessee, and the Republicans expelled Bright. Bright and Thomson's successors, David Turpie and James Wall, served about a year and were then replaced by Republicans.

Things were not much better outside of Congress. Among governors of states remaining in the union, four in the Border states, plus John Whittaker of Oregon and John G. Downey of California, were the only Democrats in office in 1861. Here, too, there was a quick turnover. By the end of 1861 only three governorships remained in Democratic hands. In other words, the seasoned Democratic officeholding leadership had been all but wiped out by the events of the fifties and the secession of the Southern states. The focal point of party leadership in the sixties had come to rest among the few congressmen with more than a brief smattering of experience and the even fewer prominent Democratic state officials in the largest states.[2]

The leading congressmen were not totally without some party standing. Richardson had long been recognized as Stephen Douglas's primary lieutenant in the House, and Clement Vallandigham had chaired the national Democratic campaign committee for Douglas in 1860. Most crucially, the whole paraphernalia of the Democratic organization remained intact. Although he was out of the country for most of the critical year 1861–1862, August Belmont led the national

1. There were Democratic representatives in only eight of the twenty-two Northern and Border states. The three Ohio Valley states—Ohio, Indiana, and Illinois—sent seventeen of the Democratic congressmen. Twenty-two others represented four states in the Northeast bloc: New York, New Jersey, Connecticut, and Pennsylvania. The other three were from Missouri. This analysis is based on data taken from *The Biographical Directory of the American Congress, 1774–1971* (Washington, D.C., 1971).

2. This material is taken from the *New York Tribune Almanac for 1862.*

committee throughout the war and was active in behind-the-scenes encouragement of Democrats and in urging the reforming of battle lines. Many of the state party organizations were also in good shape and functioning despite their problems in 1860.[3]

These men were not resting. Their correspondence early in the war was filled with invitations to informal strategy meetings, references to the need for fundraising, and details of all sorts of other partisan activities. As time went on, they rebuilt their communications and electioneering network everywhere where there were Democrats. As political activity quickened, they commissioned the writing of campaign pamphlets, arranged for the reprinting of speeches and state and local platforms, and established means to send these out to the faithful everywhere. In 1863 and 1864 the newly organized Society for the Diffusion of Political Knowledge became the center of a nationwide structure of Democratic propaganda activities. It printed and distributed thousands of copies of separate speeches and similar materials underscoring the iniquities of Republican policies. At least "three reliable men" were sought in each population center, to establish "an active auxiliary society" to the Society for the Diffusion of Political Knowledge, to receive "read, diffuse and discuss" its handouts and other party material.[4] Party leaders also established formal and informal financial networks to raise money for candidates everywhere in the nation. In 1862 the New York State party leadership asked Samuel L. M. Barlow, a prominent lawyer and financier, and Samuel Tilden to head the effort to raise $10,000 in New York City for the state campaign of that year. A year later Barlow was asked to send money for Clement Vallandigham's campaign for the Ohio governorship.[5]

3. There is some discussion of the Democratic organization in Irving Katz, *August Belmont* (New York, 1968).

4. The Society's founding is discussed in its first pamphlet issued in 1863. There are copies of all of its pamphlets in the Cornell University Library. See also Katz, *Belmont*, pp. 120–21; Alexander C. Flick, *Samuel Jones Tilden* (New York, 1939), pp. 140–41. The first two quotes are from Charles Mason (secretary of the Society) to James Sterling Morton, April 26, 1863, James S. Morton Papers, Nebraska Historical Society, Lincoln, Neb. (microfilm edition, Cornell University Library); the second is from the title page of each of the Society's pamphlets.

5. Dean Richmond and Peter Cagger to Samuel L. M. Barlow and Samuel Tilden, September 27, 1862, S. S. Cox to Barlow, December 3, 1863, Samuel L. M. Barlow Papers, Henry E. Huntington Library, San Marino, Ca.

The Democrats' party press was still widespread and vigorous. There were party papers in the major urban centers, state capitals, and most county seats throughout the North. Their editorials and news stories, widely circulated to the faithful, performed a most critical act of electoral communication: reminding the voters of their past commitments, exhorting them to turn out on election day, and reestablishing in every Democratic mind the negative images of the opposition. The Democratic press received an important addition in September 1862 when a consortium of party leaders headed by Barlow bought the New York *World,* formerly an independent, religious newspaper. Under the strong direction of Manton Marble, then an experienced twenty-seven-year-old editor, the *World* became the leading national organ of the party, promoting the Democratic line throughout the 1860s and beyond.[6] It was the apex of a structure that spread the party's message everywhere in the Northern states. It was also at the center of a functioning Democratic machine. Nineteenth-century party organizations were never very elaborate structurally. They were certainly not highly centralized. But what did exist—newspapers, party bureaucrats, legislative leaders, and campaign apparatus—were all capable of a great deal of vigorous and sustained activity aimed at influencing legislation, executive actions, and, most of all, the outcome of elections. That tradition continued in support of the Democrats in the 1860s.

The center of gravity amid this organizational vitality was unclear at the beginning of the war. The Democracy was no longer the party of Buchanan or Douglas or the Southern phalanx. No one person stood above all others in 1862 as the acknowledged leader or a national symbol of the party. New power blocs, particularly among the articulate Westerners who were the heirs of Douglas, emerged alongside other parts of the network in the Eastern states, often themselves led by relatively new men. Some of these emerging leaders were surprisingly young.[7] None of them necessarily deferred to the others. The

6. George McJimsey, *Genteel Partisan: Manton Marble, 1834–1917* (Ames, Iowa, 1971).

7. Cox was thirty-six when war broke out; Barlow, thirty-four; Belmont, forty-four. Conversely, Vallandigham and Horatio Seymour were fifty; Dean Richmond, fifty-seven.

fractiousness of the Democracy had been an important factor in party affairs even in the days of a more clearly defined leadership and well-recognized succession patterns. The potential for conflict among relatively equal power blocs was high in the early 1860s. But, despite their inexperience and the lack of well-established hierarchial patterns, the new leaders had an organizational framework on which to build. They also had clear guidelines and goals to help shape their behavior: their loyalty to their party as an institution, their desire to see it regain power, and their devotion to the party's creed.

The Strategic Perspective

By the fall of 1862, the Democratic party was fully in the field against its political enemy. It appeared to be a very good time for the Democrats to make a concerted bid to regain power. The war had been going on for over a year with no signs of victory, and with increasing unhappiness and frustration expressed by uneasy Republicans as well as by Democrats. In addition to the lack of military success, the immediate issues fostered by the war—the limits on civil liberties, the preliminary Emancipation Proclamation issued in September 1862, and the stringencies created by the war effort—added to the Republicans' problems. The administration was, in fact, ripe to suffer for its responsibility for unsuccessful and provocative public policies. Both Democrats and Republicans recognized the situation for what it was. Come what may, James Bayard wrote his son, early in 1862, "I am satisfied the fate of the Republican party is sealed. . . . The next election destroys them in the House of R[epresentatives] as they already are in the confidence of the country." John Hay, one of Lincoln's secretaries, could only agree. On a visit to Illinois in October he noted how poor Republican prospects appeared to be. The army's failure, he concluded, had had a "bad effect" on their electoral hopes.[8]

It was not only the current catalogue of errors that the Democrats saw working for them. They were also acutely committed to the idea that long-range elements in the political structure ran in their favor as

8. James A. Bayard to Thomas F. Bayard, January 6, 1862, Thomas F. Bayard Papers, Library of Congress; John Hay to John G. Nicolay, October 28, 1862, in *Lincoln and the Civil War in the Diaries and Letters of John Hay,* ed. Tyler Dennett (New York, 1939), pp. 51–52.

well. Some of them realized how close the election of 1860 had been, and how deceptive was the Republican majority. They believed the Republican victory was but a temporary derangement from a normal and natural Democratic national majority. They did not think that most Northerners would continue to support Republican policies and candidates once the ultimate aims of the party were starkly revealed. Recent political activities indicated to them that there were at least five groups in the electorate: the Republican party was dominated by radical elements, but also contained a conservative wing; former Northern and Border State Unionists and Whigs, plus War Democrats and regular Democrats completed the list. All but the Radical Republicans were people to whom the Democrats believed they could appeal with some hopes of success. In the case of some, such as the former Democrats now in the Republican party, or the War Democrats, there was the hope that they could be brought back to revitalize the old Democratic majority of the pre-1854 period if the accidental or temporary problems that had devastated the Democratic party could now be disposed of. In the case of the others, the increasingly radical behavior of the Lincoln administration would bring them over. There was, in fact, Democrats believed, a conservative majority in the country, made up of all but Radical Republicans, that could be galvanized against the sectionalist, abolitionist Republican bloc.[9]

In every state were Whigs, Native Americans, and Constitutional Unionists: men who had not supported either the Democrats or the Republicans in 1860 but who were potential counterweights to what Democrats saw as Republican radicalism. In several of the large states, these men formed a base vote large enough to tip the balance between the closely competitive major parties. Their strength was something not to be ignored, as the Conservatives themselves delighted in pointing out.[10] All of these voters were potentially open, party leaders believed, for conversion to the Democrats on a conserva-

9. Benjamin Stark to S. L. M. Barlow, March 27, 1862, Barlow Papers; George S. Converse to S. S. Cox, May 25, 1862, Samuel Sullivan Cox Papers, Brown University Library, Providence, R.I.; Albany (N.Y.) *Atlas and Argus,* November 1, 7, 1862; Springfield *Illinois State Register,* September 29, 1862; New York *World,* February 26, 1863.

10. Hiram Ketchum to Reverdy Johnson, March 7, 1863, in Reverdy Johnson Papers, Library of Congress. The Constitutional Union party continued to hold state conventions in a number of key states in 1861 and 1862.

tive platform. That majority only had to be made to see that the political conflict now under way was, as Horatio Seymour said in October 1862, "not merely a conflict between the Democratic and Republican organizations, but . . . a struggle between the conservative and radical classes of our citizens." Therefore, "let all democrats and conservative men unite . . . in the most vigorous constitutional measures for the suppression of this rebellion."[11]

There were clear signs that this was happening. Certainly, the Border State Unionists had allied with the Democrats in Congress and in the public arena since the winter of 1860–1861. In addition to the uncommitted Unionists, Democratic hopes were also whetted by the information they were receiving about the more conservative Republicans' unhappiness with the administration. As Lincoln looked "to the radical wing of the Republican party for the sole support of his administration," experienced politicians and original Republicans such as Thurlow Weed and Caleb Smith communicated their unhappiness to individuals who passed it on to the Democratic leadership. The army, as well, was reported increasingly disaffected.[12] The abolitionist policies of the Lincoln administration were "drawing together conservative men in defense of the Constitution." The Republican party, therefore, was "growing smaller by degrees and beautifully less," an editor enthused as early as February, 1862.[13]

The Democratic leadership, conscious of the possibilities present, threw open the doors to these conservatives as widely as possible. In

11. Horatio Seymour, Speech at Cooper Institute, October 13, 1862, in *The Public Record of Horatio Seymour*, comp. Thomas W. Cook and Thomas W. Knox (New York, 1868), p. 67 (hereafter, *Record of Seymour*); *Illinois State Register*, September 9, 1862.

12. *Illinois State Register*, October 10, 1862; August Belmont to S. L. M. Barlow, September 27, 1862, Barlow Papers; "Position Paper" of the Maine Democratic Gubernatorial candidate, August 6, 1863, in *The American Annual Cyclopaedia and Register of Important Events 1863* (New York, 1863), p. 603 (hereafter *Appleton's Cyclopaedia*); T. J. Barnett to Barlow, December 20, 1862, Caleb B. Smith to T. J. Barnett, August 17, 1863, August Abend to Barlow, January 17, 1863, Barlow Papers. There is much discussion of conservative and Democratic consultations in the John J. Crittenden Papers, Library of Congress. See also, Albert Kirwan, *John J. Crittenden: The Struggle for the Union* (Lexington, Ky., 1962).

13. Concord *New Hampshire Patriot*, October 1, 1862; *Illinois State Register*, September 27, 1862; *Atlas and Argus*, May 14, 1862; *York* (Pa.) *Democratic Press*, February 21, 1862.

August 1862 it publicly announced itself "ready to unite with all patriotic citizens without reference to former party combinations who agree in sustaining the government in the prosecution of the existing war against the rebellion . . . for the purpose of restoring the Union as it was and maintaining the Constitution as it is." The leaders' invitations to meeting were framed to include "conservative men not heretofore in the Democratic organization." Some Democrats joined ex-Whigs and Unionists in local political committees formed to mobilize this conservative vote.[14] Most of all it was through the substance of their campaign argument against the Republicans that Democrats saw the best means of uniting all of the conservative elements.

Only one thing could prevent the emergence of a new conservative party, Democrats believed, the enduring anti-Democratic prejudices, rooted in past conflicts, on the part of antiadministration, conservative Republicans and Whigs. Only the Democratic party was capable of mobilizing all of these disaffected elements together in a united movement. But, the continued power of "party trammels" might keep non-Democrats in the ranks of the enemy.[15] Fortunately, this danger also seemed to be passing in the face of the terrible threats confronting the country from radicalism. Unionists in Congress, most of them former Whigs, made it clear that they were ready to work with the Democrats to unseat the abolitionists in control in Washington. The results of elections since the war's outbreak confirmed the trend and underlined how great an opportunity existed. The Democrats believed they had picked up uncommitted and conservative votes in the 1861 local elections. In the 1862 elections, they made their best showing in the North since before the realignment of the 1850s. Clearly, men who had always "stood in opposition to the Democracy, [had] joined the party of the people." These "glorious" results were not "mere party triumphs" but due to the concerted actions of all conservatives. This was "not a vote against the war, but against the

14. *Atlas and Argus,* August 14, July 9, 1862; Thomas Massey and others to John J. Crittenden, December 10, 1862, Crittenden Papers; printed circular, September 26, 1862, calling a meeting of "the Constitutional League," in New York City, Barlow Papers.

15. Robert McClelland to Franklin Pierce, January 15, 1862, Franklin Pierce Papers, Library of Congress.

Republican party." The administration had been condemned for dividing the nation and for usurping the Constitution. In its place, the nation had opted for a "great conservative party" which now "commands the situation."[16]

"We Are . . . Vibrating Between Anarchism and Despotism"

The Democrats were sure about what separated them and other conservatives from the Republicans and how deep the chasm between the parties actually was. As the *New York World* said in 1864, the "differences between the ideas of the Republicans and Democratic party is still heaven-wide, antagonistical, irreconcilable."[17] The party's leaders had to articulate this difference clearly and crisply. They were convinced that all conservatives, regardless of past partisan commitments, would then find their way to the support of the Democratic party, the core of all opposition to what they all saw as Republican radicalism.

From 1862 on, the Democratic leaders developed an extensive critique of the Republican administration. Their arguments grew out of an ideology rooted in their traditions and experiences and the perceptions developed in their past about the role and power of government, about the nature of the Constitution, and about the direction of racial and social policy within the nation. Whatever new problems the war introduced into American life, the Democrats responded in their usual ways. There was, therefore, a timelessness, a static quality to their arguments. A new Republican outrage during the

16. *Illinois State Register,* November 5, 1862; James Thompson to Jeremiah Black, November 7, 1862, Jeremiah Black Papers, Library of Congress; *Boston Post,* November 10, 1862; New York *World,* October 25, 1862; *Record of Seymour,* p. 75.

The Democrats picked up thirty-five seats in Congress, elected Horatio Seymour governor of New York, won majorities in eight statewide races across the North, and succeeded in making dramatic gains everywhere. Their greatest gains were in the crucial large states of the Middle Atlantic and old Northwest regions, where they increased their share of the popular vote by 5 percent over 1860 and added thirty-one of their new congressional seats. This was partially offset by their continued poor showing in some New England and Western states, but the general pattern was of a Democratic resurgence to a position quite close to the Republicans in the states where the next presidential election would be decided.

17. New York *World,* November 11, 1864.

war provoked additional violent rhetoric but the overall structure of the Democratic argument remained basically the same from the first day to the last.[18]

At the same time, thanks to these traditional sources of their ideas, the Democrats were quite united in their critique of the Lincoln administration. No matter who spoke or wrote, former Breckinridge men or Douglasites, Copperheads or supporters of the war, the national party or different state organizations, there was a noticeable congruence of ideas. Whatever differences continued to exist among them were papered over when Democrats condemned Republicans or defended a conservative constitutional position. After the defection of the War Democrats in 1861–1862, the issues provoked by Republican policies did not divide those Democrats who remained in the party anew, nor reawaken echoes of past factiousness.

The Democratic state and national platforms set forth the party's record, presented a view of the Republicans, and offered reasons, therefore, for voting Democratic. Platforms served an important purpose in American party warfare in the nineteenth century. They were deliberately written to furnish signals to the voters, to remind them of the congruence of the party's stance with their needs. Although party leaders may not have expected that the formal argument of their platforms and other literature would be read all the way through or clearly understood by all readers, they did provide enough guides for most to understand what was being argued. The use and repetition of favorable symbols, the reduction of complex policy matters to easily understood phrases, the development of negative images of the other party, all were aspects of the technique of mobilizing voters into desired channels flowing toward election day. Speeches, pamphlets, and newspaper editorials followed up the guidelines set in the platform, profusely repeating and clarifying the signals emitted.[19]

18. They found that they had "no new principles to enunciate, no new loyalty to pledge." Edward G. Ryan, *Address to the People by the Democrats of Wisconsin* (Milwaukee, 1862), p. 1; Richard O. Curry, "Copperheadism and Ideological Continuity: Anatomy of a Stereotype," *Journal of Negro History* 57 (1972): 29–36.

19. The relevance of party ideology and platform and other appeals in nineteenth-century politics is well discussed in Lee Benson, *The Concept of Jacksonian Democracy* (Princeton, 1961), pp. 216–53, in a chapter entitled, "Party Programs, Characters, and Images."

The Democrats saw all of the problems entangling them as a well-ordered whole that could be both understand and explained. Two related and traditional themes shaped all their arguments: a limited and narrow constitutionalism, originating in Jackson's day, and a bitter fear of a puritan-inspired social revolution, that grew out of their experiences in the 1850s. Democrats argued that the Republicans were carrying on the war for their own partisan purposes, "not in the interest of the Union, but in the interest of the Republican party and its greedy retinue of contractors." Lincoln "is in no hurry to end the war." He wished to continue it to solidify Republican control of the nation for a larger purpose. The Republicans contained within them the raw materials for making a revolution. Their sectionalism, their commitment to violent change, and their agitative leadership all reflected a "fell revolutionary spirit." They were intent on letting this spirit out in order to embark on the most profound constitutional and social revolution that would enthrone the most radical doctrines. "I charge the radical and abolition leaders of the Republican party," Sanford Church said in 1863, "with the deliberate design to adopt and carry out a series of measures, the effect and object of which is to subvert the union, and not to restore it, to overthrow the Constitution and not to preserve it."[20]

This subversive design was evident, Democrats believed, in everything the administration did. The Republicans had rendered civil authority subordinate to military power. The Lincoln administration used the army not to fight rebels but to suppress Democrats. Military commanders in Northern areas enthusiastically arrested a number of Democratic spokesmen in midwar for alleged seditious and traitorous activities. Several Democratic newspapers were temporarily closed or barred from the mails. Congressman Vallandigham was first arrested by General Burnside in Ohio, and then deported south of the Union's lines on direct orders from the Lincoln administration. The suppression of civil liberties in the Border states was another piece of the

20. New York *World*, September 6, 1863, February 5, 1864; *Illinois State Register*, September 25, 1862; Sanford Church, *Speech at Batavia*, October 13, 1863 (New York, 1863). Church was one of the leaders of the Democratic party in New York State.

mosaic. The Republicans had instituted a "reign of terror" against dissenters, Democrats, and Border state people. "Every man in Delaware, Maryland and Kentucky who is not [a supporter of the administration] is not a freeman." By suspending habeas corpus, establishing military control, arresting dissenters, imposing loyalty oaths, in short by trampling upon personal rights, the Republicans had proved their total disregard for the Constitution and their hostility to democratic institutions. Their actions threatened the very basis of American liberties and constitutionalism. The greatest danger that the country faced, therefore, lay not in "the injuries that might be inflicted by the armies of the enemy, but in the danger that the American people might forget those principles of freedom and self government which has been handed down to them from their fathers."[21]

The imposition of conscription in midwar only intensified Democratic anger. Whatever the military justification for drafting men into the armed service, "all conscription or other forced service of the citizen to the state is contrary to the genius and principles of republican government." It was foreign to the American experience, destructive of American liberties, and part of a larger and unacceptable commitment to state control over individuals and their behavior. If the experiment's object was "to bring the worst features of European despotisms among us" then it had succeeded. The American people were no longer free. Obviously, this was what the Republicans intended. Their conduct of war, "from the highest official to the lowest parasite of power," was "such as to be as personally offensive as possible to all conservatives." Clearly, "if the people cannot discuss public measures, read such papers and documents as they may desire, then all idea of a republican form of government is at an end. —elections a farce, the free ballot a humbug, and the electioneering of candidates mere child's play." There was no war-created necessity for such acts despite Republican claims. Democrats "utterly repudiate" the idea that in time of war the Constitution is suspended. Rather, "the war must be carried on under, and not over" the

21. Franklin Pierce to Sidney Webster, April 21, 1861, Pierce-Webster Letters, Library of Congress; New York *World*, September 13, 1864; David G. Croly, *Seymour and Blair* (New York, 1868), p. 195.

Constitution.[22] But this could never be under the leadership of the Republicans.

The fearsome thing about all of this to Democrats was what it revealed about the Republican party. Its actions were evidence of its leaders' intentions. Republicans were unable to act other than in the way that they were doing. "A most remarkable similarity exists in the actions of this Administration toward the people of the North," Congressman Samuel Randall of Pennsylvania charged in 1863, "and those that were perpetrated by the Mother Country against the colonies." To Democrats, Lincoln's government demonstrated that Republicans were "consolidationists of a more ultra type" more than anyone had heretofore thought possible, more so than either Hamiltonians, Tories, or monarchists. In particular, Republicans intended to use government power to impose rigid standards of personal behavior on the lives of individual citizens. To Randall and his colleagues, they were expanding the powers of government into every nook and cranny of being, appointing federal officeholders to supervise everyone's life and depriving Americans of their liberty. They were creating "an Absolute state asserting all the prerogatives of an infallible church."[23]

At the core of the administration's behavior, the Democrats believed, was a puritan-evangelical perspective originating in the history and traditions of New England religious beliefs. It was a perspective that fostered an aggressive and uncompromising program of government intervention to order and direct individual behavior. Puritan-dominated Republicanism had "asserted a higher law above the Constitution itself." Republicans believed that they had "a right to regulate the whole political, moral and religious world, and that God has appointed them supervisors over the conduct of their fellow men, to control even their domestic affairs." They had "sought to do in the

22. *Congressional Globe,* 38 Cong., 1 sess., p. 427; Columbus (Ohio) *Crisis,* July 22, May 13, 1863; Stephen D. Carpenter, *The Logic of History, Five Hundred Political Texts* (Madison, Wis., 1864), p. 1; *Appleton's Cyclopaedia, 1862,* p. 558. Constitutional historians have a very different view of the Republican policies from that of the Democrats at the time. See, for example, Harold Hyman, *A More Perfect Union: The Impact of the Civil War and Reconstruction on the Constitution* (New York, 1973).

23. *Congressional Globe,* 38 Cong., 1 sess., p. 2991; *Atlas and Argus,* July 28, 1863, February 14, 1865.

name of God, what could not be done in the name of the Constitution." In other words, their policies originated in "an imprudent assumption of a superior intelligence and a higher purity."[24] They did not accept the right of people to differ about social or political matters. "The most malignant and bigoted intolerance is a predominant element amongst those who follow the lead of the Puritan today." Nobody "ever could get along with the Puritan spirit of New England. . . . It was a persecuting, intolerant, hateful and malignant spirit. . . . It was sour, narrow-minded and illiberal."[25] In the 1850s, the Republicans had agitated in favor of an extensive program of coercive cultural legislation: temperance, sabbatarian, school, and prayer laws to Americanize and Protestantize immigrants and others with different values. They had denied freedom of choice to anyone who disagreed with them: nonevangelical, Irish Catholic, and Southern slaveholder. They ignored anyone's freedom of choice except their own.[26]

The war had only brought out this tendency, sharpened it, and given it free rein in the policies of the Lincoln administration. The results of Republican rule were clear, therefore. America would become an unacceptably restrictive society with a dominant, snooping, interfering government, forcing conformity to a narrow set of behavior patterns. It was the responsibility of the opposition to prevent this. "We think New England, when it tries to regulate the morals of the whole world, and prescribe them drink and diet, has undertaken a task greater than she can perform, and will only bring trouble as long as she persists in it. . . . When preachers assume to be statesmen, and direct the affairs of the country, it is no wonder that that country goes rapidly to ruin and destruction. . . . They are narrow and short

24. The Republican party was dominated by "the Constitution breaking, law defying, negro-loving Phariseeism of New England! . . . [a section whose] Marseillaise is a hymn of apotheosis to John Brown—a horse thief and a murderer." Samuel S. Cox, *Puritanism in Politics: A Speech Before the Democratic Union Association in January 1863 in New York City* (New York, 1863), pp. 4, 10. The quotes are from Ryan, *Address*, p. 23; *New York Herald*, January 26, 1861.

25. *Chicago Times*, November 11, 1863; *Cincinnati Daily Enquirer*, January 1, 1863.

26. Ronald Formisano, *The Birth of Mass Political Parties, Michigan, 1827–1860* (Princeton, 1971). See above, chapter one.

sighted in their views, and they are intolerant, illiberal and cruel in their method of carrying them out."[27]

Appearing before the Democratic Union Association in January 1863 in New York City, Congressman Samuel S. Cox rang all of the changes on the relationship and the danger in a speech entitled "Puritanism in Politics." "Puritanism is the reptile," he began, "which has been boring into the mound which is the Constitution, and this Civil War comes in like the devouring sea." The policies of the federal government were now dominated by the "arrogant, selfish, narrow and Puritan policy" of New England. This was not temporary. It was something "bred in the bone" thereof, and therefore harder to master. New England bigotry "ever strives to cure men's morals by legal penalties." Puritans could not leave anyone or any institution with which they disagreed alone. Rather than yield their demanded "censorship over the morals" of the South, they precipitated Civil War. Their inflexible hatred and "insane propagandism" against slavery had led to war. Once war began they could still not leave anything be. They were using the authority of the government to centralize power and make all others conform or be destroyed. "The miserable fanatics of 1691–2, who hunted out little girls and poor old women and tried them for witchcraft . . . have their imitators in the zealots of today—those minions of power who spy about to accuse and arrest those who differ with them in politics." Their history is filled with "cruelties . . . practiced by the prejudiced dyspeptic puritans. . . ." They were zealots incapable of restraint, flexibility, or compromise, and in a pluralist society they were destroyers. This was the malignant force that had to be destroyed before the Union could be restored and the nation made free again.[28]

Prolonged and loud cheering greeted Cox's remarks in the hall. His words were a battle cry summarizing a belief that had shaped the Democratic creed for the past decade: the threat to individual social and political liberties set by the meddling, interventionist, puritan fanatics now controlling the Republican party and who used the government to further their designs. The trouble with the Republican

27. *Cincinnati Daily Enquirer*, January 1, July 2, 1863.
28. Cox, *Puritanism in Politics*, pp. 6–9.

party, the *New York World* summed up, "is that it not only claims to discuss, but to decide; not only to tell a man that smoking is a nasty pernicious practice, but to knock the cigar out of his mouth." Obviously, if the Republicans continued in power they would ultimately destroy every shred of democratic choice and free behavior in the name of their conception of the right. That was the ultimate threat. As Vallandigham put it, "nothing but convulsion can come of this despotism." If Lincoln were to be reelected, "our Republican government is gone, gone, gone, and ere it is again revived we must pass through anarchy in its worst form." But the Republicans did not care. "I believe old Lincoln feels as Sampson did at the gates of Gaza willing to destroy his country, his party, himself, if he can his opponents."[29]

"The Constitution Is as Binding in War as It Is in Peace"

All of this underscored, the Democrats argued, the correctness of their decision to resume opposition. "If we see the money of the nation squandered, the Constitution trampled upon, the laws disregarded, public liberty endangered, the right of suffrage taken away, the freedom of speech and of the press restricted and punished, the Union for which we are bleeding laughed at as a thing of the past," we cannot hesitate and "find no fault with those who do these wrongs, ask for no reform, seek no change. . . . Such abject submission is only fit for a slave, wholly unfit for a freeman." Their mission was clear. Since "the contest between central and self-government will always go on," the Democrats had to be "fearlessly vigilant against the encroachments of power," to show that this rebellion could be subdued by constitutional means, "faithfully and honestly applied."[30]

Fortunately, the restoration of the Union "without a star being lost" and with "the right of man to govern himself" was still possible,

29. New York *World,* June 30, 1864; Clement L. Vallandigham to Manton Marble, May 15, 1863, Manton Marble Papers, Library of Congress; Allan Pinkerton to E. H. Wright, October 11, 1964, George B. McClellan Papers, Library of Congress; Henry J. Gardner to S. L. M. Barlow, November 10, 1862, Barlow Papers.

30. *Congressional Globe,* 38 Cong., 1 sess., p. 1972; *Atlas and Argus,* January 5, 1865; Samuel S. Cox, *Eight Years in Congress from 1857 to 1865* (New York, 1865), p. 309; *Address of the New Jersey Democratic State Central Committee to the Voters of the State, October, 1862* (Trenton, 1862).

but only under the aegis of the opposition. If the Democracy won control of the government, "the ruinous course" of the Republicans could still be checked. "The salvation of the country now depends more upon the ballot box . . . than upon the armies we have in the field." There "a Democratic victory will be a salvation," a "signal for peace and reunion," while an abolition triumph will be a signal for eternal "damnation."[31]

In responding to the Republican threat, the Democrats ground themselves in the response they had long ago developed as the "nonintervention" party in the country. The Democratic party "since its formation, steadfastly denied that circumstances should affect the application or enforcement of the cardinal doctrines it professed." The war did not change anything fundamental. The Democrats "believe that the Constitution is as binding in war as in peace." The war was to be fought "not to crush and conquer the south," nor to destroy its social system, but "simply to subdue, destroy, and scatter the rebel armies, leaving the rights of northern citizens and the property of Southern slaveholders just where the Constitution leaves them." This remained the Democratic platform throughout the war. The Democrats "can cheerfully 'sustain the government' in all honorable and constitutional means to suppress the rebellion and to restore the Union." While they believe "this can be better and more successfully accomplished by peace and wise statesmanship than by war and the best generalship, they have never refused to support the war." But, they opposed "perversion of the war to any purpose of party aggrandizement, to any purpose of revolution, to any purpose other than its originally declared object, to preserve the Constitution, Government and Union." The only hope for the Union lay in bringing the war back to "the simple and naked issue" of restoring the Union. "THE UNION IS THE ONE CONDITION OF PEACE: WE ASK NO MORE." In short, "all other issues should be ignored."[32]

31. *Congressional Globe*, 37 Cong., 2 sess., p. 406; ibid., 38 Cong., 1 sess., pp. 1297, 1622, 386; *Detroit Free Press*, February 11, 1863; New York *World*, June 15, 1863.

32. New York *World*, February 25, 1864; *Chicago Times*, October 11, 1863; *Cincinnati Daily Enquirer*, October 7, 1862; John Dean Caton, "The Position and Policy of the Democratic Party. A Letter to Hon. Horatio Seymour, December 18, 1862," in *Miscellanies* (Boston, 1880), p. 19; *Chicago Times*, November 3, 1863;

The Democrats, therefore, could not support the administration in "violating or ignoring the constitution; trampling under foot State rights, and industriously subverting every principle of civil liberty guaranteed us by the Revolution. These are not necessary to suppress the rebellion." Nor would they accept the need to expand the government's power. "The one thing which the Democratic party has steadily and persistently done from the beginning," The New York *World* reminded its readers in 1863, "is to resist the accumulation of power by the federal government." In Sunset Cox's words, "UNDER NO CIRCUMSTANCES CONCEIVABLE BY THE HUMAN MIND WOULD I EVER VIOLATE THAT CONSTITUTION FOR ANY PURPOSE." That is why, even as particular issues lost their importance, the Democrats kept on fighting, for their principles "can never become obsolete for it is in the very nature of power to encroach on liberty."[33]

The Democrats did not confine themselves to a sad litany of abstract problems, however. They vigorously communicated to the electorate the terrible implications of all that was happening to the country. They verbalized their ideology in order to fight elections and personalized their argument to make it concrete to the individual elector. They believed that many voters could be won on all the issues the administration was presenting to them. "The authorities at Washington are . . . foolish enough to give us constant instances of disregard of personal rights. The more the better." But it would take time. "Our people are not yet half educated. . . . It takes a large amount of tyranny to teach the world the blessings of freedom."[34] To do this the Democrats had to keep constant pressure on in the most personal and most easily understandable terms. Only in that way could the country be redeemed.

To make their point, the Democrats usually resorted to extreme rhetoric. They tried to scare people into voting for them. The Republicans "seek to make peace impossible and war perpetual." All hope of

---

Congressional Globe, 38 Cong., 1 sess., p. 1078; New York *World,* October 2, 1863; George F. Comstock, *Speech Delivered at the Brooklyn Academy of Music* (Brooklyn, 1864), p. 8.

33. *Chicago Times,* November 3, 1863; New York *World,* January 25, December 25, 1863; Cox, *Eight Years in Congress,* 102.

34. Horatio Seymour to Manton Marble, November 11, 1862, Marble Papers.

"public liberty, for the reconstruction of the Union, for full restoration of Constitution and law" was gone unless we hurled "usurping
federal abolitionism from the high places of the government." There
will be "crossed boyonets at every poll," the "political and financial
ruin of the republic and the sacrifice of ten million white men." What
has been the result of almost two years of rule by "this radical party,"
Congressman Samuel Cox asked. He answered his own question. It
had been the disruption of the Union, war, loss of property and
revenue, increased debt, heavy taxation, emancipation and social
revolution, loss of personal liberties, the death of 150,000 young men,
increased centralization, and the "set back" of civilization for "a half
century by the demoralization incident to these unhappy events." The
result of continued Republican control of the government will be that
"burdensome taxation, suffering wretchedness, will come to the
dwellings of the common people."[35]

The Democrats reserved their most violent abuse for the antislavery policies of the administration. Their early suspicions about
abolitionist control of the Republican party became certainties as the
new government recognized the Negro Republic of Haiti, abolished
slavery in the District of Columbia, repealed the fugitive slave law,
and then issued a more general emancipation proclamation. Those
policies, the Democrats charged, were not constitutional. The federal
government had no right to interfere with slavery which was guaranteed by the Constitution as a local institution. "If the Constitution
recognizes slavery, it is not a subject of federal politics. . . . The
general government has nothing to do with it except in its mere
property nature." Nor could slavery be ended by amendment, for to
do so was to abolish "our peculiar form and structure of government." Such action would destroy "the 'balance of powers on which
the perfection and endurance of our political fabric depends.' " For
the first time in American history a change would be made in our
Constitution which would "interfere with the reserved rights of the
States." The Republicans' pressing of antislavery legislation, therefore, was one more confirmation of their disregard of constitutional

35. *Atlas and Argus*, January 8, 1864; *Illinois State Register*, July 16, March 4,
1863; New York *World*, July 8, 1864; *Record of Seymour*, p. 75; Cox, *Eight Years in
Congress*, p. 261.

limitations for the sake of their own social and political vision.[36]

The Democrats let none of this pass without tremendous outcries of horror and constant reminders that this, a white man's country, was in imminent danger of collapse, social revolution, and destruction, all brought on by the policies of the now thoroughly abolitionized Republicans.[37] Historians have offered a great deal of evidence in the past decade illuminating the extent of racism among Americans in the Civil War era and their resistance to obvious black advances in the society.[38] Democrats shared these attitudes, and certainly articulated them far more intensely than did most other Northerners. They defamed Negroes in the most scurrilous language. Negroes were "vicious, indolent, and improvident." Attempts to improve their status ran "counter to the laws of race, the laws of nature." The Union, the Pennsylvania Democracy resolved in state convention, was "made for white men; . . . the men who made it never intended, by anything they did, to place the black race upon an equality with the white." Tales of threatened miscegenation, "but another pet object of the Lincoln party," and Negro bestiality, complete with evidence, ran rampant throughout Democratic rhetoric. Lincoln and his "nigger-crazed counselors" planned to let "hordes" of slaves overrun the

36. New York *World*, January 6, 1865; *Congressional Globe*, 38 Cong., 1 sess., pp. 2096, 2938; ibid., 2 sess., p. 239.

37. Michael Les Benedict has argued effectively that the major thrust of Republicans and Republican policy was never radical in the 1860s but dominated by a basic conservatism, in turn supported by a majority of Republican Congressmen. The Republicans were unwilling to encroach on the power of the states over individual rights. Historians, he argues, "might characterize Republicans' final decision in 1877 to cease attempting to protect citizens' rights in the South through national power more aptly as a consequence than a betrayal of their principles of 1865–1868." See "Preserving the Constitution: The Conservative Bases of Radical Reconstruction," *Journal of American History* 61 (June 1974): 90.

But, as he also notes, this kind of distinction did not matter to the Democrats. They saw all Republicans as imbued flatly with a spirit of radicalism. They recognized few nuances and drew little comfort from any Republican arguments that they were not doing radical things. See also, Benedict, *A Compromise of Principle: Congressional Republicans and Reconstruction, 1863–1869* (New York, 1974).

38. V. Jacque Voegeli, *Free But Not Equal: The Midwest and the Negro During the Civil War* (Chicago, 1967); C. Vann Woodward, "Seeds of Failure in Radical Race Policy," *Publications of the American Philosophical Society* no. 110 (February 18, 1966), pp. 1–9; Forrest Wood, *Black Scare: The Racist Response to Emancipation and Reconstruction* (Berkeley and Los Angeles, 1968).

North, taking up the soil, competing with white labor, and, worst of all, mixing the races. Americans had to stop the war fought "for the visionary purpose of abolishing slavery" whose effect will "certainly be to destroy the free institutions under which you have enjoyed so many blessings," and to establish the "social equality of black and white." The Republicans will arm the Negroes and the result will be another Sepoy rebellion. The use of Negro troops in the Union army was only to be the beginning. "Another four years of abolition rule, and negro generals will command white soldiers." For the white man "it is really a case of life or death" to resist all of the Republican plans for racial equality.[39]

Nothing stopped the Republicans in their "insane course" because they had "nothing except 'nigger on the brain.'" In short, a "spirit of intermeddling and false philanthropy" dominated the government. The administration had changed the character of the war from an "avowed and just purpose" to restore the Union to "an abolition war—a war for general emancipation." In fact, "the republican idea of the war has centered down to this, that its only importance is that it is an opportunity for the blacks." We take it, one Democratic congressman argued to his Republican colleagues across the aisle, that "it is not the intention of the opposition to have peace until every negro is free." For the Negro "you will destroy the country; for him you will allow the liberties of the white man to be stricken down, and every sacred guarantee of liberty in the Constitution put under foot without a whimper of a censure." The Emancipation Proclamation "draws the line between those who wished to see the Constitution preserved and those [who] wish to see it destroyed." Enough of "experimental legislation, ending no man can tell in what unforeseen disaster." Emancipation is a "ruin breeding word." We have "more

39. *Congressional Globe,* 37 Cong., 2 sess., *Appendix,* p. 245; Charles Biddle, *Address to Philadelphia Democrats,* August 1863, quoted in Nicholas Wainright, "The Loyal Opposition in Civil War Philadelphia," *Pennsylvania Magazine of History and Biography* 88 (July 1964): 306; *Appleton's Cyclopedia, 1862,* pp. 703–704; James F. Pederson and Kenneth Wald, *Shall the People Rule?: A History of the Democratic Party in Nebraska Politics, 1854–1972* (Lincoln, Neb., 1973), p. 29; *Congressional Globe,* 37 Cong. 2 sess., *Appendix,* p. 243; ibid., 38 Cong., 1 sess., p. 712; Church, *Speech; Illinois State Register,* September 30, 1864; Columbus (Ohio) *Crisis,* January 29, 1862.

to fear today from the prejudices of an American congress as to negro emancipation than from the bayonets of a rebellious and insolent foe."[40]

As the war continued, matters grew worse. Perhaps nothing was met with more horror by the Democrats than the enlistment of Negro troops in the Union forces. To give Negroes guns threatened every attitude and belief of the country and portended a social revolution of inutterable consequences. It suggested "a madman . . . attempting to extinguish a flame by continually throwing on fuel." Nor did the American people "require . . . help from the negro" in restoring the Union. If the Union could "not be preserved by the white man . . . there are no conditions upon which it can be saved." Arm Negroes, the Republicans were warned, and all "all hope of . . . peaceful settlement . . . is washed away like some tracings on the sea shore at the turn of the tide." Yet the administration had done so. In the North after the issuance of the Emancipation Proclamation, "that masterpiece of folly and treachery . . . further enlistments of white soldiers became almost impossible," because they would not fight in an abolitionist war. As a result, the Republicans had needlessly prolonged the war for their own base and selfish motives.[41]

Democratic campaign appeals increasingly centered on the impossibility of restoring the Union under the conditions established by Republican adolitionist policies. Peace and restoration were possible only if the North reassured the South and established the conditions for a peaceful and Constitutional reunion. The coming into power of a sectional party was bad enough, for it had split the Union and caused a war. Still, the war could be brought to an end if the Union sentiment in the South were allowed room to develop and bring sense back to the bulk of the Southern people. "The fundamental condition of the problem . . . is the creation of a strong and predominant Union party

40. *Boston Post,* February 18, 1862; *Congressional Globe,* 38 Cong., 2 sess., pp. 858, 530; ibid., 1 sess., pp. 2940, 2954, 1484; ibid., 37 Cong., 2 sess., p. 2175; ibid., 3 sess., *Appendix,* p. 77; *Address of New Jersey Democrats, 1862,* 4–5; *Detroit Free Press,* June 10, 1863; T. J. Barnett to S. L. M. Barlow, December 30, 1862, Barlow Papers; *Atlas and Argus,* February 3, 1865.

41. *Congressional Globe,* 38 Cong., 2 sess., *Appendix,* p. 55; ibid., 37 Cong., 2 sess., pp. 3204, 3206; ibid., 3 sess., p. 1270; Sam Ward to S. L. M. Barlow, April 29, 1862, Barlow Papers.

in the South. If this be impossible, reunion is impossible, and all talk about it is gross absurdity." But this was not what had happened. The North had to "let slavery alone." The Republicans had not done so, however, because they valued too "many things above the Union." In fact, "everything being done is calculated to drive the Union men of the South into the arms of the secessionists." The Emancipation Proclamation intensified "the spirit of resistance in the South." The Republicans had made "the emancipation of the slave population a paramount consideration to the preservation of the country." It was clear, therefore, from the beginning, James A. Bayard believed, that the Republicans intended to make the war "one of extermination" of the South because the South would not give in.[42]

Before the policy of a war fought only to restore the Union was changed, and the Proclamation issued, "there was a strong attachment to the Constitution in many of the seceded states. . . . But [it] was entirely dispelled by the Proclamation of Emancipation." The Proclamation had prolonged the war, led to atrocities on both sides, and ultimately "strengthened the South and weakened the North." The South now fought harder because of the Northern policy of abolition.[43] The "doom of the Union is sealed unless the abolition policy is renounced." Republican "*control* of what is left of the Union is incompatible with its reconstruction, as all their notions are in direct antagonism to the prejudices, feelings and interests of the South." So long as the government was "run according to puritanical or New England ideas, we may bid farewell to any Union except one founded on a centralized sectional despotism, with *rulers* in one section and *subjects* at the other." In short, Cox lamented, "Abolition

42. New York *World*, September 24, 1864; John A. Dix to F. P. Blair, December 1861; John A. Dix Papers, Columbia University Library, New York, N.Y.; *Official Proceedings, Democratic National Convention, 1864* (Chicago, 1864), p. 23; David Davis to Joseph Holt, April 28, 1862, Joseph Holt Papers, Library of Congress; *Congressional Globe*, 37 Cong., 2 sess., p. 1360; James A. Bayard to Thomas F. Bayard, December 4, 1861, Bayard Papers.

43. Thurlow Weed to John Bigelow, April 16, 1863, in John Bigelow, *Retrospections of an Active Life* (New York, 1909), 1: 632; H. T. Utley, *The History of Slavery and Emancipation, Speech Delivered by H. T. Utley Before the Democratic Association in Dubuque, Iowa, February 12, 1863* (Philadelphia, 1863); *Congressional Globe*, 38 Cong., 2 sess., p. 40; Cox, *Eight Years in Congress*, p. 266; Charles J. Ingersoll, *A Letter to a Friend in a Slave State* (Philadelphia, 1862), p. 59.

has made the Union, for the present, impossible.''[44]

Ultimately, the Democrats warned, the very social fabric of the society, the basic bedrock of personal and institutional relationships, would collapse. ''Such social terrorism, such intolerance of opinion, as we have endured, had never before been practiced in any community speaking the English language.'' As a consequence of Republican behavior, there was a growing contempt for all law. ''The primal sin of disobedience is not only the immediate cause of this war, but its spirit has also sapped and weakened the foundations of our . . . authority in every part of our land. . . . Obedience is the basis of all family, political and religious organizations. It is the principle of cohesion that holds society together, without which it crumbles into atoms. Yet we have seen a disregard of this vital principle. . . . We have heard disobedience to laws taught in our pulpits, and commended by the press.'' The social fabric has consequently been rent irreparably. We are, in fact, ''vibrating between anarchism and despotism.'' Let none of us, Congressman J. C. Allen of Illinois concluded, ''in our effort to destroy slavery . . . destroy the fundamental law of our Government, and leave our own race a prey to anarchy or despotism. If slavery must needs be buried, let its burial be conducted without revolution or fraud, that the public authority may not be brought into contempt.''[45]

Throughout the war, Democrats, and the rest of the country too, knew exactly what the party believed about the policies of the Lincoln administration. The party's communications network never let up. Every newspaper, speech, and pamphlet incessantly drummed their arguments to the nation. Congressmen in debates pressed the message against their opponents as well. The challenge to the Lincoln administration on these matters was total.[46] The intensity of the attack

44. *Congressional Globe,* 38 Cong., 1 sess., p. 1295; New York *World,* February 16, 1863; John Dowling to S. L. M. Barlow, September 30, 1862, Barlow Papers; Cox, *Puritanism in Politics,* p. 4.

45. *Record of Seymour,* p. 33; *Congressional Globe,* 38 Cong., 1 sess., p. 1739; ibid., *Appendix,* p. 108; William Reed, *A Paper Containing a Statement and a Vindication of Certain Political Opinions* (Philadelphia, 1862), p. 20n.

46. An editorial in the New York *World* a few days before the elections in 1862 effectively spelled out all of the components of their argument. ''This election,'' the

varied. The frustrations and bitterness of the war made the Democrats rhetorically more violent at certain times, as in the spring and summer of 1863, and in the presidential campaign of 1864. But they knew from the first what was wrong and articulated their concern.[47]

When the Democrats were talking about was constitutional change of an unparalleled nature, or revolution as they called it, and they did not find it acceptable. The Republicans had confirmed all of their worst fears. "The time has come," George Pendleton summed up, "the vail [sic] is drawn aside. We see clearly. The party in possession of the powers of the government is revolutionary. It seeks to use those powers to destroy the Government, to change its form, to change its spirit. . . . It is in rebellion against the Constitution, it is in treasonable conspiracy against the Government." Let the Constitution alone, Samuel Randall went on, "it is good enough." But the Republicans had not. They had usurped states' powers, trampled on individual rights, promoted corrupting financial policies, attempted to change the social structure, "by edict and bayonet, by sham election and juggling proclamation." This now had to be stopped; American politics had to be returned to the control of conservatives. Only then would peace and prosperity replace Republican-induced war, waste, and destruction.[48]

---

editor wrote, "virtually determines the question whether our lives and liberties are to be under the protection of iinpartial courts of justice, which punish the guilty but liberate accused innocence. It decides whether we are to have free speech, a free press, free political gatherings, and free elections. It decides whether meritorious generals in the field are to be supported or thwarted. It decides whether loyal laborers are to be defrauded of from one third to half of their honest earnings by compulsory payment in depreciated and irredeemable currency. . . . This election also decides whether a swarthy inundation of negro laborers and paupers shall flood the North, accumulating new burdens on our tax-payers, cheapening white labor by black competition, repealing immigration, and raising dangerous questions of political and social equality." New York *World,* November 4, 1862.

47. In July 1864, as the parties were girding for the fall presidential election, one that would determine "not simply whether we have a Union, but whether we have a Constitution," congressional Democrats issued another address similar in nature and style to that of 1862. It ran on two full pages of the New York *World,* encompassing seven columns. Under such headings as corruption in government, conscription, constitutionalism, and the corruption of race, the address repeated every charge in the Democratic assault on the Republican administration for what they had done, were doing, and planned to do. Ibid., July 19, 1864.

48. *Congressional Globe,* 38 Cong., 1 sess., pp. 2105, 2991, 712.

Their attitudes and commitments, and the pitch of their opposition, showed a persistence and a continuity throughout the war period. Their perceptions about the extent of change or the amount of constitutional infringement were not accurate. But far from being merely highly charged in temper and irrational in content, these expressed fears clustered together in a view of the world that was coherent to Democrats and sharply differentiated them in their approach to politics and government policies from the Republicans. The Democrats believed they were in a battle between two cultures, two nations. They feared the disruption of politics, assailed the sectionalism, the social plans, and the principles of the Republicans. Their filter prevented them from seeing nuances in the situation, and how restrained the Lincoln administration was on many of these matters. Their fears were all part of a conception of the Union, its people, its government and its powers, and of its social processes, that Democrats had been committed to for years. If anything, the events of the 1850s and early 1860s had made them more traditionalist than ever. Faced with war, a Republican administration, and what they saw as their opponents' ideological commitments, they, in effect, dug in their heels. Their heels remained firmly entrenched despite the rise of new issues and problems. Democratic traditionalism in rhetoric and in belief was the most dominant aspect of their response to the war, the Lincoln administration, and their own minority status.

During the war, then, the Democrats were able to reach down and find the common symbols and ideas that united them. The fact that there were differences within the Democrats' coalition is a well-recognized aspect of Democratic party affairs during the Civil War. But they were clearly united in what Harold Hyman has called "an idiom of antipathy to marital ways. . . , of obeisance to the Bill of Rights . . . and a quest for static federalism racially ordered."[49] The Democrats, themselves, had their own familiar battle cry in regard to the revolutionary times in which they lived. They wanted "the Constitution as it is, the Union as it was." They thus met the first imperative of party: ideological unity. They were able to define and agree on what differentiated them from the enemy and then to present these differences clearly and starkly to the electorate.

49. Hyman, *A More Perfect Union,* p. 77; *Atlas and Argus,* May 21, 1862.

At the same time, they believed that what they argued was good politics. Election results in the late 1850s and 1860 had indicated that they were no longer the majority party in the Northern states. In a time when most people were deeply committed to their party and rarely willing to defect on election day, such minority status posed grave dangers. But Democrats believed that they had successfully established during the war the means to attract voters beyond their own partisans. They had been able, because of the repulsiveness of the Republicans, to draw a sharp and distinct line, but, they believed, not a partisan one, between conservatism and Republicanism. Their tactics already looked effective to them. Many who identified themselves as conservatives in this period and who had spent much of their lives opposing the Democrats, men such as John Jordan Crittenden in Kentucky and Robert Winthrop in Massachusetts, did become increasingly drawn toward the Democrats in the latter's guise as the party of conservative restoration. It appeared also that these conservatives brought with them many other former Whigs and Constitutional Unionists. That certainly seemed so in the elections of 1862. Along with Democratic popular strength already manifested, these would be enough to bring conservative statesmen, led by the Democrats, back into national power.

But there was another matter which clouded Democratic hopes even as they developed an electorally effective conservative argument. Divisions quickly emerged among Democrats over how that appeal should be made, as well as over the shaping of concrete policies based on their common general conservative attitude. How much did they have to disguise their own partisan roots in order to continue to attract, and win over permanently, these others who were not Democrats, in fact who had been anti-Democratic throughout their political life? Given the depths of Democrats' commitment to their own traditional beliefs could they develop an appeal to the non-Democrats without sacrificing basic ideological tenets of their own and thus run the risk of disrupting their own party? These questions confounded the party leadership from the beginning of the war.

4

"The Oddities and Absurdities" of Particular Groups: The Democrats Confront Each Other, 1861–1864

IN THEIR BID to end the threatened puritan-abolition revolution, the Democrats' major weapon was their long history of standing together in pursuit of their cause, fortified by their strong agreement on a conservative ideology. All agreed on the need to oust the Lincoln administration. But, unfortunately for their hopes, and despite the strength of their common outlook the wartime Democrats found it difficult to agree on the best means of accomplishing that. The most rational way for a political party to act in any era is to do everything in its power to attract to it the greatest possible number of voters. It should, therefore, promise them what they want and demonstrate continually a willingness to achieve what is promised, and to rule the country effectively and efficiently.[1] This was particularly necessary for a minority party trying to win over normally hostile or uncommitted, albeit restless, voters.

But, obviously, it is never that simple. Because of internal constraints, particularly a commitment to specific principles, party spokesmen and candidates cannot promise everything. Often their commitments preclude reaching out as far as necessary to disaffected nonparty members. The difficulty of working out suitable tactics within such restrictions can also cause internal problems. So it was

1. Party behavioral norms are well discussed in Nelson Polsby and Aaron Wildavsky, *Presidential Elections: Strategies of American Electoral Politics*, 4th ed. (New York, 1976); and Gerald Pomper *Elections in America* (New York, 1968).

with the Civil War Democrats. From the first, they were beset by the constraints of their own partisan commitments and by important tactical differences over how to proceed. As a result, their communal sense was often strained. There was tremendous anger and bitterness between different Democrats despite their common views concerning the dangers facing the country.

"No Antiwar Party Could Succeed With The People"

The Democracy continually had to confront the root question of its own legitimacy as an opposition party in time of war. Democrats were caught in one of the most difficult of all political situations. They were endeavoring to work out an active and uncompromising opposition to the government at a time when the Union was in the most extreme danger. In the early days of the conflict, Stephen A. Douglas warned his fellow Democrats against seeming to oppose the Union's efforts to subdue the rebellion in their zeal for partisan warfare against the excesses of the administration. They needed, he warned, to dissociate themselves from the rebelling South even as they assailed the policies of an administration which, with little trace of political ingenuousness, trumpeted itself as the sole defender of the Union and the guardian of the country's salvation. As another Democrat put it in 1863, "while we all agree in the purpose of utterly annihilating the Lincoln administration and its policy we must also agree in standing by our constitutional government . . . and in an unfaltering determination to maintain the Union, under the Constitution."[2]

Opposition to the government had rarely been popular (although always present) in previous American wars. Democrats still used such epithets as "Blue Light" and "Hartford Convention" Federalists against the Whigs a generation after the War of 1812. The Whig objections to the Mexican War caused them much embarrassment as well. Previous experience had shown that opposition parties could only operate effectively within certain limits during wartime. They could not appear to be extremist or seem to be going beyond legitimate

2. For Douglas, see above, chapter two. Joseph K. Edgerton to S. S. Cox, April 8, 1863, Samuel S. Cox Papers, Brown University Liberty, Providence, R.I.

limits in their opposition.[3] The Democrats' lot, therefore, would not be easy. They had the "sad & difficult role" of opposing a "weak and wicked ruler without harming . . . [the] country."[4] In the middle of a civil war when people hungered for stability and reassurance, wanted to believe in the legitimacy of their government, and felt the bitterness of an internecine conflict, successfully developing a policy of responsible opposition could be beyond reach.

The Democrats hastened to make it clear from the outset that the sine qua non for ending the war had to be full restoration of an unimpaired Union. No Democrat "asks that we shall consent to a peace involving disunion." As the only national party in existence and the only one that appreciated the value of the Union, the Democracy would never accept, Congressman Cox vowed, its "mutilation or dismemberment." Democrats realized that most Northerners did not want a war for abolition but did "demand its continuance until the Confederates consent to return to the Union." Democrats agreed with that. Between a war "for the single purpose of maintaining the Constitution and the Union, a peace overthrowing them, we understand that all Democrats are for the former."[5]

Such statements were unexceptional. Almost all Democrats subscribed to the Unionist quality in the party's rhetoric. Nevertheless, an important distinction between Democratic groups soon emerged concerning the war itself. It was evident in the public arenas of politics such as Congress, where the debates frequently indicated differences in perspectives between Vallandigham or Fernando Wood on one hand, and Sunset Cox among others on the other. These differences carried over into some of the actual roll-call voting on various bills and resolutions offered during the war. Generally, all Democrats voted in positions different from the Republicans. But, in his study of the

3. They could not, in V. O. Key's words, "so threaten accepted policies and practices" as to arouse "widespread anxieties" about the nation's ultimate victory. V. O. Key, *The Responsible Electorate* (Cambridge, Mass., 1966), pp. 78–79. See also Samuel Eliot Morison, Frederick Merk, and Frank Freidel, *Dissent in Three American Wars* (Cambridge, Mass., 1970).

4. William H. Wadsworth to S. L. M. Barlow, December 16, 1862, Samuel L. M. Barlow Papers, Henry E. Huntington Library, San Marino, Ca.

5. *Chicago Times*, November 20, December 4, 1863, April 7, 1864; *Congressional Globe*, 37 Cong., 3 sess., p. 683; New York *World*, April 20, 1864.

Thirty-seventh Congress (1861–1863), Leonard Curry identified two distinct Democratic blocs separated from each other on certain votes on emancipation, the coercion of the South, and other war-related policies.[6] Similarly, Michael L. Benedict, in a very thorough examination of voting patterns in the Thirty-eighth Congress (1863–1865), also found some Democratic division. In the House of Representatives, for example, in the first session all but a few stragglers were either in one bloc of forty-four representatives including such men as George Pendleton, Daniel Voorhees, and Wood, all of whom Benedict labels "extreme Peace Democrats" or in a second bloc of twenty-eight "moderate Peace Democrats" including Cox. The issues dividing these men from each other ranged from how one voted on an amendment that no troops be raised under the conscription bill until the president offered an armistice, to reactions to a resolution that the president appoint a peace commission to negotiate with the Confederacy, to another on whether to support a resolution of thanks to General Philip Sheridan.[7] Such differences revealed some critical problems in the way Democrats viewed their opposition role.

The War Democrats were gone. But there were echoes of at least some of their assumptions in the stance taken by one group of party members remaining in the Democratic organization. They supported the war effort, arguing that the "sober, honest, intelligent thought of these Northern states is in favor of sustaining this Republic by force of arms." They agreed with Buchanan's dictum of late 1861 that "the government must be supported with men & money in the prosecution of the war."[8] Perhaps most Democrats did not go as far as national

6. Leonard P. Curry, "Congressional Democrats, 1861–1863," *Civil War History* 12 (September 1966): 213–29; and his *Blueprint for Modern America: Nonmilitary Legislation of the First Civil War Congress* (Nashville, 1968).

7. Michael Les Benedict, *A Compromise of Principle: Congressional Republicans and Reconstruction, 1863–1869* (New York, 1974), pp. 339–41, 344–45, 391–92. This discussion is based on my interpretation of Benedict's lists and charts, not his.

8. George L. Miller to James S. Morton, April 10, 1863, James S. Morton Papers, Nebraska Historical Society, Lincoln, Neb. (microfilm copy, Cornell University Library); James Buchanan to John Adams Dix, December 10, 1861, John Adams Dix Papers, Columbia University Library, New York, N.Y.; *Address of the New Jersey Democratic State Central Committee to the Voters of the State, October, 1862* (Trenton, 1862), p. 16. George McJimsey, *Genteel Partisan: Manton Marble,*

chairman Belmont who, on the Fourth of July 1862, said, "there is no sacrifice too great, none we should not most cheerfully make in order to help the government at this moment. We want more troops, more money and everything good and loyal citizens can give to their country in this hour of danger." But they made it clear in their private correspondence that, although they were unhappy that the war had to be fought, and that they preferred some means of negotiating a restoration of an unimpaired Union, on balance, if a war to restore the Union had to be fought, they were animated by a commitment to what John Van Buren later called a "sound war spirit."[9]

The attitude persisted for another reason as well, that of electoral strategy. An important group of party members believed that they must never let their pro-war, Union-restoring position be muted or distorted or neglected. They realized that it was not only what the party believed and said it stood for, but also the image that it projected to the public that would determine electoral success. They wanted, in short, to establish the party's legitimacy clearly in the minds of the people, despite its opposition stance in a time of national crisis. They believed that "while the war lasts, no party can succeed that does not make its energetic prosecution the paramount object" of its program. They had, therefore, to "lose no opportunity . . . to clear [their] skirts from the suspicion of sympathy with secession." If they did not, they were "sure to be defeated." The American people "will rush to the support of your candidate and platform," the Democratic National Convention was told in 1864, "provided you will offer to their suffrage a tried patriot, who has proved his devotion to the Union and the Constitution, and provided that you pledge him and yourselves to maintain that hallowed inheritance by every effort and sacrifice in your power." But, "any attempt to stem the popular tide, and to throw

---

1834–1917 (Ames, Iowa, 1971); David Lindsey, *"Sunset" Cox: Irrepressible Democrat* (Detroit, 1959); and Irving Katz, *August Belmont: A Political Biography* (New York, 1968), are good introductions to some of the most prominent Democratic Legitimists.

9. August Belmont, *Letters, Speeches and Addresses of August Belmont* (New York, 1890), p. 134; John Van Buren to Samuel J. Tilden, September 4, 1863, in *Letters and Literary Memorial of Samuel J. Tilden,* ed. John Bigelow (New York, 1908), 1: 185.

cold water on the patriotism of the people when they feel the destiny of the nation is at stake, will always prove abortive." It "may reasonably be demanded of an opposition party that it shall be patriotic. It has no right to embarrass the government in the discharge of necessary duties. When the country is engaged in a just, or even an unjust war, a patriotic opposition will not permit the honor of the country to suffer, or its safety be imperiled, by withholding necessary supplies." This was the linchpin of their commitment and their strategy. They knew that "no antiwar party could succeed with the people."[10]

At the heart of their position, of course, was their desire to maintain an effective opening to unhappy and disenchanted conservatives who were not Democrats. They had a vision of the electorate as conservative, Union, pro-war, and potentially pro-Democratic if everything worked out correctly. The election of 1862 had confirmed that "there were not enough old Democrats to give us the victory," Judge John Caton of Illinois told Horatio Seymour right after the election. "We must get, and did get, accessions from the Republicans." Democratic leaders maintained all sorts of contacts with the conservatives, both publicly, in such forums as Congress and in the newspapers, and privately, in correspondence, even with conservative members of the Lincoln administration. They knew that there were major differences between themselves and the other group. Undoubtedly, Democrats were in "advance of the mass of conservative men" who supported them in 1862. But it was neither "necessary nor desirable . . . to emphasize . . . differences. We desire to emphasize . . . points of agreement."[11]

10. New York *World*, November 5, 1863; August Belmont to S. L. M. Barlow, October 17, 1862, Barlow Papers; Belmont, *Letters*, p. 141; C. H. Bond to S. S. Cox, February 19, 1862, Cox Papers; New York *World*, February 17, 1864; John Caton, "The Position and Policy of the Democratic Party. A Letter to Hon. Horatio Seymour," in idem, *Miscellanies* (Boston, 1880), p. 22.

11. Caton, "Position and Policies of Democrats," p. 23; New York *World*, February 26, 1863; James F. Barlow to S. S. Cox, November 22, 1863, Barlow Papers. Samuel Barlow, for one, had an extensive correspondence with Montgomery Blair and T. J. Barnett, both members of the Lincoln administration. Similarly, many Democrats kept in touch with the secretary of war, a Democrat, Edwin M. Stanton, at least for a while. For one fruit of some of these contacts, see Herman Belz, "The Etheridge Conspiracy of 1863: A Projected Conservative Coup," *Journal of Southern History* 36 (November 1970): 549–67.

There was certainly a great deal of evidence that non-Democratic conservatives, among them Republicans and original administration supporters, shared the feeling that Lincoln's policies had hurt the war effort and made peace all but impossible. Manton Marble was told of conservatives who had "never been a member of the democratic party," who were now "convinced that there is now no hope of ending this deplorable war and restoring the Union but by and through that party." They were now willing to join openly with their traditional Democratic enemies because of their fears. The Constitutional Union party in New York State, which had retained its separate organization after 1860, indicated in 1862 that it now favored joint nominations with the Democrats for governor and other state offices. Finally, even the doyen of anti-Democrats, Thurlow Weed, was reported as being "secretly for us." As a result, "all conservative men are coming to us daily thus increasing the conservative strength in our party rendering the future more hopeful."[12]

But this promising opening to the conservatives would work only if an association with the Democracy would not open them to charges of treasonable conduct. In 1862 conservatives saw that Democrats "were as earnestly engaged in the prosecution of the war as was Mr. Lincoln himself." So they voted Democratic. If the party would continue to hold "all the reflective, substantial conservatism of the nation" in its ranks, it "must show no lukewarmness or hesitancy in sustaining or prosecuting" the war. Therefore, the Democracy's mission was to continue to preserve the national honor and not speak of peace until the restoration of the Union was assured.[13]

To further this strategy, these Democrats took every opportunity to demonstrate their vigorous devotion to saving the Union. They did their best to repress ambiguous or unfriendly actions and statements about the war from party meetings and other sources. At the New York state convention in 1861, for example, it was reported that a delegates'

12. G. S. Millard to Luke F. Cozans, June 30, 1863, Manton Marble Papers, Library of Congress; S. L. M. Barlow to George B. McClellan, September 12, 1864, George B. McClellan Papers, Library of Congress; J. D. Eaton to Sanford Churchill, in Churchill to Horatio Seymour, January 28, 1863, Horatio Seymour Papers, New York State Library, Albany, N.Y.

13. Caton, "Position and Policy of Democrats," pp. 28, 30–31; S. S. Cox to Manton Marble, June 17, 1864, Marble Papers.

dispute was settled by throwing out one group whose seating might make the party seem antiwar. Numerous resolutions of thanks to soldiers were passed and included in party platforms. In Congress, most Democrats clearly established a record of war support in their votes for appropriations and supplies, for "all men and means required for the vigorous prosecution of the war." They accepted restrictions on their freedom such as agreeing to swear oaths of loyalty to the Union. The editorials in their newspapers and the speeches of their candidates and congressmen always included affirmation of the need to fight the war and the denial of any peace based on any other terms but the restoration and reaffirmation of the Union. Statements that they were unconditional Union men, and were, as Allan Thurman of Ohio suggested, "for the Union—one and inseparable," filled their public declamations. Never, one typical statement summed up, "has a Government been sustained with such ample resources of means and men as the people have voluntarily placed in the hands of this Administration. . . . As Democrats we are determined to maintain this patriotic attitude, and despite . . . adverse and disheartening circumstances to devote all our energies to sustain the cause of the Union; to secure peace through victory."[14] In sum, as the editor of the Albany (N.Y.) *Atlas and Argus* wrote in 1862, "No Democrat in Congress has impeded the progress of legislation to put down rebellion. No Democrat, out of Congress in these Northern states has failed to support the Government by men and money in its struggle for existence." They could do nothing more.[15]

At the same time, the Legitimists did keep up their opposition to the administration. Unlike the War Democrats, their commitment to legitimacy did not include any confusion about the difference between opposition to the government and support of the Union. It may be "reasonably . . . demanded of an opposition party that it shall be

14. Columbus (Ohio) *Crisis,* July 8, 1863; Erastus Corning et al. to Abraham Lincoln, May 19, 1863, *The War of the Rebellion, A Compilation of the Official Records of the Union and Confederate Armies*, Series II (Washington, D.C., 1899), 5: 654; New York *World*, April 20, 1864; Springfield *Illinois State Register*, October 13, 1862; *Congressional Globe*, 38 Cong., 1 sess., p. 458.

15. *New York Herald*, September 6, 1861; *Congressional Globe*, 38 Cong., 1 sess., p. 1531; ibid. 2 sess., p. 275; *Detroit Free Press*, December 19, 1863; Albany (N.Y.) *Atlas and Argus*, June 12, 1862.

patriotic.'' But after it had voted supplies to support the war, "it is its *right,* it is its DUTY to hold the administration responsible for a wise and honest application of these resources.'' That distinction they kept clear in their minds and their public stances as well. But, in keeping with their electoral strategy, their opposition was couched in tones of a general conservatism which was also, they felt, quite compatible with normal Democratic attitudes. ''The Democrats discriminate between the constitutional and unconstitutional measures of the administration, zealously supporting the former and vigorously repudiating the latter.'' They reminded everyone that political opposition contributed substantially to the proper functioning of the government because there was ''no period when the public interest requires the government to be watched with greater vigilence or held to a stricter accountibility than in the midst of a great war.'' The opportunity for excess, mistakes, and corruption was then expanded immeasurably. It was ''the proper business of a patriotic opposition to check such abuses, and to insist that the war shall be conducted with prudence, wisdom, and such economy as is consistent with vigor.''[16]

The Legitimists were as ideological as any other Democrats. They never advocated that the party abandon or even temporarily suspend its principles. Rather, they wanted those principles encased in something else as well. As one of Cox's correspondents put it in early 1862, speaking of a local Democratic newspaper, ''the 'Watchman' ought to have gone in for a vigorous prosecution of the war, and at the same time given the abolitionists 'hail Columbia.' '' This the Democratic leaders tried to do as clearly as they could. Thus, ''the true issue between the abolitionists and democrats has nothing to do with the continuance of the war; the issue is, the purposes and objects for which it is continued.'' A ''vote for the Democratic state ticket . . . is not a vote against sustaining our gallant soldiers in the field, as the Republicans try to make out, but will have the effect to stimulate the administration to more vigor in the conduct of the war, and thus bring about an early and honorable peace. Let it be remembered that the failures of the administration were when it had no opposition and that it has done

16. New York *World,* February 24, 1863, February 17, 1864; J. D. Eaton to S. Churchill, in S. Churchill to Horatio Seymour, January 28, 1863, Seymour Papers.

better in every way since the reorganization of the Democratic party.''[17]

These were all shrewd arguments, for they were directed at both Republican ideological intransigence and the administration's inability to solve the crisis of the Union. But there was a weakness in the Legitimists' argument, one that brought them a great deal of trouble within the party. There were limits to Democratic attempts at simple vote maximization. A party, particularly a minority one, is always in a state of tension between its devotion to its principles and its need to win over votes from outside the party. If it sticks rigidly to its traditional principles, does it offer the uncommited outsider anything? If its leaders wished to win such men to them, did they not have to adopt a more flexible stance in regard to candidates and policies? But at the same time, how far could they go toward the outsiders in their effort to win them over without causing restlessness in their own ranks? If the Democracy became too much of a ''me-too'' party, would it not run the risk of losing some of its own supporters who would choose either to bolt to a third party possibly, or to sit it out on election day? Should the party members, for example, nominate non-Democrats for elective offices, tone down their espousal of the more provocative Democratic principles, and mute their opposition in areas where conservative consensus did not exist? Did not, in short, any Legitimist-conservative coalition have a potential weakness in it if there was some sacrificing of Democratic principles, in the name of legitimacy and cooperation with the conservatives?

The answer was that no Democratic leader could ignore the things that made the party distinctive (and traditionally inhospitable or repellent to non-Democrats). Everyone had to operate within defined parameters set by the party's traditions, its principles, and its distinctive outlook. The whole course of midnineteenth-century political history, the deeply ingrained suspicions and differences between party cultures saw to that. The Legitimists, in their overtures to the conservatives, always made it clear that cooperation had to be on Democratic terms, usually with Democratic candidates, and within the Democratic organization. In midwar, conservative leaders com-

17. C. H. Bond to Cox, February 19, 1862, Cox Papers; *Detroit Free Press*, October 11, 1863; New York *World*, November 2, 1863; *Illinois State Register*, August 28, 1862.

plained that Democrats "never resort to expedients to increase their vote" such as the nomination of non-Democrats or the tempering of outright Democratic platform planks and policies.[18] Such behavior roused, in itself, old partisan antagonisms and made wartime movement toward conservative cooperation difficult even in the face of common fears and enemies. And it did not resolve the internal conflict within the Democracy growing out of the resistance by many party members to the Legitimists' perspective.

"There Is No Room for a Second-Hand War Party"

There were in the Democratic party a number of "hot headed fools who would ruin everything" (in the words of an angry party opponent), because they had a different vision and ordering of priorities from the Legitimists.[19] They never hesitated to assert themselves strongly in party councils and elsewhere. To begin with, there were Democrats who from the very outset of the war spoke strongly against the conflict as "one of the saddest, blackest pages in the history of this country," which would lead only to "ruin and devastation North and South." Particularly strong among Border State Democrats, but with support elsewhere as well, they spoke intensely against the war even as their voices were often drowned in a sea of defenses of the conflict. They had not changed their minds about the way to reunite the country with the outbreak of the fighting, as so many other Democrats had done. They had opposed the destructive tendencies of Northern sectionalism before the war; they continued to do so once war commenced. To them the South was right constitutionally and all that had happened had changed nothing. They were unconditionally and reflexively antiwar.[20]

18. R. F. Stevens to R. B. Connolly, January 20, 1863, Seymour Papers.

19. J. D. Eaton to S. Churchill, in S. Churchill to Horatio Seymour, January 28, 1863, Seymour Papers. The best introductions to the Peace Democrats are Frank L. Klement, *The Limits of Dissent: Clement L. Vallandigham and the Civil War* (Lexington, Ky., 1970); idem, *The Copperheads in the Middle West* (Chicago, 1960); Wood Gray, *The Hidden Civil War* (New York, 1942); Charles Ray Wilson, "The Cincinnati *Daily Enquirer* and Civil War Politics: A Study in 'Copperhead' Opinion," (Ph.D. diss., University of Chicago, 1934). See also, *Proceedings of the Great Peace Convention Held in the City of New York, June 3, 1863; Speeches, Addresses, Resolutions and Letters from Leading Men* (New York, 1863).

20. *Congressional Globe*, 37 Cong., 1 sess., p. 244; James A. Bayard to S. L. M. Barlow, May 16, 1861, Barlow Papers; *New York News*, April 15, 1861.

As the war progressed, another group of antiwar Democrats joined them. Most of these originally supported a war to restore the Union, but grew to have grave doubts about the impact the conflict was having on the country. Like other Democrats, they too wondered how best to achieve the triumph of their party's brand of conservative constitutionalism. Prominent party leaders such as Clement Vallandigham of Ohio, Thomas Seymour of Connecticut, and Fernando Wood of New York agreed with many other Democrats that the Union was in the greatest danger, that the revolution was upon them, and something had to be done to overthrow the administration in power. In fighting to restore the Union and preserve the Constitution they bitterly attacked, as did their Legitimist brethren, the centralization of power, abolitionism, and the Republican party which had been, Fernando Wood charged, "feeding the flame of rebellion ever since its existence." They too reminded everyone of the traditional Democratic cry, "the rights, the inalienable, indestructible state rights that guard our firesides and homes." These "sacred local rights" had to be maintained as strongly as one would "the domestic purity of . . . families," for "it is this idea of a strong government . . . which has destroyed us."[21]

Then, however, their vision changed somewhat from that of other Democrats. Differences emerged over the relationship of the war effort to the threat they saw to the Union. The Legitimists argued that negotiations between North and South to end secession were preferable, but that the war was necessary to preserve the Union. Their antirevolutionary campaign could go on, however, even in the context of fighting the war. The pro-peace group had no patience with the Legitimists' stance. The latter focused so much attention on the problem of party legitimacy that they lost sight of the revolutionary situation in which the country was caught. The pro-peace group, on the other hand, saw the war as the major element distorting and misshaping the Union. So long as the war was supported in the North, no negotiations would ever take place. Moreover, its fighting fed the demands for ever more centralization of authority, ever more revolutionary policies that allowed the government to proceed on its

21. *Congressional Globe*, 38 Cong., 1 sess., p. 1535; William B. Reed, *A Northern Plea For Peace* (London, 1863), pp. 19, 36.

way doing what it wanted. Therefore, war was part of a revolutionizing policy, not separate from it. It was "multiplying the genius of a terrible social change and revolution. The most radical, revolutionary, and disorganizing doctrines" were "brought into vogue by the war; doctrines which sweep away the whole fabric of our institutions." If we continue the war, Vallandigham argued in his famous speech of January 1863 defining his peace stance, "I see nothing before us but universal political and social revolution, anarchy and bloodshed, compared with which the Reign of Terror in France was a merciful visitation."[22]

Many of the most prominent peace men did couple their position with an argument that peace could not come at any price. It had to be on the basis of the restoration of the Union in its entirety. As James Buchanan said during the campaign of 1864, "peace would be a great, a very great blessing; but it would be purchased at too high a price at the expense of the Union." Let us "renew our efforts to procure peace; but if failing, let us preserve our *nationality.*" In sum, among the peace people, one observer wrote, "there is an inconquerable desire for union—there is also a profound yearning for peace; the former overriding the latter with overwhelming power."[23]

Unfortunately, the war could not restore the Union, its one reason for being waged; such an idea was "sheer hallucination." Only negotiations between the sections would bring the South back. Continued war would have the opposite effect. First, it could not help but become a war of total destruction against the South. It was clear that the Republican radicals intended to destroy the South's social system. The Confederacy would, therefore, have nothing to negotiate about and would, instead, never stop resisting. The government was "carrying on war to exterminate the South. . . . The [Emancipation]

22. *Congressional Globe,* 38 Cong., 2 sess., *Appendix,* p. 56; Vallandigham's speech is in ibid., 37 Cong., 3 sess., *Appendix,* pp. 52–60; *Cincinnati Daily Enquirer,* September 6, October 29, 1863.

23. James Buchanan to J. Buchanan Henry, September 22, 1864, in *The Works of James Buchanan,* ed. John Bassett Moore (Philadelphia, 1910), 11: 372; E. J. Henry to John White Stevenson, March 15, 1863, John White Stevenson Papers, Library of Congress; Frank Freidel, Introduction to *Union Pamphlets of the Civil War, 1861–1865* (Cambridge, Mass., 1967), p. 38; Richard O. Curry, "The Union As It Was: A Critique of Recent Interpretations of the Copperheads," *Civil War History* 13 (March 1967): 38.

proclamation . . . shut the door on conciliation'' and it was naive to talk of saving the Union with its present form of government and constitutional liberty unimpaired. Even if the Lincoln administration succeeded in conquest, it would only make things worse. ''One half [of the Union] held in the union by force of military power . . . will not make a free Republic.'' Rather, it would ''constitute a military despotism.''[24]

If war was the source of all of the country's present and future problems, then there could be no such thing as Democratic support for the conflict. The peace group was convinced that the Legitimists deluded themselves if they believed it possible to support the war and still preserve the Constitution. Actually, all that the Legitimist position ultimately did was to destroy all that the Democratic party stood for. ''I believe,'' Fernando Wood argued, that ''the Democratic party, as far as this immediate question is concerned cannot be an abolition war party. There can be no such thing as a War Democrat, because when a man is in favor of the war, he must be in favor of the policies of the war as it is prosecuted by the party in power, with its unavoidable tendency to destroy the Constitution and the Union.'' In other words, the distinction the Legitimists drew between opposing the administration while supporting the war was invalid—it could not be drawn. If a Democrat supported the war, ''although he protests against the means employed, he is engaged in encouraging the main policy of the Abolitionists notwithstanding his protests.'' Such men could make ''no issue'' on which to challenge the Republicans. Each side would try to outdo the other in its commitment to vigorous prosecution, and the war would only increase in fury, as would the revolution of American life. In short, ''there is no room for a second-hand war party.''[25]

Ohio's Vallandigham became identified as the most forceful and

24. James A. Bayard to S. L. M. Barlow, February 4, 1864, Barlow Papers; Bayard to Thomas F. Bayard, January 8, 1863, Thomas F. Bayard Papers, Library of Congress; M. Birchard to S. S. Cox, March 10, 1964, Cox Papers.

25. *Congressional Globe*, 38 Cong., 1 sess., p. 1537; James Wall to William Henry Hurlbert, n.d., Barlow Papers; James Buchanan to Nahum Capen, January 27, 1864, in *Works of Buchanan*, ed. Moore, 11: 355; *Cincinnati Enquirer*, December 29, 1863.

notorious spokesman for this viewpoint. He spoke persistently and everywhere, pinpointing the relationship between peace and conservative constitutionalism. "I am for the Constitution first, and at all hazards; for whatever can now be saved of the Union next; and for Peace always as essential to the preservation of either," was the way he began. As the war progressed and he increasingly became a symbol of the antiwar forces, his mind did not change although he further clarified his position. In a speech in his hometown of Dayton in August 1862, he reiterated that he was for

obedience to all laws and constitutions. No man can be a good democrat who is not in favor of law and order. No matter how distasteful constitutions and laws may be, they must be obeyed. I am opposed to all mobs, and opposed also—inexorably opposed above everything, to all violations of constitution and law by men in authority—public servants. . . . Those parts of our constitutions and laws which command or restrain the people must be obeyed; but still more must those also which limit and restrain public servants, from the President down. . . . I am for suppressing rebellion—I am. I always have been. Perhaps my mode is not that of other men; but I have the right . . . of judging for myself of the true and proper mode. I think mine would have prevented it at first; and even after it began, would have ended it long since. . . . I repeat it: I am for suppressing all rebellions—both rebellions. There are two—the Secessionist Rebellion South, and the Abolition Rebellion, North and West. I am against both; for putting down both.

Let those who wish, he told the Democratic state convention in Ohio that July, fight the rebels. And "let Democrats fight the unarmed, but more insidious and dangerous Abolition rebels of the North and West, through the ballot box." The problems that he himself had with the government, he saw as the result of "no crimes save Democratic opinions." It proved that the government was out to suppress civil liberties, particularly of their political opponents.[26]

In Congress Vallandigham worked assiduously to find ways to

26. Clement L. Vallandigham to R. H. Hendrickson and others, May 13, 1861, in *Speeches, Arguments, Addresses and Letters of Clement L. Vallandigham* (New York, 1864), p. 305 (hereafter, *Speeches of Vallandigham*); "State of the Country," in ibid., pp. 398, 408; "Speech Before the Democratic State Convention, July 4, 1862," in ibid., p. 388; Clement L. Vallandigham to "The Democrats of Ohio," May 22, 1863, Barlow Papers.

conciliate the sections and to convene a peace conference. His resolutions introduced in December 1862 typified his efforts and his stance:

1. *Resolved,* That the Union as it was must be restored and maintained one and indivisible forever under the Constitution as it is . . .

2. *Resolved,* That if any person in the civil or military service of the United States shall propose terms of peace, or accept or advise the acceptance of any such terms, on any other basis than the integrity and entirety of the Federal Union, and of the several States composing the same, and the Territories of the Union, as at the beginning of the civil war, he will be guilty of a high crime. . . .

4. *Resolved,* That the unhappy civil war in which we are engaged was waged in the beginning, professedly, not in any spirit of oppression or for any purpose of conquest or subjugation, or purpose of overthrowing or interfering with the rights or established institutions of those States, but to defend and maintain the supremacy of the Constitution and to preserve the Union with all the dignity, equality and rights of the several States unimpaired, and was so understood and accepted by the people, and especially by the Army and Navy of the United States; and that, therefore, whoever shall pervert, or attempt to pervert, the same to a war of conquest and subjugation, or for the overthrowing or interfering with the rights or established institutions of any of the states, and to abolish slavery therein, or for the purpose of destroying or impairing the dignity, equality, or rights of any of the States, will be guilty of a flagrant breach of public faith and of a high crime against the Constitution and the Union. . . .[27]

Finally, he blasted any suggestions that his course, or that of his party colleagues, was treasonous, reminding his audience of the politics of the situation as well:

We sympathize with treason and traitors! We, who have stood by the Constitution and the Union from the organization of the party, in our father's day, and in our own day, in every hour of trial, in peace and in war, in victory and in defeat, amid disaster and when prosperity beamed upon us—we to be branded as enemies to our country, by those whose traitor fathers burned blue lights for signals for a foreign foe, or met in Hartford Convention to plot treason and disunion fifty years ago![28]

As the war progressed, the anger and frustration of these men became increasingly bitter, leading some of them into more and more extreme rhetoric. By 1864, men such as Wood, William B. Reed of Pennsylvania, and Alexander Long, another Ohio congressman, all

---

27. *Congressional Globe,* 37 Cong., 3 sess., p. 15.
28. *Speeches of Vallandigham,* p. 387.

lamented their original support for the war effort back in 1861. The commitment of some of them to no peace without reunion weakened considerably. They argued that Union was now lost anyway, and pled for an end to coercion at any price. "I now believe," Long said in early 1864, "that there are but two alternatives, and they are either an acknowledgment of the independence of the South as an independent nation, or their complete subjugation and extermination as a people; and of these alternatives I prefer the former." Others were becoming similarly anguished and unable to deal with the situation created by the war, the Legitimists' acceptance of it, and the problem of rebuilding the Union as a complete whole. We should "deceive no one who is for the war" as a means of restoring the Union, J. Sterling Morton wrote in his diary. "Peace might restore it. War cannot & makes disunion."[29]

In all of this, Vallandigham and his fellow peace men, like their Legitimist colleagues, were acutely conscious of the demands and opportunities of politics and electoral campaigning. They naturally believed that "a Peace candidate for President on a Peace platform would sweep through the country like a hurricane."[30] But their vision was more complex than that. Their conception of proper electoral strategy differed markedly from that of the Legitimists. Although they too believed that there was a conservative majority in the country, they saw both danger for the party and no real necessity for the Democrats to make too many concessions to win the portion of the antiradical vote outside the party. "In politics and in war," one wrote, "battles are won by fighting and not by giving ground when you are in the right." They believed that the Legitimists were too concerned to reassure the non-Democrats, even to the point of absurdity.[31] Parties in America were now divided into Democrats and abolitionists, "nothing else." Conservatives, therefore, would, should, and had to support the Democracy.[32]

29. *Congressional Globe*, 38 Cong., 1 sess., p. 1502; James C. Olsen, *J. Sterling Morton* (Lincoln, Neb., 1942), p. 129. On Reed, see Arnold Shankman, "William B. Reed and the Civil War," *Pennsylvania History* 39 (October 1972): 455–69.

30. *New York News*, January 18, 1864.

31. Morris I. Miller to Thomas Hart Seymour, November 26, 1862, Thomas Hart Seymour Papers, Connecticut Historical Society, Hartford, Conn.

32. *Crisis*, December 31, 1862; Reed, *A Northern Plea*, p. 14; *Atlas and Argus*, February 16, 1863.

These men were essentially purists in politics. Sharing with the Legitimists a commitment to certain deeply ingrained traditional Democratic beliefs about limited government, the Constitution, and conservative social policy, they were most suspicious of any weakening in the presentation of those ideals to the public. Compromise on principles was not an acceptable political strategy.

Austin Ranney has recently sketched a persistent theme of internal distinctions within any political party, a theme that has existed throughout a large portion of our political history. Many of these internal differences have not necessarily been over ideology (which most of the time different factions of the same party share in large measure with one another), but over what constitutes proper political behavior. One group has argued that the party's crucial need is competitive: to mobilize effectively all of the party's resources for winning elections. The party's principles will get nowhere unless it first achieves victory. This group thinks, primarily, therefore, in terms of vote maximization, compromise of difficult and controversial problems when necessary, and of keeping the party united. The other group has, however, what Ranney calls an "expressive" view of a party's function. The party's first duty is "to express the nature and will of its members. . . . The essence of politics is not the mere competition for office among parties and interest groups; it is standing up and being counted for what is right regardless of whether it is popular."[33]

So it was with the peace element within the Democratic party in the Civil War. A contemporary observer once described Purist meetings as ones with "longhaired fanatics in the ascendent." More calmly, Clement Vallandigham's biographer has painted him in terms that could be applied to the others of this group as well. "Once he had accepted a proposition, he hung on tenaciously. Once he had occupied a position, he was most reluctant to desert it. He regarded vacillation as a weakness and pussyfooting as cowardice. He chose to ignore expediency."[34] Politics was fought not simply for spoils, nor even only for victory. It was a continuing struggle between good and evil.

33. Austin Ranney, *To Cure the Mischief of Faction: Party Reform in America* (Berkeley and Los Angeles 1974). The quotes are on pages 134, 139.
34. *New York Herald,* October 18, 1864; Klement, *Limits of Dissent,* p. 62.

Vallandigham's speech in 1855, part of which forms the epigraph of this book, well expressed Purist attitudes toward party principles and toward compromise. "No party," the Ohioan said then, "is at all times equally pure and true to principle and its mission. And whenever the Democratic party forgets these, it loses its cementing and power bestowing element; it waxes weak, is disorganized, is defeated till, *purging itself of its impurities* [italics added] and falling back and rallying within its impregnable intrenchments of original and eternal principles, it returns . . . with irresistible might and majesty, to the conflict. . . . It is this recuperative power . . . which distinguishes the Democratic party from every other, and it owes this wholly to its conservative element, FIXED POLITICAL PRINCIPLES."[35]

The relationship between the two elements, party and principle, was clear enough to the Purist. "An honest Democrat's attachment to his party is strong. . . . But his love of his principles is also strong and he cannot see what use a party is to him or his country, if the principle be thrown away." Obviously, "for the sake of harmony and completeness of action, it is proper that concession and accommodation should be made in matters merely mechanical; but not even for the sake of unanimity should a principle be sacrificed." Unfortunately, "it is assumed by gentlemen who embark in party manipulations, that the sole end of a party organization is to get its members into office, and that it only answers the purpose of its creation when it gains possession of political power. Not so do we understand it. Usually the least valuable service performed by a party is the elevation of individuals; and the possession of power in the State, and its judicious exercise, are things not always intimately associated. A party is, or should be, a moral power perpetually existent and effective, and this it may, independent entirely of the accidents of majority and minority." In short, "a party without a principle is substance without a soul."[36]

The Purist attitude toward campaigning, victory, and defeat followed from such considerations. They looked upon considerations of party image and excessive concentration on how to win elections as

35. Vallandigham, "History of the Abolition Movement," October 29, 1855, in *Speeches of Vallandigham*, p. 99.

36. *Crisis,* September 21, 1864; *New York News,* June 25, 1863; *Cincinnati Enquirer,* February 1, 1864.

first steps in the degradation of all that the party stood for. They refused to compromise on policies or make cosmetic adjustments in their public stance for the sake of votes. The Democratic party could always accept defeat. "So long as it stands upon its principles a score of defeats will neither disband it nor discourage its true men. But it can not afford to betray itself nor to be betrayed, to sell out nor to be sold out by any—to have the opinions, feelings, thoughts and convictions of its members put as so much stock in a mere office-seeking enterprise." It is "better to be beaten in a bold and uncompromising defence of principle and a fearless maintenance of honor than to be successful in a contest where either principle or manly courage are bartered for victory." No party is ever stronger "than when it is parting with its compromises—the representatives of its moral weakness, its conservatism of personal interests, its cowardice."[37]

Second, they wanted bald, straight-out, uncoated presentation of everything the party stood for. "We sincerely believe," one said, "that the best way to deal with the people in order to secure their support to a just cause, is to place before them the true issue, in the distinctest manner." They denied a key tenet of the Legitimist argument. "No election was ever carried on the flimsy basis of a choice of evils—nor the trash of argument called a *half loaf.*" Resort to "political subterfuges and dodges to catch men of all opinions can no longer serve the purposes of tricksters. The people have resolved on plain talk and honest dealing. Our platform and candidate must be for War or for Peace. There is no middle ground. There can be no half-way house." Party leaders should not "court the votes of the vacillating by leaning toward every point of the political compass, and steering their boat up

37. *Cincinnati Enquirer,* January 1, March 11, 1864; *Chicago Times,* October 18, 1863; *Crisis,* September 7, 1864.

As Ranney points out, this kind of attitude has recurred throughout our history. In very recent times, its echoes have been heard. Hubert Humphrey was quoted in early 1976 as commenting that "liberals are very demanding, they want to see you suffer to prove your purity." Another commentator referred to " 'litmus test' liberals" who "have sometimes demanded a high and nearly suicidal degree of ideological purity." Finally, a Democratic pollster reported on a group of Democrats at an issues conference who wished to capture the White House but "appeared unwilling to adjust their convictions to attain that goal." *New York Times,* November 24, December 24, 1975, March 25, 1976.

the stream and down the stream at the same time."[38]

Most of all, "the Democratic party should not be tempted by hopes of partisan success into an abandonment of ancient principles or an adoption of modern chimeras. A party governed by no principle is a nuisance and a curse—a mere combination of political brigands, maintained by the hope of plunder. The Democracy, instead of abandoning old issues and old principles should adhere to them more closely than ever because they are more vital and important now than ever." Therefore, Vallandigham told the Democratic district convention in his Ohio constituency in 1862, "the vindication of Democratic principles and the Democratic cause is, at this time especially, of far more importance than mere success in any election. . . . Do right; and trust to God, and truth, and the people. . . . Perish offices, perish honors, perish life itself, but do the thing that is right."[39]

"We Carry Weights"

These different viewpoints about conceptions of electoral tactics, the impact of the war on basic Democratic principles, the electorate's position, and the nature of party behavior caused some vicious intraparty sniping during the war. There was much unhappiness among the contending groups of Democrats, particularly when each's election strategy and conceptions ran at cross purposes. The Purists' attitude toward other Democrats who did not accept the ideals of purity of purpose was predictably angry. They could not understand their party colleagues who watered down party principles, weakened party stances, and compromised on critical matters concerning party ideology. If any Democrat became "equivocating, doubting, moderating," if any tried "to transfer the party over to Abe Lincoln's war and its criminal desolations," he was destroying the party, not helping it. But that the Democratic party was "to be sold out, root and branch, if some of its present professed leaders can do it," they had "the very best reasons for believing." Ultimately, Fernando Wood argued that the peace men were "the only Democrats; all others are bastards and

38. *Cincinnati Enquirer,* January 30, 1864; *New York News,* September 9, 1861, July 16, 1864.

39. *Crisis,* December 28, 1864; Freidel, *Union Pamphlets,* 2: 705.

impostors; there is no such thing as a War Democrat, for that is a contradiction in terms."[40]

The Legitimists answered in kind. They believed they were being misrepresented concerning their alleged lack of devotion to party principles and their willingness to compromise. They considered themselves as devoted to traditional Democratic principles and policies as any Purist. But they never forgot that the need to win elections limited what a minority party could engage in in its quest for votes. Anyone who opposd a union of conservatives in the present crisis was, in Samuel Tilden's view, "a traitor to the country." That union could only come about if the Democracy put legitimacy in a prominent place in its advocacy alongside its traditional conservative principles. They saw, therefore, the peace-Purists as "a drag on the democracy" and its electoral fortunes. "How," one asked, "are we ever to carry a presidential election against the enormous patronage of the government, if particular cliques insist on dividing the party by raising unseasonable issues and attempting to force on it a creed in opposition to the judgment of the majority?" Vallandigham was "the most serviceable man to the administration in the country" because he is an "indiscreet denouncer of the war." Legitimists went out of their way to repudiate the more extreme statements of the peace men, and worked behind the scenes to counter and reduce the impact of the Purists on the Democrats' electoral chances.[41]

There was, therefore, much tension within the Democratic party during the war: anger, bitterness, and internal sniping. By midwar, both sides had worked out and articulated their stances. Each clung closely to its conception of what constituted correct tactics. Neither wanted to give in. Neither was tolerant of "the oddities and absurdities" of the opposing group.[42] Each believed that the other side was

40. C. M. Ingersoll to Thomas Hart Seymour, February 24, 1864, G. W. Hungerford to Seymour, August 4, 1862, Fernando Wood to Seymour, February 19, 1863, Thomas Hart Seymour Papers; *Crisis*, March 16, 1864, December 21, 1862, February 25, 1863; Omaha *Nebraskan*, September 25, 1863, quoted in Olsen, *Morton*, p. 126; *Cincinnati Enquirer*, January 3, 1863; Noah Brooks, *Washington in Lincoln's Time* (New York, 1895), p. 115. Wood's comment, according to Brooks, was allegedly made to Lincoln. Even if it was not, it still catches the flavor of the group.

41. *New York Herald*, September 8, 1863; New York *World*, May 6, June 2, 1863.

42. New York *World*, June 2, 1863.

going about the game of politics in quite the wrong way and harming, therefore, the principles each side said it was fighting for. Each tried to force as much of its perception of the proper Democratic advocacy on the party as it could, because they were struggling for both the soul of the party and the future of the country. Neither was happy when the other side achieved dominance and despaired of the result when such happened. In 1863, for example, the peace men were riding on a wave of popularity. Recent military defeats and a number of repressive actions by the Lincoln administration gave new impetus to their point of view. Vallandigham's martyrdom by General Burnside had raised a rash of protests, not only from Peace Democrats, about the dangers to civil liberties and the threat of domestic repression as a consequence of the war. The Purists swept a number of key nominations in some crucial and competitive states. In the spring elections for the Connecticut governorship, the Democrats nominated Thomas H. Seymour, an identified Peace Democrat. Later in the year they nominated two others of the same group, George Woodward and Vallandigham, for governors of Pennsylvania and Ohio, respectively.[43]

The Purists were jubilant. They believed they had turned a corner. Not only was "the substantial, reliable mind of the Democratic party" for peace and a peace platform, but that they were also witnessing "a political revolution" among the people generally in favor of peace. The Legitimists, however, were not happy. "I despair of success," Cox wrote after the Vallandigham nomination. He and others still read the political signs differently. They pled with the Purists not to let the party be suspected of antiwar tendencies or let conservatives fear for the Union if they supported the Democracy. Cox tried to get General George McClellan to run for governor in Ohio to strengthen the Legitimist focus of the party's appeal, but Vallandigham swept all before him among the Democrats of Ohio thanks to his martyrdom. Seymour's race in Connecticut became the focus of heavy peace involvement. Men came from all over to campaign for him.[44]

43. "It is useless to attempt to conceal the fact that Vallandigham is the most popular man of his party in Ohio." R. G. Dun to S. S. Cox, February 18, 1863, Cox Papers.
44. S. S. Cox to Manton Marble, June 14, 1863, Marble Papers; New York

"We are making a fierce fight," Cox wrote in August 1863, "but we carry weights." The election results confirmed the pessimism. Seymour, Vallandigham, and Woodward all lost. The reason was clear enough to the Legitimists. The American people were disgusted with the Lincoln administration and its policies. They were ready for a change of government. "Victory was in our grasp," Cox lamented. But the "unfortunate position" of the peace men cost the Democracy its advantage. The nomination of men tainted with peace sentiments "afforded a plausible" pretext for Republicans to divert attention away from the real issues of the canvass. The Democracy, therefore, "groans and sweats under the consciousness of being beaten without reason."[45]

Clearly there was irritation, even hatred, here. It was very hard to contain because the war exacerbated tensions so much. Furthermore, there was in the Purist approach to politics an impatience, more, a rigid hostility, to the Legitimists' arguments. But there is more concern here than simply recording that bitterness. These divisions had an impact on the fabric of the party. They helped, most of all, to explain certain aspects of party behavior during the war years. The peace men did not always have their own way in party councils. In 1863, they were particularly strong in states such as Ohio and Pennsylvania where critical state elections occurred. But that was not always the case. At other times, even in states where the peace men were strong, the Legitimists took a share of party nominations or had their way in the resolutions of local and state party conventions.

It is difficult to evaluate precisely the sources or the actual strength of the two factions. There was a heavy Middle Western element in the

World, 6 June 1863; S. S. Cox to George B. McClellan, May 31, 1863, McClellan Papers; George Pendleton to J. S. Morton, May 29, 1863, in Olsen, *Morton,* pp. 119–20; Fernando Wood to Thomas Hart Seymour, March 23, 1863, Marcellus Emery to Seymour, August 24, 1863, George Pendleton to Seymour, September 5, 1863, Henry Clay Dean to Seymour, November 8, 1863, Thomas Seymour Papers. The 1863 campaigns are well covered in Klement's *Limits of Dissent* and his *Copperheads in the Middle West;* and Joanna D. Cowden, "Civil War and Reconstruction Politics in Connecticut, 1863–1868" (Ph.D. diss., University of Connecticut, 1974).

45. S. S. Cox to Manton Marble, August 16, 17, September 24, October 21, 1863, Clement L. Vallandigham to Marble, October 4, 1863, Marble Papers; New York *World,* October 16, November 5, 1863.

Purist group. The bloc's most prominent leader, Vallandigham, was joined in his outspokenness by a number of his Ohio contemporaries as well as by other Democratic politicians from neighboring Indiana and Illinois. But the movement was never simply a sectional one. There were men opposed to these peace-Purist doctrines from the same Midwestern states. At the same time, men such as Reed and Woodward of Pennsylvania, Seymour in Connecticut, and Joseph Wall of New Jersey also supported this position with others from their states, as did sizable blocs of Democrats in other Eastern states. Even in New England, according to ex-President Franklin Pierce, most Democrats did not favor a vigorous prosecution of the war. On the other side, a New York City group led by Belmont, Barlow, and Marble were the most prominent of the Legitimists, but they were strongly opposed even within their own state and could find support in the Western states.[46]

There was often a great deal of sectional rhetoric in the advocacy of the Purists. They never let up on the old theme that the Republicans belonged to an unacceptable, sectionalist party rooted in New England, or the relationship between Republican policies and the party's sectional home. Purist attacks on New England were frequent and intense through the war years. However, none of this necessarily distinguished Purists from other Democrats. Members of the party who could not be labelled pro-peace also used sectional rhetoric, as, for example, Congressman Cox, or Governor Seymour of New York. Such rhetoric was in the air and not the exclusive preserve of only one

46. Franklin Pierce to John J. Taylor, June 14, 1864, Pierce Papers. In the voting blocs in the House of Representatives in the first session of the Thirty-eighth Congress, for example, there were twenty-two Midwesterners, eighteen Easterners and four Border state Democrats in the extreme peace group; nine Midwesterners, thirteen Easterners and six Border state Democrats in the moderate group. Benedict, *Compromise of Principle*, pp. 339–40. There were some tendencies here but they were not very clear cut. Further analysis of the precise socioeconomic bases of the cleavages within the party would be an interesting and informative addition to our knowledge about the social basis of the Democratic party and about the sources of political and attitudinal cleavages generally. Such meticulous local studies need to be undertaken. But for our purpose here, that of delineating and understanding the way the Democratic party behaved in the Civil War era, the importance of this division is somewhat different. See Curry, "Union As It Was."

group of Democrats.[47] Votes for candidates in conventions or for specific planks in party platforms are not sure guides either because there were all sorts of other matters, ambiguous language, prevote compromises, and cross pressures at work in such votes.

What is clear is that neither set of ideas dominated the party entirely. Each faction appeared powerful enough so that its views had to be taken into account when the party considered its campaign strategy and electoral appeals. As a result, things did not always go smoothly for either bloc. Something had to be given to each in intraparty decisions if the party were to stay together and operate as a united organization. If unity were a goal, however, the differences in the party, and the internal balance of power, could diffuse the Democrats' electoral stance into a position different from the one either the Legitimists or the Purists wanted. So there continued to be an ambiguous set of relationships within the party and therefore something of an ambiguous public stance on the war by the Democracy. Yet there still remained the forces that led them all to consider themselves Democrats. The spirit of community and the partisan imperative remained part of the equation shaping party operations. These forces were working to keep the party on the path to victory despite the internal problems and bitter confrontations of the wartime years.

47. *Crisis,* July 8, 1863; William B. Reed, *A Paper Containing a Statement and a Vindication of Certain Political Opinions* (Philadelphia, 1862), p. 27; *Chicago Times,* November 11, 1863; Samuel S. Cox, *Puritanism in Politics;* Stewart Mitchell, *Horatio Seymour of New York* (Cambridge, Mass., 1938), p. 348. See above, chapters one and two, for earlier evocations of the sectional, anti–New England theme.

5

"There Was Too Much at Stake to Quarrel": The Democrats' Fight for the Presidency, 1864

THE DIVISIONS WITHIN the Democratic party during the war years often seemed quite serious. There was a great deal of internal tension at all times. Much of it was expressed privately. But much bitter comment also reached the public forum, exacerbating matters still further. Nevertheless, the disagreements and bitterness were only one part of the story of the Civil War Democracy, and one easy to overestimate in terms of consequences for the party. Factional disagreements, even violently divisive ones, were not unusual in the history of American political parties. They did not necessarily lead to disruption or impotence.[1] The Civil War Democracy was painfully aware of its internal differences. But it continued to be as strongly aware of the basic principles, common perspectives, and historical memories Democrats shared with one another, all of which differentiated them from the Republicans. Democrats had very good reason to stay together. Only the victory of their party could change the nefarious policies of the government. To achieve that victory the Democrats had to emphasize their spirit of community and retain their unity. That was the critical thing. "A party is like an army," one observer noted

---

1. The Republicans during the Civil War are a major case in point. For a number of intelligent remarks about their unity despite intense factional infighting, see Michael Les Benedict, *A Compromise of Principle: Congressional Republicans and Reconstruction, 1863–1868* (New York, 1974); David Donald, "The Radicals and Lincoln," in idem, *Lincoln Reconsidered. Essays on the Civil War Era* (New York, 1956).

to McClellan in late 1863. "The strength of the enemy is now, apparently greater than ours, and he has the choice of ground. We should, therefore, combine every element of strength." No one must be allowed to "divide the Democrats of the East from the Democrats of the West."[2]

"By Jesus, Don't Ask Too Much"

The forces promoting unity and memories of common experiences, therefore, exerted great influence in a situation otherwise complicated by important internal differences about priorities and tactics. But, of course, despite all of the pragmatic considerations and ideological communalism, effective cooperation was not automatic. Both sides had to accept the need for compromise, recognize each other's strength, and work hard to soften their own stances in the interest of unity. The Legitimists took the initiative in arguing the case and in finding means of cooperation despite differences. They desired, as the New York *World* said in 1863, "to emphasize . . . points of agreement, not . . . differences."[3] They never let up on the theme. We "must bring to the altar of our country," Belmont argued, "the sacrifice of prejudice, opinions, and convictions—however dear and long cherished they may be—from the moment they threaten the harmony and unity of action so indispensable to our success." All good Democrats should "try to tolerate each other's peculiarities and act in harmony." They should make no policy declarations that would exacerbate the differences. Opinions must be "waive[d]." Or, as New York State Democratic chairman Dean Richmond put it, more pungently, "by Jesus, don't ask too much." Anyone who "counsels faction and disorganization" must be "summarily swept into limbo by the imprecations of a righteous and determined people." It is more important that the Democratic party should be "strong, united and

2. George W. Morgan to G. B. McClellan, November 30, 1863, George B. McClellan Papers, Library of Congress; New York *World*, February 26, 1863; August Belmont, *A Few Letters and Speeches of the Late Civil War* (New York, 1870), pp. 108–09; *Chicago Times*, July 2, 1864.

3. New York *World*, February 26, 1863; Manton Marble to James Wall, March 30, 1864, Manton Marble Papers, Library of Congress.

harmonious, than that it should in this election adopt either a war or a peace platform."[4]

The Purists often responded in kind. Even Vallandigham hoped that "a united Democratic party will yet save the Constitution, the Union and Liberty." Purists, too, seemed to accept that "there must be sacrifices of individual opinions, feelings and preferences" in order to keep the party united.[5] Nor were such efforts confined to rhetoric. Throughout the war there were indications that both sides were willing to find ways to work out their differences and cooperate with each other. As Manton Marble wrote to Thomas Hart Seymour when the latter was running for governor of Connecticut in 1863, "I am anxious to give you all the help in the coming election which the *World* is capable of rendering." Meetings were held to get the Purists to moderate their position in the interest of unity and victory. After one such at Albany in March 1863, among Cox, Vallandigham, Horatio Seymour, and William Bigler of Pennsylvania, Cox wrote that Vallandigham "has agreed to abate his hostility to the war for the sake of the party." In late 1863, even the perpetually warring New York City Democratic factions agreed to work together, due, in the words of Mozart Hall, to "the exigencies of our country."[6]

In other words, the will to remain united was obviously there. As bad as internal factional differences might be, there was much more distance between all Democrats and all Republicans than between different blocs of Democrats (or Republicans). Democrats, therefore, sought to work out campaign appeals in every election during the war emphasizing the elements of conservative constitutionalism all groups

4. Belmont, *A Few Letters and Speeches*, p. 109; *Chicago Times*, August 8, 1864; *New York Herald*, September 9, 1863; New York *World*, February 26, June 2, 5, August 17, 1863, March 29, August 1, 1864; Springfield *Illinois State Register*, in New York *World*, August 23, 1864; New York *World*, September, n.d., 1863, in Manton Marble Collection, Scrapbook 3, University of London Library; Elon Comstock to Franklin Pierce, July 10, 1863, Franklin Pierce Papers, Library of Congress.

5. Clement L. Vallandigham to Manton Marble, May 21, 1863, Marble Papers; *Chicago Times*, April 12, 1864. See also Frank L. Klement, *The Limits of Dissent: Clement L. Vallandigham and the Civil War* (Lexington, Ky., 1970), pp. 135–36.

6. Manton Marble to Thomas Hart Seymour, February 24, 1864, Thomas Hart Seymour Papers, Connecticut Historical Society, Hartford, Conn.; Samuel S. Cox to Erastus Corning, March 13, 1863, Horatio Seymour Papers, New York State Library, Albany; *New York Herald*, September 3, 9, 1863.

in the party agreed to, and which distinguished all Democrats from all Republicans. Still, differences among Democrats did remain. Many Purists remained intransigent, many Legitimists impatient. As a result, there was an appearance of careful walking on eggs through all of the party's activities. At the end of 1863, despite the rhetoric and the will to work together, it was still unclear how much effective cooperation was possible in the tests to come.

"The Democracy Must Defeat Themselves If Now Defeated"

The presidential election campaign of 1864 provided a sharp test of the extent of the Democrats' determination to function together as a party and the comparative power of the different forces within the party. The political situation once more looked promising, even more so than in 1863, due to another year of frustrating and inconclusive war, government interference, and Negro advances, all of which seemed to be attracting to the Democrats more and more of the formerly hesitant. The Republicans' divisiveness, their occasional panic over politics, and the impact of the draft, all made the Democrats optimistic about their chances. It was reported that "scores of the rank and file of the republican party" were "declaring that they have got enough of Old Abe, and will vote for any person nominated . . . [by the Democrats] if he is not an ultra peace man." The only hitch was the Democrats' own situation. "Old Abe is quite in trouble just now. . . . The Democracy must defeat themselves if now defeated."[7]

Internal Democratic factional rhetoric in the months before the crucial presidential election of 1864 echoed the lines taken by the different groups over the previous two years. The Legitimists were particularly angry about the party's losses in 1863. They were quick to draw the lesson of the stinging defeats of that year. They believed that the party had been in a flourishing condition and on the verge of victory after the successes of 1862. But the Democracy had behaved wrongheadedly in 1863. "Victory was in our grasp." But the "foolish peace principles of Mr. Vallandigham and his immediate

7. Cyrus Hall McCormick to Manton Marble, August 17, 1864, Marble Papers; *New York Herald*, August 28, 1864.

followers afforded a plausible pretext for charging the Democratic party with opposition to the war.'' Legitimists recognized the essential unionism of most of the Purists and the latter's right to formulate alternative party policies. But they also saw how the Republicans ignored subtleties and the real truth in the matter to attack all Democrats viciously as traitors. That strategy had worked in 1863. ''Hundreds of votes were lost among that class of persons having every desire to record in an election their utter disapprobation of the conduct and policy of the administration, yet unable to see that peace men are not disloyal men.'' Without that onus, the Democracy might have won. Therefore, as before, they reiterated their conviction that the party ''must plant itself'' immovably ''on the war footing.''[8]

But the Legitimists were not alone in articulating demands of the party. The Purists made it very clear that they had no intention of giving up what they believed in and that there were limits to the amount of compromising they were prepared to do for the sake of party harmony. Giving in on questions of principle had been the bane of the party, the thing that ''has dragged the Democratic party down from its high estate & made it a football for gambling politicians.'' Thomas Hart Seymour received a flood of correspondence in the spring of 1864 warning him that if the Peace Democrats gave up their principles they would ''humble and disgrace themselves for nothing.'' The coercion of the South was ''a folly'' and a policy of ''intense wickedness.'' Democrats were ''more and more inclined to peace.'' This was ''a positive fact.'' Why hide it?[9]

''What a good party wants,'' James Bryce wrote late in the nineteenth century, ''is not a good president but a good candidate. The

8. New York *World*, October 16, 1863; S. S. Cox to Manton Marble, October 21, 1863, Marble Papers; T. J. Barnett to Samuel L. M. Barlow, June 6, 10, 1863, Henry Stebbins to Barlow, January 20, 1864, Samuel L. M. Barlow Papers, Henry E. Huntington Library, San Marino, Ca.; New York *World*, March 19, November 5, 1863; S. L. M. Barlow to George B. McClellan, August 3, 1864, McClellan Papers; C. M. Gould to S. S. Cox, October 15, 1863, Samuel Sullivan Cox Papers, Brown University Library, Providence, R.I.; J. N. Baldwin to Manton Marble, October 14, 1863, Marble Papers.

9. Samuel F. B. Morse to Thomas Hart Seymour, May 2, 1864, John Cotton to Seymour, May 15, 1864, Marcellus Emery to Seymour, April 10, 1864, H.B. Whiting to Seymour, April 12, 1864, Thomas Seymour Papers; *New York News,* August 19, 1864.

party managers have therefore, to look out for the person likely to gain most support, and at the same time excite least opposition.''[10] Since 1863, the most powerful Legitimists had been pushing General George B. McClellan as the Democratic presidential candidate who most closely met Bryce's ideal. McClellan seemed to possess all of the required assets to legitimize the Democrats' protest against the government. He was both a general and a committed Democrat. With him at the head of their ticket the Democrats could hardly be characterized as a peace party. As a general, in fact the General in Chief earlier in the war, there could be no question of McClellan's loyalty to the Union, support for the war, and desire to defeat the South. Nor could Purist Democrats, Legitimists believed, challenge his ideological bona fides of Democratic commitment. He was a good Democrat who could attack the Lincoln administration for its execution of policy without casting doubt on his own support for the ends of that policy. He stood as a dramatic example of the mishandling of the war by the Republican administration. All of these strengths could only help the party in its electoral quest. ''With any other man we utterly lose the army votes.'' Further, thousands of Republicans would support him, but not any other nominee. ''I really cannot believe,'' said one Legitimist, in conclusion, ''that any true friend of the party, who wishes success, will oppose McClellan.''[11]

But many Purists disagreed and poured great obloquy on the notion of nominating McClellan. He offended them as a general who had conducted war operations and as a commander who they believed had suppressed civil liberties in the Border states in the interest of security earlier in the war. ''We have sacrificed too much in defence of state rights,'' one wrote, to give votes to a man both ''pledged

10. James Bryce, *The American Commonwealth*, 3rd rev. ed. (New York, 1906), 1: 187.

11. Samuel L. M. Barlow to Manton Marble, August 21, 27, 1864, Marble Papers; J. D. Hoover to Franklin Pierce, January 5, February 16, 1864, Pierce Papers. See also William B. Reed to S. L. M. Barlow, May 26, 1863, S. S. Cox to Barlow, November 21, 1863, Barlow to Reverdy Johnson, January 25, 1864, Barlow to S. B. Parsons, February 1, 1864, Barlow Papers; D. Salomon to Manton Marble, November 12, 1863, S. S. Cox to Marble, July 25, 1864, Marble Papers; Joel Parker to George B. McClellan, August 27, 1864, S. S. Cox to McClellan, April 22, 1864, McClellan Papers. On McClellan, see William Starr Myers, *General George Brinton McClellan* (New York, 1934).

to destroy those rights'' and willing ''to wage this war until 'armed rebellion' is put down.'' There could be ''no union of the party on a war platform or a war candidate.'' In such a situation ''an Administration man is preferable to a War Democrat.'' Or, run a peace candidate and be beaten rather than win with someone who is really ''half dem[ocrat] & half abo[litionist].'' In other words, as a Connecticut Democratic editor put it, ''if we cannot have a peace candidate on a State Sovereignty platform, we had better show the country the eloquence of *silence* at the polls.''[12]

So bitter did exchanges between factions become early in 1864 that there was some strong feeling that no compromise was possible. The Democrats seemed too deeply split.[13] Still, circumstances can alter behavior, even among Purists. As the convention neared, in fact, some of them indicated a willingness to compromise somewhat. They recognized how dangerous the country's situation was. Like the Legitimists they despaired for the nation. They were unhappy, had a deep sense of foreboding, a feeling that 1864 might be their last chance. There were indications that for the first time many of them shared with the Legitimists a strong belief, as one put it, that ''there was too much at stake to quarrel'' with each other. Before the convention, the *Chicago Times* urged that Democrats and all other conservative men ''cultivate that spirit of concession solely by which its deliberations can be harmonious and its nominations successful.'' The recent elections in Connecticut ''proved the impolicy of committing the party to any declaration which involves even indirectly, the cessation of hostilities until the insurgent States acknowledge the authority of the Constitution.'' Perhaps, most critically, the editor of one newspaper anticipated Bryce's later observation about candidates. ''The convention will not be called upon to consider who is the best man for the Presidential office,'' he wrote, ''but who is the best man that can be elected to the office. It will not be called upon to consider what are the best measures for the country, but what are the best

12. Marcellus Emery to Thomas Hart Seymour, February 29, April 10, 1864, M. B. Whiting to Seymour, April 2, 1864, C. W. Harris to Seymour, April 13, 1864, C. M. Hawes to Seymour, December, n.d., 1863, Thomas Seymour Papers.
13. This is certainly the occasional feeling that erupts in the correspondence exchanged within each of the Democratic camps.

measures which can be practically enforced . . . Its action, to become effective, must be indorsed by the people, and must, therefore, be of a character which will command itself to the popular feeling and judgment. Without this, its labors will be in vain."[14]

Many said in advance that they would abide by the decision of the national convention even if the results there were other than they wished. After the convention, "there can be no such thing as a war democrat or a peace democrat. There can only be democrats with but a single duty to perform—to support the action of the convention." A "majority of the party is the whole party . . . the minority must unfalteringly abide by and support the action of the majority." Even Vallandigham, it was reported, intended to stay within the party because he opposed the idea of a separate ticket.[15]

The Purists' actions matched their rhetoric. Many of them wrote and spoke in favor of local Democratic candidates and platforms despite differences in viewpoints. In the Ohio convention it was a Vallandigham delegate who early in 1864 moved to make the election of a delegate-at-large unanimous after Vallandigham himself had been defeated for the position.[16] Still, there was always a sting in their behavior, even among the more flexible. They retained their conditions. They did not believe that the coming national convention would be "so regardless of the interests of the nation and the democratic party as to nominate a man who has no hold upon the hearts of the people, or place its nominee upon a platform so narrow that the entire conservative strength of the nation may not safely rally upon it." It had better not be. It was possible that General McClellan will "receive the regular nomination. In that event the Peace party will support him upon a Peace platform, and none other." Nevertheless, there were indications in the spring of 1864 that Purists could be negotiated into active party support, that a certain amount of their rhetoric was posturing and maneuvering into a position where their claims would be recognized.[17]

14. *Chicago Times*, April 17, June 23, August 8, 19, 24, 29, 1864; *Cincinnati Daily Enquirer*, September 12, November 5, 1864.

15. *Chicago Times*, August 8, 29, 1864; Klement, *Limits of Dissent*, p. 282.

16. A. Banning Norton to S. L. M. Barlow, March 25, 1864, Barlow Papers.

17. H. B. Whiting to Thomas Hart Seymour, April 12, 1864, Seymour Papers; *Chicago Times*, August 8, 1864; *New York News*, August 11, 1864.

The Legitimists were acutely sensitive to the needs of the situation. They were deferential to the Purists because they correctly assessed their strength and importance. They knew they had to take into account the growing anger and frustration against the war and its impact felt by many Democrats everywhere. They did not want to create unnecessary friction. As Barlow summed up, "my battle is to be fought in November and not in August." Nor did the Legitimists want any missteps that would exacerbate things. To them the core of their preconvention strategy was that the Democrats needed to keep both wings of the party working together if they were to win. If union and harmony attend the deliberations of the convention, "its nominees will almost certainly be elected." Therefore, "our efforts should be directed to pouring balm into the hearts of the . . . Peace Democrats. Let them understand they are of some account in the making of our organization for 1864."[18]

Nevertheless, the Legitimists continued to believe there were limits to flexibility. If the Democrats wrote "an ultra platform or nominate[d] an unavailable candidate," they would lose. Fortunately, "our friends understand what is necessary so fully that they will not allow any mistakes that can be prevented." Although concerned about the platform, their main focus in the months before the convention was in keeping with the spirit of Barlow's comment that "our elections are always carried by men more than by abstract principles." Realizing the strength of the peace-Purist wing, some feared an initiative to nominate someone unacceptable such as Fernando Wood and moved to head it off. "The nomination at Chicago of an out and out peace ticket, will result in the reelection of Lincoln. But give us McClellan and a true man from some one of the border states for the Vice-Presidency" and Democrats would win.[19]

Still, the nomination had to be nursed along carefully because of the strength of the peace men and the need to reassure them about

18. Samuel L. M. Barlow to Washington McLean, August 16, 22, 1864, S. S. Cox to Barlow, December 13, 1863, Barlow Papers; S. S. Cox to Franklin Pierce, March 17, 1864, Pierce Papers; James S. Rollins to Cox, August 19, 1864, Cox Papers; *New York Herald*, February 25, 1864.

19. Samuel L. M. Barlow to Washington McLean, August 16, 1864, Barlow Papers; Barlow to George B. McClellan, August 29, 1864, McClellan Papers; Barlow to S. S. Cox, June 13, 1864, James Rollins to Cox, August 19, 1864, Cox Papers.

McClellan. George W. Morgan warned McClellan, for instance, against taking "the actions of a New York multitude [in favor of vigorous prosecution of the war under Democratic leadership] as the index of the wide-spread country." He had better pay attention to the sensibilities of the Purist wing if he wished to win the nomination. McClellan's West Point speech (viewed as a strong endorsement of the war) "will give you the election," Cox told the general, "but it does not help to [give you] the nomination." McClellan was also advised, again by George Morgan, that "a letter from you . . . declaring in favor of an armistice would double our chances at Chicago." He should also say something, Cox thought, about "the necessity of using all rational methods at every honorable chance for peace and union." Such was needed not for his election so much "as for his nomination." Cox was quoted as being grateful for McClellan's public support for the Purist George Woodward in the Pennsylvania gubernatorial election of the year before. "It was necessary. He never could have gotten the nomination without it."[20]

Many of the Legitimists were optimistic about their chances at the national convention. Surveying the scene well before the convention, Samuel L. M. Barlow found everything falling into place. "The mission of the democratic party is," he wrote, "to make war, to preserve the national honor and territory and to aggrandize its power. Such a party cannot make peace or speak of peace, unless these objects are obtained. I think the so-called peace men here and in Washington all understand this now, and that they will not attempt in our National Convention, either by a candidate or a theory, to pervert the true sentiment of the people."[21]

"I Feel So Anxious for Harmony"

The cynical and battle-weary editor of the *New York Herald* once referred to national conventions as "great congregations of unscrupulous politicians, among whom bargaining takes the place of

20. George W. Morgan to G. B. McClellan, August 4, 12, 17, 1864, S. S. Cox to McClellan, August 4, 1864, McClellan Papers; S. S. Cox to Manton Marble, August 7, 1864, Marble Papers; Tyler Dennett, ed., *Lincoln and the Civil War in the Diaries and Letters of John Hay* (New York, 1939), p. 143. On McClellan's "Woodward Letter," see George B. McClellan to Charles Biddle, November 12, 1863, McClellan Papers.

21. Samuel L. M. Barlow to H. G. Stebbins, February 1, 1864, Barlow Papers.

principle and expediency is substituted for patriotism."[22] This had an element of truth but was incomplete. National (not to mention state) conventions were critical arenas for the nineteenth-century party system as places where more activity than the *Herald* described occurred. "The national convention was a secularized, protracted revival meeting," a historian has recently written. Here the party faithful "gathered to demonstrate that they were of the flock, to remember their saints and martyrs, revive their party spirit, enunciate their party creed," and choose their candidate.[23] But it was even more than that. The end product of each party's struggle with its internal conflicting groups was the product of much bargaining, mediation, and ultimate compromise.

The national convention was one of the major places where negotiations occurred. It was the meeting ground of the many different interests within the party, each seeking to have its influence recognized and its demands satisfied by the nominations the party made and the platform it constructed. The candidates finally nominated and the platforms developed usually were the best the party could present, given the strength of its various factions. The function of the delegates was to agree sufficiently about both candidates and platform so as to maintain both party unity and electoral effectiveness. It was sometimes done handily, through compromise and conciliation. Sometimes it was done with great difficulty, in which case bitterness was the main end product. Through it all remained always the primary need to offer attractive and potentially successful candidates and issues.[24]

So it was with the Democrats in 1864. The ninth Democratic National Convention convened, after one postponement, in Chicago on 29 August, the latest meeting ever. Both major groups within the party looked to it as the focal point of their activities, the place to force as much of their demands as they could consonant with the hoped-for

22. *New York Herald*, April 25, 1864.

23. Robert D. Marcus, *Grand Old Party, Political Structure in the Gilded Age, 1880–1896* (New York, 1971), p. 260.

24. For good discussions of the function of the convention, see Gerald Pomper, *Elections in America* (New York, 1968), pp. 150ff; Nelson W. Polsby and Aaron B. Wildavsky, *Presidential Elections: Strategies of American Electoral Politics*, 4th ed. (New York, 1976), pp. 69–121.

unity of the party. Andrew Jackson once referred to the delegates attending a national convention as "fresh from the people." The more than two hundred delegates arriving in Chicago in 1864 were that. Selected by state conventions and state party committees, they well represented the different perspectives present in the party after three years of war. Most of the leading figures in the fights of the past few years were there, from Vallandigham and Fernando Wood to Manton Marble and Horatio Seymour, along with the less prominent.[25]

Before they met there was a great deal of backstage maneuvering to insure each faction's success. The Purists were in close touch with each other in their efforts to forestall Legitimist domination. Secret meetings and public assemblies both applied pressure against their opponents. Their numbers and activities frightened the Legitimists. Belmont wrote from Chicago that "the Vallandigham spirit is rampant & his being placed on the Comm[ittee] of Resolutions will give trouble." An outside Republican observer commented that at Chicago Vallandigham "was the hero of the occasion." The Legitimists, therefore, consulted constantly with each other, weighed every rumor, anticipated every piece of opposition, and tried to assuage every fear. Running through their consultations was their awareness of the inability of either Purists or Legitimists to dominate affairs entirely and the need to find means of keeping the Purists together with them and, more importantly, eagerly fighting for victory.[26]

25. Andrew Jackson to James Gwin, February 23, 1835, in *Niles National Register*, April 4, 1835; *Official Proceedings of the Democratic National Convention Held in 1864 at Chicago* (Chicago, 1864).

26. August Belmont to S. L. M. Barlow, August 29, 1864, Barlow Papers; Barlow to McClellan, August 29, 1864, McClellan Papers; Barlow to Manton Marble, August 21, 1864, Marble Papers; Klement, *Limits of Dissent*, pp. 267–68, 282. The activities of Belmont and Marble at Chicago are well covered by their biographers. See George McJimsey, *Genteel Partisan: Manton Marble, 1834–1917* (Ames, Iowa, 1971); and, Irving Katz, *August Belmont, A Political Biography* (New York, 1968).

There is no clear explanation as to why the convention's meeting was postponed. People in each faction expressed suspicion of the action. Perhaps the best explanation was by Dean Richmond. He said it was done to keep the Democrats working hard together. Everyone was, but a nomination "may cool off some." Richmond to Manton Marble, June 16, 1864, Marble Papers. See also William Cassidy to Marble, June 25, 1864, ibid. There was also a chance that electoral conditions would become better for the Democrats if they waited due to increasing war weariness. See S. S. Cox to G. B. McClellan, June 9, 1864, McClellan Papers; Fernando Wood to Edmund Burke, June 23, 1864, Edmund Burke Papers, Library of Congress.

There were available ways out of their dilemma, however. It was known that the Purists were divided over exactly what to do: fight within the convention, think in terms of compromise where necessary, or perhaps form an independent party. The Purists might be conciliated through reasonable platform concessions. They were, after all, opposed to the Confederacy and committed to peace on the basis of the reunion of all of the states. "The *ne plus ultras* of our party," Manton Marble suggested, "will take Peace and Union, if we don't insist on War in our platform." There were already rumors before the convention met that in the interest of unity there would be a war nomination and a peace and Union plank. The platform "is, I suppose, already definitely arranged," one commentator wrote to Barlow a few months before the convention. Although it had not been, Legitimist leaders worked assiduously behind the scenes to forge a compromise. They seemed ready to go as far toward the Purists as necessary. "I am so bound up in your nomination and election," Cox wrote to McClellan early in August, "that I am, perhaps, too ready to make all the proper concessions to secure both." It was claimed, just as the convention met, that the McClellan men had given "assurances" that "an amicable compromise will be effected to unite the whole party on one man and one platform; a split in the Convention is not entertained for a moment."[27]

Despite some trepidation about the consequences of doing so ("I fear there may be trouble as to the platform," Barlow wrote in late August), there is evidence that ultimately the Legitimists were willing to concede the Purists the lead in drafting the platform, perhaps partly because their eyes seemed so fixed on the candidate, partly because they had to concede the Purists something due to their relative power within the party, and partly because they believed a reasonable deal could be worked out.[28] But the Legitimists never lost sight of their

27. *New York Herald,* August 29, 30, 1864; S. L. M. Barlow to August Belmont, 15 June, 1864, John Pruyn to Barlow, June 18, 1864. Barlow Papers; S. S. Cox to George B. McClellan, August 4, 1864, McClellan Papers; *Official Proceedings,* p. 34; *Cincinnati Enquirer,* August 29, 1864. It was "well known," the *New York News* later claimed, that those opposed to McClellan gave up their opposition "in consideration of the general consent to certain clauses in the platform" (September 24, 1864). The Purists may have believed so, but there was more to it. See below.

28. Samuel L. M. Barlow to George B. McClellan, August 29, 1864, Barlow to Benjamin Stark, July 28, 1864, Barlow Papers.

belief that the party must "not only support by their platform and action the war for the restoration of the government over all the states, but they must [also] pursue such a course in Congress and by their presses as will compel the people to believe that this is their *true* object in seeking the possession of power." We must say to the peace men, argued Barlow, that "our only safety lies in success, and that with McClellan, peace is certain. This ought to make them willing to so frame a platform as to enable all who are in opposition to Mr. Lincoln's policy to unite with us, as after all, mere platforms, cannot control as against events, either for peace or war." This could be done, as Barlow pointed out, if the party "will avoid all unnecessary irritation on the subject of war or peace, expressing themselves in favor of a Union of the States." If "they choose to insert a plank with reference to negotiation & reconciliation, I have no doubt that it will be well received by the masses of the people." So long as the restoration of the Union remained in full view the drafters of the platform could do "no harm by advocating [a] . . . convention or any other . . . extraordinary measures looking to peace." Surely, even "the most violent representative of the peace party would not today assent to separation and all that they claim is, that war is not necessary to secure reunion."[29]

The response of the Purists to all of this proved prickly and then reasonable. At Chicago there was balking at McClellan by some who argued they could never support a general associated with the attempted military subjugation of the South. Others emphasized the price of their support. Fernando Wood told Barlow that, although he wanted Democratic success, it was "with a man who will close the war without more fighting and without disunion." He was willing to take McClellan only on those terms. George Pendleton warned New York Congressman Francis Kernan that McClellan's nomination would cause trouble and pleaded for another candidate. "I feel so anxious for harmony in our councils at Chicago." Some of the peace men led a brief flurry to block the nomination in favor of either

29. S. L. M. Barlow to Manton Marble, August 21, 1864, Marble Papers. Barlow to Benjamin Stark, July 28, 1864, Barlow to ?, n.d., 1864, Barlow Papers; Noah Brooks, *Washington in Lincoln's Time* (New York, 1896), pp. 182–83; George W. Morgan to George B. McClellan, June 20, 1864, McClellan Papers.

ex-Governor Thomas Seymour of Connecticut or his cousin, Governor Horatio Seymour of New York. Both were clearer symbols of opposition to the war policies of the administration. But such efforts did not last long. A meeting called to drum up support for another candidate proved to be, in the words of the *New York Herald*'s Chicago correspondent, "a fizzle." A resolution to bolt the ticket if McClellan were nominated was defeated by a two-to-one margin of the very few people (about thirty) reported at the meeting.[30]

For one thing, there was much sentiment for McClellan everywhere, even among the Western delegations where the Purists were supposed to be strongest. The Illinois and Indiana delegations, containing many Purist-peace men, but also many Legitimists, favored him. At its caucus at the convention, the forty-two delegates in the Ohio delegation split, seventeen for McClellan, four for Horatio Seymour, and twenty-one for Thomas Seymour.[31] More critically than the support by the Legitimists in these delegations, many Purists seemed genuinely committed to not splitting the party over the nomination. Pendleton's comment to Francis Kernan about his anxiety for party harmony was echoed in the behavior of the other main leaders of the faction. Vallandigham's deportment at the convention was reported as being "considerably toned down" and "very moderate." In a speech to a Chicago crowd before the convention opened, he was reported as saying that "he would support the nominee of the Convention, whoever he might be." More to the point, when McClellan came under attack in the convention, Vallandigham argued that "from the first moment we assembled here to the last, I have been animated by but one sentiment . . . in this Convention peace to the end that there may be peace in the land."[32] They appeared to be, in short, in the

30. Fernando Wood to S. L. M. Barlow, June 15, 1864, Barlow Papers; George Pendleton to Francis Kernan, August 21, 1864, Francis Kernan Papers, Cornell University Library, Ithaca, N.Y.; *New York Herald*, August 28, 1864 et seq.; Columbus (Ohio) *Crisis*, August 3, 1864.

31. *New York Herald*, August 26, 1864; Klement, *Limits of Dissent*, p. 282.

32. *New York Herald*, August 27, 1864; *Official Proceedings*, p. 47. There is a useful discussion of the machinations by some of the peace men to nominate Horatio Seymour at the convention in William F. Zornow, "McClellan and Seymour in the Chicago Convention of 1864," *Journal of the Illinois State Historical Society* 43 (Winter 1950): 282–95. Zornow, I believe, overdoes the extent of the peace revolt at the convention and ignores the forces working for unity, including Vallindigham's motion

aftermath of the Democrats' losses in 1863, more willing than they had been to find a means of cooperating with their colleagues.

The Democrats nominated McClellan on the first ballot with only a very few scattered votes cast against him. Vallandigham moved to make the nomination unanimous. This willingness to find a way to unity was also present in the drafting of the platform. The Purist leadership was very involved there. Vallandigham later said he had "confined his efforts almost exclusively to the question of the platform" at the convention. But he did not go as far as some Purists wanted. He drafted a plank embodying a declaration in favor of a peace policy which was more moderate than many of his supporters cared for. The Legitimists on the platform committee, whatever their desires may have been for an unequivocal war platform, went along. The Legitimist James Guthrie of Kentucky, who had beaten Vallandigham for chairman of the Committee on Resolutions, had (with Samuel Tilden of New York) the job of drafting resolutions that would satisfy all. Their end product included the nub of Vallandigham's ideas.[33]

For the first time since 1844 the platform did not include the usual Democratic litany on such policy matters as tariffs, banking policy, land distribution, or foreign affairs, all of which were now replaced by a general attack on the degradation of the Constitution during the war. Its tone had been established in Belmont's opening speech to the convention: "Four years of misrule by a sectional, fanatical and corrupt party, have brought our country to the very verge of ruin." The focus of most of the platform was on the impact of the war on the civil and individual liberties of the American people, and how these liberties had been circumvented, abrogated, and reduced by the administration without cause or reason. Everywhere, speech and assembly had been suppressed, states' rights disregarded, all designed to prevent the restoration of the Union and a government "deriving its just powers from the consent of the governed." The interference in

---

to make the nomination unanimous. But he is good on the disquiet felt by some at the convention.

33. Vallandigham's claim is in his letter to the *New York Herald,* October 27, 1864. The story of the resolutions committee is in the *Herald,* September 5, 1864. Also see Klement, *Limits of Dissent,* pp. 283–85.

free elections in the Border states was "revolutionary." The whole administration policy resulted in "the administrative usurpation of extraordinary and dangerous powers not granted by the Constitution." In other words, the Democrats reiterated the essentials of their appeal since the late 1850s, emphasizing the revolutionary and, to them, now well-demonstrated destructive intent of the Republicans.[34]

The Legitimists' concerns were met in three planks. The first affirmed the Democrats'

unswerving fidelity to the Union under the Constitution as the only solid foundation of our strength, security, and happiness as a people, and as a framework of government equally conducive to the welfare and prosperity of all the States, both Northern and Southern.

Another plank extended the "sympathy" of the party to the nation's armed forces, along with assurances that when they came to power, they would extend "all the care, protection, and regard that the brave soldiers and sailors of the republic have so nobly earned." In addition, a final clause deprecated "the shameful disregard" by the administration of Union prisoners of war left "in a suffering condition" in Southern prisons.

The Purist plank was the national platform's second resolution:

Resolved, That this convention does explicitly declare, as the sense of the American people, that after four years of failure to restore the Union by the experiment of war, during which, under the pretense of a military necessity of war-power higher than the Constitution, the Constitution itself has been disregarded in every part, and public liberty and private right alike trodden down and the material prosperity of the country essentially impaired, justice, humanity, liberty, and the public welfare demand that immediate efforts be made for a cessation of hostilities, with a view of an ultimate convention of the States, or other peaceable means, to the end that, at the earliest practicable moment, peace may be restored on the basis of the federal Union of the States.

The Republican newspaperman, Noah Brooks, reported later that as this resolution was read, "S. S. Cox clasped his hands in his lap and dropped his head, a picture of despair. August Belmont . . . also looked profoundly sad."[35] Perhaps, but both the public and the

34. The platform is conveniently reprinted in Kirk H. Porter and Donald Bruce Johnson, *National Party Platforms, 1840–1972* 5th ed. (Urbana, Ill., 1973).

35. Brooks, *Washington in Lincoln's Time*, pp. 184–85.

behind-the-scenes reaction of the Legitimists was not despairing at this point. They were euphoric at holding the party's first united and successful convention in eight years, getting their apparently strongest candidate nominated without too much rumbling, and drafting a platform that seemed to contain the right Legitimist elements: "the present wording is quite a concession to us," Belmont wrote. The New York *World* saw the platform as a "vigorous, patriotic, and conciliatory declaration of principles" designed "to remove the main obstacles to the formation of a Southern union party" by its moderate tone. Other editors agreed. This platform "opened a way of communication to the South. It offered peace, within the Union, on the basis of the Constitution." Lincoln had stood against reunion, but now the South would see it could renegotiate with the North once more. The Democrats were not running on either a war platform or a peace platform. "Union with peace, if possible, but Union and the Constitution at all hazards, are its declarations." With that platform fully carried out, there would be no war for abolition, subjugation, and confiscation, nor any peace that divided the Union.[36]

"Thus far," the old Whig Edward Everett commented during the convention, "more success than could have been expected has attended the efforts to unite the two wings of the Democratic party." Others echoed Everett's surprise.[37] But given their desire for harmony and the realization that they had much in common holding them together, particularly their hopes, fears, and enemies, the important men within the party on both sides worked assiduously to keep it united. There is no way of knowing for sure whether or not a fullblown arrangement had been worked out by Democratic leaders before the convention: candidate in return for platform. The evidence is not conclusive. But there certainly was a recognition of the realities of power within the party and the desire of most Democrats to stay together. The Legitimists helped the process by their willingness to

36. New York *World,* September 1, 1864; Albany (N.Y.) *Atlas and Argus,* September 9, 1864; *Detroit Free Press,* September 6, 1864; *Boston Post,* September 3, 1864.

37. Edward Everett to Charles Frances Adams, August 30, 1864, Edward Everett Papers, Massachusetts Historical Society, Boston, Mass.; *New York Herald,* September 1, 1864.

compromise and their great emphasis on the proper candidate. Coupled with their feeling that the platform would not be too far out of line and could be tempered by interpretation a smooth convention became possible.[38]

The Purists, too, were happy with the result. Benjamin Wood, editor of the *New York News*, exulted that "we accept the platform . . . as a great triumph for the peace party." McClellan was not the Purists' choice, but he would "receive our earnest support" anyway. He was a Democrat and therefore certainly better than any Republican. The fact that they would be most likely to emphasize principles, and therefore the platform first, helped promote unity, as did their lack of an obvious front-rank candidate espousing their position. Unlike McClellan, no Purist leader or candidate in the aftermath of the 1863 elections was regarded as an obvious choice for the nomination in 1864. (One wonders how much more trouble the Democrats might have had about their ticket if Vallandigham or Thomas Seymour had been decisive winners in 1863.) Now, even Alexander Long of Ohio, who had been censured by the House of Representatives for his bitter peace-at-any-price sentiments, said that although he considered McClellan "the worst man" for the nomination, "having the name of a democrat, I would still choose him before Lincoln or Fremont, and cast my vote with my friends." Perhaps a greater sense of realism stimulated by the stinging defeats of 1863 was the cause. It may also have been, however, that the Purist leaders felt they were getting what they wanted: a strong condemnation of the administration's war as the means of reuniting the Union. In such a situation their purism was not affronted by the nomination or the temporizing language. They had gotten their principles enunciated. Their candidate had to run on those principles.[39]

Each Democratic faction could move, therefore, towards the other in 1864, both had the will to do so, both wanted to find a way to work together against the Republicans. At the convention, both sides believed "there was too much at stake to quarrel, and they must har-

38. August Belmont to George B. McClellan, September 3, 1864, McClellan Papers; Samuel L. M. Barlow to Washington McLean, September 2, 1864, Barlow Papers.

39. *New York News*, September 1, 1864; *Official Proceedings*, p. 39.

monize in some way."[40] This willingness was reaffirmed in the nomination of the vice-presidential candidate. James Guthrie of Kentucky was supposedly the first choice of the Legitimists for the post, but "some of the New York leaders" thought it best to be "magnanimous to Ohio," center and symbol of the peace-Purist perspective. So Congressman George Pendleton became the near-unanimous choice.

"They Are the Fiercest Party Disciplinarians"

The first outside reactions to the Democrats' actions were positive. The convention, the *New York Herald* noted, "sustains the integrity of the Union." The main feature of the convention, according to this same source, was "the utter and final defeat" of the rabid peace men. Only a few Democrats seemed unhappy with the results. A group of peace men reaffirmed their dislike of McClellan. They also did not think the peace plank went far enough. But the vocal opposition of the extremist and small minority of peace men could only be thought to be a plus for the image of a Legitimist, conservative party.[41] But euphoria dissipated quickly. Before the convention, those pushing compromise had been warned that "you will ruin your candidate by the load you will put on his back" in the platform. The Legitimist response had been to "let the candidate be his own platform." To their horror, they discovered he could not. The platform was a responsible one in the Democrats' view. But it could be made to appear otherwise, and quickly was in the days and weeks after the convention. The Republicans, it was reported, were taking advantage of the party's "omission to declare that *we will insist on the Union under all circumstances.*" There was disappointment that the peace men had pushed so hard for their plank and so forgot "that the real battle and the only hope of victory is at the polls in November and not in the Convention."[42]

40. *New York Herald,* September 1, 5, 1864; *Official Proceedings,* p. 55.

41. *New York Herald,* September 1, 1864; *Crisis,* September 7, 1864.

42. "The platform is not acceptable to many Democrats as well as those who are being estranged from Lincoln; and these last must be looked to." A. Stephens to George B. McClellan, September 2, 1864, McClellan Papers; Durbin Ward to Samuel S. Cox, August 2, 1864, Cox Papers; *New York Herald,* September 5, 1864; Washington Hunt to Manton Marble, September 8, 1864, Marble Papers; S. S. Cox to George B.

Something had to be done. It was not done at the convention because "it would have involved a fight and probably rupture." To restore the situation now, the Legitimists wanted a clarifying letter from McClellan when he accepted the nomination. Samuel Barlow was deluged with warnings that "many thousands of votes depend on . . . McClellan's" response to his nomination. On the other hand, the pro-peace men were also quick to warn Barlow that they wanted McClellan's acceptance letter to be circumspect. One peace sympathizer warned that the platform should be left as it was. Otherwise, "you cannot carry Pennsylvania on a war policy immediate or remote." If there were attempts to change the meaning, the Democracy would lose a body of men they could not afford to lose, "and who are worth more than the migratory and uncertain semi-democrats of Maine and Connecticut." In deference to the divisions within the party and the relative strength of the different pressures on him, McClellan wavered, for a time, as to what to do. Still, as the reactions added up, the need for a stronger stance seemed the more crucial consideration. Coupled with that was a feeling that, no matter what, the peace men would stick.[43]

When McClellan's letter came, the Legitimists' spirits revived. The candidate made it clear that in his view the union was the paramount consideration and that there would be no peace, not even a temporary armistice, until reunion was assured.[44] As a result, McClellan was reported as having a good chance of carrying the six largest states of the central belt between New York and Illinois. Even General John McClernand, a leading War Democrat, was reported as having

McClellan, September 7, 1864, George T. Curtis to McClellan, September 1, 1864, James Dixon et al to McClellan, September 8, 1864, August Belmont to McClellan, September 3, 1864, S. L. M. Barlow to McClellan, September 3, 12, 1864, McClellan Papers.

43. William Cassidy to S. L. M. Barlow, September 5, 1864, Andrew Morris to Barlow, September 2, 1864, Amasa J. Parker to Barlow, September 5, 1864, William B. Reed to Barlow, September 1, 4, 1864, Robert Randall to Barlow, September 13, 1864, Barlow Papers; Clement L. Vallandigham to George B. McClellan, September 4, 1864, McClellan Papers. See also Charles R. Wilson, "McClellan's Changing Views on the Peace Platform of 1864," *American Historical Review* 38 (April 1933): 498–505.

44. Samuel L. M. Barlow to William B. Reed, September 9, 1864, Barlow Papers. McClellan's letter is in Wilson, "McClellan's Changing Views."

come out for him. Purists, however, were angry. Their newspaper spokesmen quickly lashed out at their candidate. "General McClellan has blown the party to pieces as by a bombshell." His repudiation of the platform was "a breach of party discipline" and an "unjustice." Purist sensibilities revived vigorously. "No election was ever carried on the flimsy basis of a choice of evils—nor the trash of argument called a *half loaf*." Remember, one summed up, although "an honest Democrat's attachment to his party is strong . . . his love of principles is also strong and he cannot see what use a party is to him or his country, if the principle be thrown away. This . . . is the big trouble now."[45]

Still, the imperative fostered by the party's communalism continued to hold them together. Though unhappy, the Purists stuck with the party. Vallandigham, for one, was certainly not prone to fight about McClellan's nomination, even after the letter of acceptance. In a mid-September speech in Dayton, Vallandigham called for party unity and said he would support the candidates of the Chicago convention as the only means of saving the country. He was not alone. Pendleton was quoted as saying that "he will say or do nothing calculated to harm." One by one, other dissenters came around, reluctant and unhappy in some cases though they seemed. The Columbus *Crisis*, organ of the Ohio extreme group for so long, finally, if grudgingly, put the ticket on its masthead. Even the *New York Daily News*, which argued at first that the duty of Democrats was to support all but the top of the ticket, eventually admitted that hundreds of thousands of "honest and conscientious peace men" would support the Chicago ticket. In the first place, their very Purism and commitment to the party kept them in place. As S. S. Cox had argued long

45. *New York Herald*, September, 13, 24, October 12, 1864; *New York News*, September 13, 16, 25, 1864; *Crisis*, September 7, 21, 1864; W. B. Lawrence to Franklin Pierce, October 17, 1864, Pierce Papers; S. L. M. Barlow to William B. Reed, October 19, 1864, Barlow to William Cassidy, September 22, 1864, Barlow to Washington McLean, October 15, 1864, Barlow Papers; S. S. Cox to Manton Marble, September 6, 1864, August Belmont to Marble, September 13, 1864, Marble Papers; John Horatio(?) to Thomas F. Bayard, September 11, 1864, Thomas F. Bayard Papers, Library of Congress. There was some talk of a meeting of Purists to take action against McClellan. See Charles O'Conor et al. to Jeremiah S. Black, September 10, 1864, Jeremiah S. Black Papers, Library of Congress.

before, "they are the fiercest party disciplinarians and they dare not bolt." In addition, the Democratic leaders had not challenged their stance beyond repair. They had cooperated at the convention, and McClellan's letter was not an extreme war statement by any means. Democrats had successfully, if somewhat painfully, established a situation in which peace men, Legitimists, and other conservatives could all agree in a situation where they all wanted to agree. As Vallandigham's brother said, what was important was that "between Mr. Lincoln and General McClellan, the latter was greatly preferable."[46]

The Democrats thus entered the campaign intent on making "vigorous exertions for victory," and with high hopes due to their unified determination to beat the Republican revolution. Despite continued distrust between the groups in the party, exacerbated by charges that some Purists were sitting it out, things looked good indeed. Their organization was well developed and constantly pressed to work harder. At the national level under the aegis of Belmont and the National Committee, tracts were published and distributed, finances were raised, and priorities established for their effort. The Society of the Diffusion of Political Knowledge under the leadership of Samuel F. B. Morse issued a range of pamphlets to counter the work of the Republican Union League clubs.[47] The Democrats mounted their attack along their already well-established lines of constitutional preservation and social conservatism, the issues they believed separated them from the Republicans. All of the concerns they had voiced since 1862 were repeated in profusion. Democrats, conservatives, and Republicans were left in no doubt that the Democratic campaigners believed that the Lincoln administration was strangling the Constitution, building up the power of the federal government to a dangerous level, and forcing a social policy on a reluctant country that would

46. S. L. M. Barlow to William B. Reed, September 2, 9, 13, October 19, 1864, Barlow Papers; *New York News,* September 30, October 22, 27, 1864; Edward McPherson, *The Political History of the United States During the Great Rebellion* (Washington, D.C., 1864), p. 64; *New York Herald,* September 25, 1864; S. S. Cox to S. L. M. Barlow, November 21, 1863, Barlow Papers; James L. Vallandigham, *A Life of Clement L. Vallandigham* (Baltimore, 1872), p. 367.

47. Katz, *Belmont,* and McJimsey, *Marble,* have good discussions of the activities of the Democratic organization during the campaign.

only lead to disaster. The Democrats argued nothing new in 1864. They worked at a higher, more intense pitch than ever to get across a familiar argument.[48]

Most of all they aimed their fire, once more, beyond the party faithful. In a series of fiery exhortations, the Democrats appealed to all dissatisfied conservatives to forget past differences and remember that "the last hope for the Union—and for Constitutional liberty—will be destroyed if Lincoln is elected." Particular attention was paid to the Republicans. They expected that not merely Democrats, but conservative Republicans too, would rally to the support of the ticket. In other words, for the sake of the country, "whether you call yourselves Republicans, Whigs, or Democrats, sink party now deeper than plummet can sound, say good bye to by gones . . . and elect McClellan. . . . In the name of country vote for him!" So far as the issues of the war were concerned, they argued the subtlety of their position. Their point was that the platform called for peace on the basis of the union's integrity. Their theme was well stated by August Belmont. Both McClellan and Pendleton, he argued, had declared for the restoration of the Union "at all hazards . . . peacefully if we can, forcibly if we must."[49]

The extent and vigor of their united efforts underscored how well the Democrats had weathered a most significant test in 1864. As one newspaper dramatically put it, "when the day of trial comes, it will be found that the ranks of the party are as firm and serried as were those of the old Macedonian phalanx."[50] They had worked together effectively as a party despite their internal differences in order to win the presidential election. Their ability to cooperate showed the continued importance of the partisan imperative in structuring their thought and behavior. Tensions continued to exist. Differences remained sharp. The opposing factions confronted one another repeatedly. Each was

48. See chapter three, above, for the structure of their wartime argument. The campaign, as a whole, is succinctly treated in Harold M. Hyman, "Election of 1864," in *History of American Presidential Elections, 1789–1968*, ed. Arthur M. Schlesinger and Fred L. Israel (New York, 1971), 2: 1155–1246; and James A. Rawley, *Turning Points of the Civil War* (Lincoln, Neb., 1966), pp. 169–204.

49. S. L. M. Barlow to Thomas Pratt, September 22, 1864, Barlow Papers; *Boston Post*, July 15, August 18, September 9, 1864; *New York Herald*, September 25, November 5, 1864.

50. *Chicago Times*, October 8, 1864.

acutely aware of the seriousness of their disagreements over how the party should behave in the crisis of war. But the things that united them remained alive as well. Whatever the differences among Democrats, a long tradition of fear and loathing of Republicans as well as the administration's immediate policies, confirming all their fears, held them together. They shared the same ideology and demonology. Parties must often cope with polarized policy demands among their supporters. But policy polarization has not always been strong enough to outweigh common ideals, traditional loyalty, and adherence to the party. Everyone probably gave the party the benefit of every doubt. All groups, no matter what the errors or provocations within the party, wished to stay in the organization. It was their home and the only place where truth was heard and a return to right was possible. Because of this partisan imperative they preserved their unity during the Civil War despite all their strains and internal tensions.

Nevertheless, there was a tightrope here. No one was happy when his beliefs clashed with the current stance of his party. If the differences were too sharp a partisan might sit out the election or vote for the other party. No one can now know if some Democrats, particularly the Purists, would have bolted the party in 1864 in disagreement with the platform or the candidate. There were indications of that possibility. Still, this was never tested, for party leaders on all sides acted rationally in terms of organizational imperatives. They recognized their differences as well as the things that united them. Although each faction tried to win as much as it could, each's simultaneous awareness of the other's limits and needs, and the desire for unity, caused them to behave in ways that minimized the possibility of a split. The Democrats thus found it within themselves to maintain their party as a vigorous and effective organization despite their disagreements with each other. Moreover, the picture they presented to the electorate was not at all ambiguous in their own eyes, but was of a partisan coalition acting in terms of a set of clear-cut ideas and commitments.

6

"To the Polls": The Shape
of Party Competition,
1861–1864

ELECTION ACTIVITY IN the United States in the 1860s was never-ending. The multiple levels of government—national, state, and local—provided many opportunities for electoral confrontation, even during a bloody civil war and despite the Lincoln administration's alleged repressiveness. In addition to the two sets of national elections—for Congress in 1862, and for the president and Congress in 1864—there were statewide elections for governor and other offices in some Northern states in every year after 1860. Some states voted annually. In New York, for example, there were gubernatorial elections in 1862, and 1864 as well as statewide elections for other posts in 1861 and 1863.[1]

The results of all of these state and national elections were critical to the Civil War Democracy. The Democrats' view of the world, their response to electoral and partisan pressures, their organizational activities, were parts of a complex structure that was the party. Another crucial element involved the voters, most particularly their reaction to the public image the party projected as a result of its internal actions. Obviously, the Democrats concentrated mightily on the electorate. Until they regained power at the polls, there was little else they could do to reverse Republican policy. Weak in numbers in Congress, they could protest vigorously but then lose every roll-call vote. With a few major statehouses in their grip, and then control of the presidency

1. In New England, governors were elected annually. Elsewhere, there were off-year elections for such officers as secretary of state, auditor, superintendent of public instruction, and attorney general.

and Congress, on the other hand, they would be able to reverse the critical situation in which they found themselves. Their attention to electoral strategy, therefore, was all but total.

The Democrats went into many of these wartime campaigns buoyant with hope and expectant of victory. They never lost faith that the Republican victories in the late 1850s and 1860 were aberrations. The Republican majority was very fragile. Issues ran in the Democrats' favor. As one editor wrote in 1864, the "tide is all one way. We hear of many Republicans being converted to Democrats, but of scarcely any Democrats turning Republicans."[2] The fact that they had been strong in 1860 in the key states of New York, New Jersey, Ohio, Illinois, and Indiana encouraged them in their belief that a breakthrough to victory was only a matter of time.[3]

Their optimism seemed plausible. The Republican majority in the Northern states in the election of 1860, however decisive, had indeed been small. Any shifting by groups of disaffected voters, or refusal to vote by Republican partisans, could alter national political control decisively. The Democrats, therefore, pulled out all stops in each election. They mobilized their troops assiduously and fought with the vigor of the committed and hopeful. Their intense persistence was nicely articulated in a series of instructions printed in the New York *World* just before election day 1864:

We entreat our friends to enter upon the great work which now devolves upon them in a spirit of harmony, to waste no time in discussions with each other, and to allow no vote to be lost to the great cause of national redemption and personal liberty that can properly be secured. . . . There must be instant and prompt organization in every election district throughout the country. Those who can afford the time, and have the cause at heart, would do well to quit work and spend the interval between now and election day in preparing for the most vital political struggle since the foundation of the government. . . .

[It] is incumbant upon the committees, clubs and citizens: 1. To urge all the voters to attend the polls at their opening, and to remain there patiently until their votes have been received . . . Let no man take the risk of waiting until after dinner. Let no man grudge to give one entire day, if necessary, to the salvation of his country.[4]

2. New York *World,* November 2, 1864.
3. See the discussion of their strength in 1860 in chapter one, above, particularly the analysis of the competitiveness of the Democracy.
4. New York *World,* November 8, 1864.

But the result of all this arduous activity was not what the Democrats wanted or expected.

"Our Numerous Strength"

Elections in most Northern states, certainly the crucial large ones, had a nerve-wracking quality to them between 1861 and 1864, thanks to the close margins in most races. Democratic electoral success, however, was at best checkered. In 1861 there was a series of statewide races across the North. Ohio, Maine, New Hampshire, and Connecticut elected governors; New York, a secretary of state; other states had local races. There were also congressional races in the spring of 1861 in three New England states.[5] Contrary to all of their hopes, the Democrats did not bounce back. They lost in all of the major states, everywhere, in fact, except in California (and there their vote fell precipitously). They averaged 41.3 percent of the popular vote in these races, a drop of 3.4 percent from their totals in the same contests in these states in 1859–1860, and a loss of 0.2 percent from their totals there in the presidential race.[6] In the congressional elections in 1861, the overall pattern differed little from the year before. Although the Democrats gained two seats in Connecticut, there was almost no shift in the average of their popular vote. They actually lost 0.7 percent from 1860.

It was clear enough that in this first set of wartime elections, the Democrats had not recovered their majority position in the country. Moreover, in some places they were, in fact, still badly offstride. To be sure, they had improved their position in a number of New England states. But these 1861 congressional elections in New Hampshire and

5. Connecticut, New Hampshire, and Rhode Island.
6. This percentage is based on Democratic totals in the following states: Maine, New Hampshire, Vermont, Massachusetts, Connecticut, New York, Ohio, Wisconsin, Iowa, and California. Wartime voting percentages are listed in Table 6.1, below.

In all of the computations in this chapter, certain decisions had to be made, for example, to combine separate Democratic tickets in a number of states early in the war (as a better indicator of Democratic electoral support), and to omit the Border states throughout, since they were frequently not free of outside (that is, administration) control. For a summary description of conditions in the latter, see Philip J. Avillo, Jr., "Ballots for the Faithful: The Oath and the Emergence of Slave State Republican Congressmen, 1861–1867," *Civil War History* 22 (June 1976): 164–74.

Connecticut took place early in the year, just as the war broke out. They occurred, therefore, when the Democrats were clearly opposing the Republican threat to the Union. The elections in the large states, on the other hand, were later in the year, an awkward time for the Democracy. The era of no-partyism was in full swing. Democratic opposition was, consequently, often confused and not sustained everywhere. In addition, the complications surrounding the War Democratic defection have to be considered in evaluating the Democrats' relatively poor showing in 1861. The Republicans actually ran a number of War Democrats for high office in several states, either to attract Democratic voters or to confuse them. Turnout decreased across the country and both parties' total popular vote dropped from both the presidential election and from the most recent statewide contests in these same states. But the Democratic vote dropped more. Most of the loss occurred in the two very large states of New York and Ohio. In both, the Democracy lost significantly more from their earlier totals than did the Republicans.[7] In short, the political world remained unsettled, particularly for Democrats. Their only consolation was their belief that these election results were deceptive, not a reliable indication of electoral strength, and that things would be different.

By the fall of 1862 the Democrats had fully reentered the field against the administration. Their organization was active and vigorous, their ideas clearly and forthrightly presented. They and their opponents fought each other energetically, playing on all of the themes each had developed against the other in previous years of confrontation. These races, then, were the first real opportunity to test the potency of the Democratic opposition. Not only were all but a handful of the country's congressmen up for reelection, but there were major races for governor in New York, New Jersey, New England, Michigan, and Oregon, and other statewide races in the Middle West, Pennsylvania, and California.

7. In New York, turnout in 1861 was 72 percent of the number of voters who went to the polls in 1860, but the Democratic vote was only 60 percent of their 1860 total while the Republicans received 83 percent of their 1860 total. In Ohio, where turnout fell to 85 percent of those who voted in 1860, the Democrats received 77 percent of their total of the year before, but the Republican vote was 97 percent of their vote in 1860.

The elections were a great triumph for the Democrats, their first good day at the polls since before the war. They won the governorships of New York and New Jersey, statewide races in Indiana and Illinois, and captured thirty-five Republican-held congressional seats. Their total popular vote across the North increased significantly over 1861, nearly back to their 1860 statewide totals in many places. Over all, they averaged 44.6 percent of the vote in the statewide races and 49.9 percent in all congressional races, even though their national average was depressed by bad showings in places such as Massachusetts and Vermont where Democrats had long been overwhelmingly outnumbered.[8] They did much better in a core of large states where the real contest for national control was being waged. "The powerful central division of the Union," from Connecticut through to Illinois, contained about 60 percent of the nation's population, 127 electoral votes, and a majority of the Union's congressmen. There, the Democrats increased their total popular vote over the year before to average 50.8 percent of the vote in the statewide races. Their percentage was a gain of 5.4 percent in these same states over the presidential election of two years before. They also added thirty-one seats in Congress. They were, in short, doing well where it counted.[9]

Perhaps the most striking of the 1862 Democratic victories was the gubernatorial race in the most populous state in the Union, New York, where Horatio Seymour defeated James Wadsworth. Although the margin between the two was close, 305,648 to 295,897, i.e., 50.9 percent to 49.1 percent, the crucial element was the Democratic gain over their 1860 and 1861 totals. Their 1862 vote was 117,000 more than the year before, and their proportion of the vote increased by an extraordinary 12 percent. Their improvement over 1860 was 4.6 percent. Elsewhere, there were other striking Democratic gains in 1862. In Pennsylvania they won the two contested statewide races and showed remarkable gains in the popular vote while doing so. Two

8. In Vermont, the Democrats received only 11.5 percent of the vote in the gubernatorial election. In Massachusetts they ran allied with the "People's" Party, and in Rhode Island they supported William Sprague's race for governor as a Unionist. In Maine, where there were two Democratic tickets, the War Democrats received 1,709 votes, the regular Democrats over 39,000.

9. The "powerful central division of the Union" reference is in the *New York Herald,* November 6, 1862.

years before, the Republicans had taken the state in the presidential race with 56.3 percent of the vote. Now the Democrats captured 50.4 percent of the statewide vote, gained fifteen seats in the state legislature, and six congressional seats for a total of twelve of twenty-four.

Even in races which the Democrats did not win in 1862, their share of the vote improved mightily over 1860 and 1861. In Maine, for example, the regular Democrats increased their proportion of the vote by over 20 percent in the governorship race from 1861—mostly at the expense of the War Democrats, as many of the latter returned to their party. Clement Vallandigham lost in his Ohio congressional district, but it was one that the Republican legislature had gerrymandered —and he substantially increased his margin in his original counties.[10]

The 1862 elections clearly marked a significant Democratic resurgence. But to what level? Closer inspection of the Democracy's vote indicates that although the party had done well there were limits to its achievements. Nowhere did the party enjoy comfortable margins. Its highest statewide total was 56.5 percent, in New Jersey. In most states in the decisive core area, Democratic totals hovered around 50 percent of the vote cast. The same was true of the congressional elections. Party candidates won many of their seats in traditionally Democratic areas by substantial margins. On the other hand, in many of the other seats they gained, their hold was at best slippery. In six Ohio seats, for example, they took between 50 percent and 52 percent of the vote, thin margins indeed. There were some wide swings in a number of states from their totals of the past two years, but these wild fluctuations were in strongly anti-Democratic states such as Vermont and Massachusetts. In the states where national power was decided, the states of the central core, the amount of vote shifting was relatively small (averaging 5.9 percent) from the most recent contests for these same seats.

Significantly, it was Republican stay-at-homes who depressed that party's proportion of the vote to the benefit of the Democracy. The Republicans' total vote fell across the country; the Democrats' did not. In such key states as New York, Ohio, Indiana, New Jersey, and Pennsylvania, for example, Democratic votes either increased or

10. See Frank L. Klement, *The Limits of Dissent: Clement L. Vallandigham and the Civil War* (Lexington, Ky., 1970), pp. 102–13.

dropped significantly less than did Republican totals from their margins in 1860 and 1861. The Democracy had made a respectable showing and demonstrated that it remained a strong minority party. But there was no great swing of the tide toward it as yet. At best, Democrats seemed to be coming back into equilibrium with the Republicans. They still faced much hard fighting to regain full national power.

In 1863 there were gubernatorial races in Ohio, Pennsylvania, Minnesota, Wisconsin, California, and the New England states, and races for various other state offices in three other states including New York. The situation at first glance seemed promising for the Democrats. As in the year before, many Republicans were in despair; Lincoln was warned by one of his secretaries that the Republicans were in danger in Pennsylvania because of ''the solid Irish vote—the chill and discouragement of the draft—the proclamation of *Habeas Corpus.*'' Horace Greeley was similarly advised of the same problems in Delaware where Republicans faced an uphill fight because of the Emancipation Proclamation. More and more non-Democratic conservatives were reported to be joining up against the Republicans. ''Where else could a disciple of Daniel Webster go,'' one asked, but to the conservative party of the Union?[11]

But, unlike the year before, the Democrats were sadly disappointed on election day. There was an increase in turnout across the country as three hundred thousand more people went to the polls than had done so in 1862 in the states having elections in both years, an increase of 13 percent in the total electorate. But the Democrats did not benefit. They won none of the statewide races (although they received a plurality of the popular vote in New Hampshire). Their share of the vote dropped significantly in such states as Illinois and Wisconsin, and fell slightly in New York and Pennsylvania. Their greatest drop, about 7 percent, was in the Middle Western states where they had done so well in 1862. This was due in large part to Clement

11. Tyler Dennett, ed., *Lincoln and the Civil War in the Diaries and Letters of John Hay* (New York, 1939), p. 134; Robert D. Hoffaker to Horace Greeley, September 15, 1863, Horace Greeley Papers, Library of Congress; Frederick W. Seward, *Seward at Washington, 1861–1872* (New York, 1891), p. 196; *New York Herald,* September 4, 1863.

Vallandigham's spectacular loss in his race for governor of Ohio, waged from exile in Canada. He was badly beaten as voter turnout increased in that one state by 113,000 votes. The Democrats received only slightly more votes than they had in 1862, while the Republican total vote increased by 110,000. The Democratic share of the vote fell to 39.4 percent, a drop of 11.4 percent from the year before and 5.9 percent from 1860. A percentage shift against them of more than 10 percent in a single state was an appalling loss for the minority Democrats.

But too much focus on the Ohio race obscures the relatively insignificant overall change in the habits of the electorate. On the whole, the Democrats did not do badly, actually maintaining a high level of national support. In Pennsylvania, where George Woodward, a peace candidate almost as notorious as Vallandigham, was the Democratic standard bearer, a surge to the polls did not go as disproportionately against them as had been the case in Ohio. Turnout increased by 89,000 votes over 1862, but both parties benefited from that to some degree. The Democratic share of the vote dropped only 1.9 percent over 1862, and gained 7.5 percent over 1860. In New Hampshire and Connecticut, the Democracy even picked up votes in 1863 over the year before. Their national total dropped slightly, to 41.8 percent of the popular vote, compared to 44.6 percent the year before. Wild swings continued in the noncompetitive states in New England, but in the central bloc there was very little gain or loss at all in their proportion of the vote (outside of Ohio) from the Democrats' very nice run in 1862. The average change from the year before, including Ohio, was only about 3 percent, both in the central bloc and overall. They did a little better in the races early in the year before the full onset of the conflict over the peace stance of some Democrats, but only slightly so.

A pattern partially indicated in 1862—of selective gains and losses, and responses to particular and local situations rather than any sustained national surge in the Democracy's favor—seemed to mark popular voting by 1863. The Democrats were able to make some gains and their vote level remained stable in many places, but all of this was counterbalanced by other losses in areas where particular problems beset them. There did not seem to be anything working as yet in the political situation to alter the underlying structure of the vote enough to favor the party. And in some places, apparently, there were immediate factors working against them which the Republicans were able to play on to hold most of their voters to them. This was confirmed in 1864.

Once more there was much optimism in the Democrats' camp, despite their defeats of the year before. They remained convinced that a "progressive revolution in public opinion" was underway due to the continuation of an indecisive war and the policies pursued by the government.[12] The opportunity to regain national power was there. In addition to the usual run of state offices, they had the chance to regain control of Congress and, of course, elect a president for the first time in eight years. The Lincoln-McClellan race for the presidency was, also, the first straight two-party national presidential fight since the election of 1828. Every participating voter had to choose one side or the other, and that, Democrats believed, would help them.

Unfortunately, the results did not bear out the Democrats' optimism. National turnout fell from 1860 by 7.4 percent (81.2 percent to 73.8 percent). McClellan and Pendleton received 1.8 million votes of the four million cast, the largest total any Democrat had ever received in the states participating in the election. But the Democratic figure was only 45 percent of the national total. They won majorities in only three states with twenty-one electoral votes. They gained more than 4 percent over their total popular vote in 1860 in the states that voted in both years. The number of wild swings in electoral support at the state level died down and the mean national voter swing was very small overall. There were a number of states where the Republicans were predominant: in New England, on the plains, and in some Midwestern areas. In the rest of the country there were some very close races. The Democrats' level of support in the very large states of New York and Pennsylvania was particularly impressive. Both they and the Republicans increased their total vote there over 1860, the Democrats by more than their opponents. But it was not enough to overcome Lincoln in either state.

12. New York *World*, October 13, 1864.

The Democrats' congressional gains of 1862 were also wiped out. They lost thirty-eight seats in the House of Representatives in 1864 from the Northern and Western states. In the new Thirty-ninth Congress there were half as many Democratic representatives as after the 1862 elections. Their total vote in the congressional races declined about 5 percent nationally from their 1862 figures. In some states their decline was very slight. In Pennsylvania, for example, the Democrats averaged 48.8 percent of the congressional vote compared to 50.7 percent in 1862. In Indiana the figures were 47.0 percent in 1864 and 52.5 percent in 1862. Yet these slight declines had a major effect on their fortunes. The Democracy had won twelve seats in Pennsylvania in 1862, but only eight in 1864. In Indiana they had won seven seats in 1862. In 1864 they won only three.

The election of 1864 revealed the same situation in regard to Democratic prospects as had all wartime elections. They remained very close to their opponents and always posed a threat. Furthermore, they were better off than their 45 percent of the national vote indicates. Much of the depression in their overall totals remained due, as in the past, to one-sided conditions favoring the Republicans in a few states in New England and in the West. Democratic gains and losses were greatest in these fringe states. But looking at the central bloc of states from Connecticut to Illinois gives a better idea of the size of Democratic strength and their promise during wartime. These states, in which the Democrats were strong, could determine the outcome of presidential elections and which party controlled Congress. In them the Democrats averaged 47.8 percent of the presidential vote, an increase of 1.4 percent from 1860. In the statewide races they did about the same as they had the year before, averaging 46.3 percent as against 47.3 percent in 1863, and 50.8 percent in 1862.[13] The patterns prompted some Democrats, such as Horatio Seymour, to comment after the presidential election that he was "entirely satisfied with the result. . . . It shows our numerous strength and that a majority of the people are with us when they act freely."[14]

13. Part of that difference was due to the absence of a statewide contest in New Jersey where the Democrats had done well in 1862.

14. Horatio Seymour to ?, November 24, 1864, Horatio Seymour Papers, New York State Library, Albany, N.Y.

Nevertheless, the election confirmed that the basic distribution of the vote still favored the Republicans. Democrats won a number of vital races but they also lost many key ones (including New York's governorship), were unable to make any significant breakthroughs in a consistent manner, and lost the biggest race of all, the presidency. The number of Democratic voters increased during the war but so did the number who supported their opponents. The Democratic overall percentage of the vote remained steady in the low and middle fortieth percentile, a promising but not spectacular figure. Their vote moved over a very small span during these years. They had maintained their relative position in most of the states remaining in the Union, except in the Border, lost some ground due to the basic Republicanism of some newly admitted small states, and all in all had managed to maintain their electoral strength. In short, they had held their own, neither gaining nor losing ground during the war.

The Competitiveness of the Democracy

These percentages offer a number of impressions about Democratic strength in the Civil War. The nature of the party's position and its meaning for two-party competition can, however, be measured fairly precisely. An index of competition for each state provides a picture of the actual condition of the Democracy in relation to their Republican opponents in the most crucial of all areas: their ability to regain national power through the electoral process. (See Table 6.1.) Comparing the wartime indices of party competition with those developed for the 1859–1860 period (chapter one above) indicates how competitive the Democrats were in the key largest states in the Union throughout the war, and therefore potentially potent nationally as well. There were, in fact, some wartime shifts in their national standing. In 1860 there were no safe Democratic states, two that were intensely competitive, and six that were moderately competitive.[15] The rest were either safe Republican, dominant Republican, or, as in the case of the Border states, areas that the Democrats could not subsequently include in their calculations due to their military control

15. As listed in chapter one, above, the definition of an intensely competitive state is one with an index of more than 95; a moderately competitive state is one with an index between 90 and 94.9; a state is one one-party dominant if the index is between 85 and 89.9, and safe if the index is less than 85.

Table 6.1
Democratic Electoral Percentages and Index of Competition 1861–1864

STATE	DEMOCRATIC PERCENTAGE						Presidential Elections, 1864	Index of Competition, 1861–1864
	State Elections, 1861	State Elections, 1862	Congressional Elections, 38th Cong.	State Elections, 1863	State Elections, 1864	Congressional Elections, 39th Cong.		
Maine	41.3	46.5	44.4	42.6	42.7	41.3	39.8	85.3
New Hampshire	47.0	48.5	46.8	53.1	45.9	49.6	47.4	94.9
Rhode Island[a]	—	—	—	41.0	41.7	35.6	37.8	78.1
Vermont	21.4	11.5	28.7	28.8	28.2	29.3	23.9	48.5
Massachusetts	32.4	39.4	36.1	29.3	28.2	27.3	27.8	63.1
Connecticut	48.8	43.6	48.3	48.3	46.2	48.6	48.6	95.0
New York	38.9	50.9	51.7	47.4	49.5	50.5	49.4	94.9
New Jersey	—	56.8	55.9	—	—	52.5	52.8	91.0
Pennsylvania	—	50.4	50.7	48.5	—	48.8	48.2	97.8
Ohio	42.3	50.8	50.8	39.4	43.5	44.0	43.7	88.9
Indiana	—	51.9	52.5	—	46.3	47.0	46.4	94.5
Illinois	—	53.2	56.5	—	—	45.2	45.6	90.6
Michigan	—	47.5	47.4	47.3	44.8	44.5	44.1	91.9
Wisconsin	45.8	—	51.7	40.9	—	43.4	44.1	89.4
Iowa	41.9	43.5	41.8	38.3	35.7	34.6	35.8	77.6
Minnesota	—	—	42.0	39.2	—	41.2	40.9	81.7
Kansas[b]	—	—	—	—	40.2	45.6	21.4	71.5
Nevada	—	—	—	—	40.0	—	40.2	80.2
California	53.2	42.1	—	41.0	—	41.6	41.4	85.2
Oregon	—	32.9	34.8	—	—	40.1	46.1	77.0

[a]In Rhode Island, the Democrats supported a conservative Republican ticket early in the war. Their own share of the vote is impossible to compute.

[b]In Kansas, the Democrats were part of an opposition ticket. Their figures here are inflated, but since the numbers do not change Kansas's position as a safe Republican state, they are included.

by the administration after 1860 and their consequent lack of free elections much of the time.

At first glance, then, the Democrats seemed to be in more trouble in 1864 than four years earlier. But a closer look at the results indicates otherwise. In the first place, there had not been much change in the intensely and moderately competitive states in terms of electoral votes. The most intensely competitive states in the Union during the war were Pennsylvania and Connecticut. In 1860, Delaware, Illinois, and New Jersey comprised this category. The moderately competitive states from 1861 to 1864 included the large ones of New York, Illinois, and Indiana, as well as Michigan, New Jersey, and New Hampshire. (See Table 6.2.) In 1864, therefore, states with 114

Table 6.2
States Listed by Competitiveness, 1861–1864
(with the number of their electoral votes)

SAFE REPUBLICAN		DOMINANT REPUBLICAN		MODERATELY COMPETITIVE		INTENSELY COMPETITIVE	
Rhode Island	4	Wisconsin	8	New Hampshire	5	Pennsylvania	26
Iowa	8	Ohio	21	New York	33	Connecticut	6
Oregon	3	Maine	7	Indiana	13		
Kansas	3	California	5	Michigan	8		
Massachusetts	12			New Jersey	7		
Vermont	5			Illinois	16		
Nevada	2						
Minnesota	4						

electoral votes were either intensely or moderately competitive. Although McClellan had won only in New Jersey, the Democrats had a good chance for victory in any given election in any or all of the rest of the states in both categories. This was a slight drop from the 127 electoral votes in these categories in 1860, but was still a majority of the Electoral College.[16]

Furthermore, in many of the large states there had been some movement toward the Democrats during the war. They increased their

16. Things were even slightly better than they looked because of some strength in the Border region. But this remained erratic and uncertain throughout the war due to military control there.

number of supporters in them more than did the Republicans. Pennsylvania, the second-largest state in the Union, had been a dominant Republican state in 1859–1860; by 1864 it was intensely competitive. (Democratic votes increased there by 80,000 votes, the Republicans by 28,000). New York, Maine, Indiana, and New Hampshire had grown somewhat more competitive during the war as well. A number of states grew less competitive during the war, particularly Ohio, where much of the Republican gain in 1863 remained with the party the following year. But the point remains that in terms of electoral strength the Democrats were in a good position in the nation as a whole. Despite their defeats during the war they remained within striking distance of their opponents.

In the races for the House of Representatives, too, the Democrats demonstrated continued strength in wartime elections. There were nineteen safe Democratic House seats and three in which they were dominant. This was a slight improvement in the Democratic position over 1860. The battleground remained the twenty-seven seats, mostly in the central belt of states, that were intensely competitive and the thirty-six which were moderately competitive. Unfortunately for the party, Democratic House seats by and large grew more competitive and Republican seats less so between 1862 and 1864. There were also a few less competitive seats than in 1860. Still, the Democrats retained a good chance for control of 85 of the 155 seats, those in the intensely and moderately competitive categories, outside of the Border states.

In sum, the Democratic party remained a reasonable position of strength during the Civil War. All told, election results indicated to the Democrats that the Republicans were wise to exert military control over the ballot boxes of the Border states and to admit two new Western states which could be counted on in the Republican column. But there was more to the Democrats' situation than that.

The Continuity of Voting Behavior

Despite the continued Democratic strength and the closeness of the vote, the pattern of wartime popular voting confirmed that the Democrats were trapped in a minority role. For the voters, despite occasional variability in their behavior, had remained steadfastly in their accustomed behavioral grooves. Whether one chooses to consider states where there were some erratic swings of electoral totals during the war, and occasional surges or drops in participation favoring one party, such as Ohio, or the most intensely competitive of all Northern states, Pennsylvania, or a number of the largest and most influential in terms of national power, such as New York, Illinois, or Indiana, the outstanding characteristic of wartime electoral behavior was the remarkable continuity in the way the electorate cast its votes. In Ohio, for one example, there was always a very high level of inter-election correlations. Annual wartime elections correlated with each other at a mean of .94, even including the confusing election for governor in 1861 in which a War Democrat was the Republican nominee.[17] Voting behavior in New York, Pennsylvania, Indiana, and elsewhere also showed similarly strong positive relationships in the way voters behaved between successive elections. In New York, correlations averaged .88 in the four elections between 1861 and 1864. (See Table 6.3.) This compares with .90 for the most stable

Table 6.3
Democratic Correlations, 1860–1864, New York

	1861	1862	1863	1864
1860	.75	.96	.96	.96
1861	—	.77	.81	.78
1862		—	.98	.98
1863			—	.98

period of the second-party system between 1839 and 1844. In Pennsylvania, the mean correlation figure for wartime elections was almost .99; in Indiana, .88; in Connecticut, .97; in New Jersey, .94. In Illinois, which showed the least stability among the states in the central bloc, the mean correlation was still a relatively high .82.

Even some elections which at first glance seem to deviate from the normal pattern do not appear to do so upon closer inspection. The election of 1862 was a normal, not a deviating, election. It was highly

17. These correlations are based on returns at the county level within each state. I am grateful to Phyllis Field, Marc Kruman, and the Cornell University Computing Center for aid in computing these figures.

correlated in every state with the other elections of the early 1860s. Similarly, the Ohio gubernatorial election of 1863, the major wartime landslide, was highly correlated with other elections in the period. Only the elections of 1861, held at a moment of unsure development of full-scale party competition, show less voter stability than do the others in the period. In fact, the wartime correlation figures in most states were depressed by the 1861 contest. Removing 1861 from the calculations in Illinois causes the mean correlation figure there to zoom to an extraordinary .98. In New York, removing the election of 1861 increases the mean correlation figure to .97. In other states the change, though not as dramatic, is still important. Throughout the Northern states, then, there was a striking pattern of stability in the voting. The mean correlation in the central bloc of states, for example, in all wartime elections was .91, a very high figure indeed. (Removing the elections of 1861 from the calculation lifts the figure to .95.) In short, the similarity of each party's percentages at the state level from one election to the next was not based on compensating swings of voters' choice.

The pattern revealed in the correlation figures is confirmed by another set of electoral comparisons. With some dramatic exceptions, there was very little movement at the county level in each state in each party's percentage of the vote between successive elections as there would be if voters were surging to one party or another all across the board.[18] There was some temporary growth or decline in each party's share of the vote at the county level throughout the war. But generally the shift was moderate. The average of all county changes in the central bloc of states between 1862 and 1863, for one example, was 4.8 percent. For the war period as a whole, the mean shift for these states at the county level between elections was 4.5 percent. In New York, the average wartime shift was 3.3 percent; in Pennsylvania, 3.1 percent; Indiana, 5.8 percent; Ohio, 8.1 percent—percentages similar to earlier periods of party stability. The largest shift in all of these

18. Correlations are best at showing the amount of interactive changes, i.e., people moving between parties, but do not catch near uniform shifts everywhere in a state toward a single party. These can only be caught by another measure, such as, as is done here, computing the percentage of county votes shifting between successive elections.

states was 11.1 percent in Ohio between 1862 and 1863, indicating a surge in this instance toward the Republicans. But generally the county-level shift figures reinforce the picture of electoral stability.

Furthermore, there was stability across office boundaries as well. There was little deviation in the vote from one contested office to the next. The size of each party's vote, the percentage each received, and the correlations between elections for governor and other officials were usually the same as congressional or presidential balloting. Compared to the twentieth century there was little split-ticket voting. Even off-year elections showed little change in the distribution of the vote. Although overall the Democrats did slightly better in "on-year" elections, as in 1862 and 1864, the real differences between the distributions of the vote in an off-year and on-year was very slight. Unlike the twentieth century again, there was only one electorate in the 1860s, one that came out to vote in generally the same proportions for each party in every kind of race, year after year.[19]

There was always some variability in voter behavior. Not every state was an exact microcosm of every other in its voting experience. But whatever variability and shifting existed, their extent and impact were not critical to the main point. The outstanding characteristic of Northern voter behavior in the Civil War years was that the electorate had neither fragmented nor become volatile. Neither the geography of each party's vote nor its size relative to the other had moved markedly. There had been little conversion of voters to new political habits. There had been an increase in the number of each party's voters, but in proportionate terms. When people cast their ballots they remained in accustomed partisan grooves, and the pattern of electoral behavior remained, therefore, quite rigid. This rigidity posed a major problem for the Democratic party.[20]

19. For a discussion of the growing importance of split-ticket voting and "roll-off" and "fall-off" in popular voting behavior, see Walter Dean Burnham, "The Changing Shape of the American Political Universe," *American Political Science Review* 59 (March 1965): 7–28.

20. Using a different method of measurement, Professor Peyton McCrary has found similar results in his study of electoral behavior in the 1860s. See his "The Civil War Party System: 1854–1876: Toward a New Behavioral Synthesis?" (Paper presented to the annual meeting of the Southern Historical Association, Atlanta, Georgia, 1976). Confirmation of this stable pattern for a number of Midwestern states can be seen

The pattern had been set in the aftermath of the realignment of the midfifties. By 1860 the electorate had become locked in.[21] From then on, voting behavior became entirely predictable, except for the important possibility of differential turnout (i.e., that more of one party's normal supporters would stay home than those of the other party). One could, and politicians of the age often did, predict the outcome of national elections from certain preliminary clues. The spring elections in Connecticut and New Hampshire for Congress and state offices were early indicators. The October elections in Indiana and Pennsylvania were even more important since they came in the middle of widespread and intense campaign activity. Political observers knew that the results in the October states foreshadowed the electoral pattern of the following month.[22] If there were the right kind of volatility in voter behavior and deviation from the normal pattern, there was real hope of a Democratic victory. If, on the other hand, there were continuity from the past in the October elections, then defeat for the Democrats elsewhere in November was foreshadowed. The stability of behavior saw to that. This was the pattern the Democrats had been unable to shake during the war.

---

in Ray Myle Shortridge, "Voting Patterns in the American Midwest, 1840–1872" (Ph.D. diss., University of Michigan, 1974).

21. Most wartime elections in the central bloc of states, for example, correlated strongly with the election of 1860. The correlation was at the .95 level in Ohio, .96 and better in Pennsylvania and New York, and only slightly lower in Connecticut, Indiana, and New Jersey.

22. There is a succinct and useful discussion of this in Robert D. Marcus, *Grand Old Party, Political Structure in the Gilded Age* (New York, 1971), chapter one.

7

"The Smell of Treason Was on Their Garments": The Dynamics of Party Competition, 1860–1864

THE DEMOCRATS HAD BEEN well and truly beaten in their wartime crusade to return the United States constitutionally to 1860. In their postmortems they underscored their indifference to soul-searching and concentrated on the calamitous consequences for the nation. "For my country's sake, I deplore the result," George McClellan wrote a few days after the election of 1864. But "for what may befall the republic in the next few years," the *Illinois State Register* continued, "no living creature can hold the democratic party responsible." The Democrats were certainly not ready to strike their colors. They reemphasized their determination to fight on with "no surrender of principles" and bravely reminded themselves once more that the Democracy, "a great, respectable party . . . though temporarily defeated, is destined to live and be the main pillar of the public safety."[1]

Underneath Democratic declamations and posturing, however, remained a critical question regarding party fortunes. Party members had believed all through the war that a majority of the country was with them ideologically and that the force of public events would ultimately work in their favor. But, despite their effective mobilization of their own partisans and sustained articulation of powerful issues, they had not been able to upset the stability of a voting pattern that

1. George B. McClellan to Samuel L. M. Barlow, November 10, 1864, Samuel L. M. Barlow Papers, Henry E. Huntington Library, San Marino, Ca.; Springfield *Illinois State Register*, November 10, 1864; New York *World*, November 19, 1864.

favored the Republicans. The results, in other words, provided the worst kind of frustration for the Democratic leaders: very close races with an occasional whiff of victory, coupled with an inability to win regularly or in the most important national contests.

But why had the Democratic onslaught, begun with such high hopes, and then carried forward with such relentlessness, failed in the end to bring the party any more than temporary victories and nothing but defeat in its quest for the major prize of all? There were a number of possible answers perceived at the time. Some Democrats, for example, focused on the alleged corruption of the voting process. Defeated partisans, whether Republicans or Democrats, usually cried fraud when an election was over. It was an old American tradition.[2] The Democrats saw in the situation in the Border states confirmation of their fears. Troops often controlled the polls and, in the Democrats' view, clearly worked on behalf of the Republican party on election day. One army officer in Maryland declared in 1863 "that no 'damned Democrat vote' would be accepted." The Democrats believed that few were. During the war, too, the army had granted a great many furloughs at propitious moments to allow soldiers to return home and vote, sometimes, according to the Democrats, not to their home states but, instead, to states with close races.[3]

Democrats were also suspicious of the way soldiers' voting occurred in the field. A number of states had enacted soldiers' absentee ballot laws for wartime elections. In most cases soldiers were allowed to vote in their camps and stations and have their ballots returned to each state to be added to its totals.[4] Many observers believed that the army contained significant numbers of members of both parties. But

2. See, for example, Thomas Hendricks to Jeremiah S. Black, November 6, 1864, Jeremiah S. Black Papers, Library of Congress; *Congressional Globe*, 38 Cong., 2 sess., pp. 858–59.

3. Quoted in Charles L. Wagandt, "Election by Sword and Ballot: The Emancipation Victory of 1863," *Maryland Historical Magazine* 59 (June 1964): 155. See also Benjamin Thomas and Harold Hyman, *Stanton: The Life and Times of Lincoln's Secretary of War* (New York, 1962), pp. 249, 293, 295; William B. Hesseltine, *Lincoln and the War Governors,* 2nd ed. (New York, 1955), pp. 271–72.

4. The standard study of soldier voting during the Civil War is Josiah Henry Benton, *Voting in the Field* (Boston, 1915). T. Harry Williams, "Voters in Blue," *Mississippi Valley Historical Review* 31 (September 1944): 187–204, is a good overview of political attitudes within and toward the army.

the Democrats feared that they would not receive their rightful share of these votes. Convinced that the army was "full of abolition spies, under the guise of tract distributors, State Agents . . . Chaplains & Sanitary Commission agents" who would propagandize against the Democracy and coerce Democratic soldiers to act contrary to their political beliefs, they made it clear, that "we have no confidence in an honest vote from the army." [5]

The way the soldier voting occurred in the presidential election of 1864, its most significant test, confirmed, to the Democrats, their worst fears about the voting process. Apparently, according to Democratic observers, only Republican campaign literature was distributed; Democratic materials and ballots were seized, thrown away, or sent back. "There is no use in talking about the soldiers' vote. We cannot get it—the officers will not permit the men to have tickets." Lincoln canvassers among the troops outnumbered those for McClellan by two to one. Further, there was "a great deal of influence exerted by some officers over the men under their command." Finally, "our commissioners tell us that Democrats were threatened to be sent to the front if they voted." There may have been something to the Democrats' perceptions. It seemed clear that the administration was not loath to use, Assistant Secretary of War Charles Dana later recalled, "all the power and influence of the War Department . . . to secure the re-election of Mr. Lincoln." [6]

5. Edward Cross to Franklin Pierce, April 14, 1863, Franklin Pierce Papers, Library of Congress; Albany (N.Y.) *Atlas and Argus,* August 27, 1863, March 25, 1864; Samuel S. Cox to Samuel L. M. Barlow, November 2, 1863, Barlow Papers; Horatio Seymour to George B. McClellan, September 30, 1864, George B. McClellan Papers, Library of Congress. See also "Plan of Democratic Campaign for October, 1864," copy in Manton Marble Papers, Library of Congress.

6. C. M. Gould to S. S. Cox, October 16, 1864, Samuel S. Cox Papers, Brown University Library, Providence, R.I.; Charles Mason to Horatio Seymour, October 10, 1864, Horatio Seymour Papers, New York State Library, Albany, N.Y.; Allan Nevins, ed., *A Diary of Battle: The Personal Journals of Colonel Charles S. Wainright, 1861–1865* (New York, 1962), pp. 472, 476; William B. Reed to S. L. M. Barlow, October 18, 1864, William H. Wadsworth to Barlow, October 24, 1864, Barlow Papers; Finley Anderson to George B. McClellan, September 6, 1864, McClellan Papers; Charles Dana, *Recollections of the Civil War* (New York, 1899), p. 261. There are good summaries and descriptions of voting by soldiers in Oscar O. Winther, "Soldier Voting in the Election of 1864," *New York History* 25 (October 1944): 440–58; and Arnold Shankman, "Soldier Votes and Clement L. Vallandigham in the 1863 Ohio Gubernatorial Election," *Ohio History* 82 (Winter/Spring 1973): 88–104.

In any event, the 150,000 soldiers' ballots went disproportionately for the Republicans by about 78 percent to 22 percent (as compared to 53 percent to 47 percent for the civilian vote). There is no doubt that the way the soldiers' vote distributed itself gave the Republicans a number of crucial states. Whether the result was entirely the result of intimidation and fraud is not clear. However, despite the disproportionate result, the soldiers' vote really did not have all that much import for the presidential race. Even if the soldiers' totals had been closer to the percentages of the home vote in the same states, little would have changed. The Republicans would still have won the presidential election in the Electoral College.

Possibly the defection of the War Democrats destroyed any chance that the Democratic party had of regaining the electoral advantage in the country. Early in the war, War Democratic organizations ran separate candidates in a few places, getting a small share of the popular vote and reducing the Democratic total. In Ohio in 1861, a War Democrat was nominated by the Republicans for governor to blur party distinctions and bring over some Democrats. In 1864, War Democratic leaders such as John A. Dix and Daniel Dickinson in New York, and John McClernand and John Logan in Illinois, among others, actively worked against their former colleagues. They reassured each other that they were pulling significant numbers of voters away from their old party. But their secession and activities, while perhaps important as an elite disruption, seem never to have had much effect on the total Democratic vote, either earlier in the war or in the presidential election. The persistence of each party's popular support despite the strains of wartime indicates that no major mass defections occurred. It is clear that the Democrats received their normal popular vote in the early sixties. If there were some small defections of War

---

There is evidence that the soldier voters, even former Democrats, while in the army were more prone to vote Republican with or without intimidation. First of all the sense of community and commitment to the Union cause was particularly strong in the army, and Republican propaganda about the legitimacy of the Democrats seems to have affected the soldiers very strongly. See Wainright, *Diary of Battle*, pp. 476–77; James I. Robertson, Jr., N.J., ed., *The Civil War Letters of General Robert McAllister* (New Brunswick, N.J., 1965), p. 518; Rutherford B. Hayes to Sophia Hayes, October 21, 1863, in *The Diary and Letters of Rutherford B. Hayes*, ed. Charles Williams (Columbus, Ohio, 1924), 2: 442.

Democrats, even in the closely contested states, it is difficult to see that they affected the final outcome of the contest for national power.[7]

Finally, there is the evidence that although differential turnout negatively affected each party at different times, it particularly hurt the Democrats. A drastic fall-off in their vote total hurt the Republicans in 1862 and the Democrats in 1861 and in 1863 in some states. The fact that voting correlations remained stable throughout the war in most places, and county percentage shifts within states were not large between elections, would seem to confirm the point that the occasional electoral landslide or abnormal pattern of voting was caused not by conversion of voters from one party to another, but either by severe drops among the party's normal voters who simply abstained, or by the short-term infusion of some new voters in the electorate who, stimulated by a momentary issue of dramatic force (as in Ohio in 1863), disproportionately voted for one party. Shifts in turnout were not widespread in the presidential year of 1864, however, when turnout and the total national vote stood at normally expected levels.[8] The important point here is that even if depressed turnout hurt the Democrats at different times, such a fall-off in numbers was an effect, not a cause. Still to be understood, therefore, was what caused Americans to vote the way they did during the war years. In short, whatever the possible effects of the soldiers' vote, War Democrats' defections, or fall-off in turnout, there was much more contributing to the rejection of the Democratic party. The crucial element in the equation concerned the nature of the partisan imperative in the United States and how the parties, particularly the Democrats, had to behave as a result.

7. On the War Democrats, see above, chapter two. On their activities in 1864, see John A. Dix to Abraham Lincoln, November 12, 1864, John A. Dix Papers, Columbia University Library, New York, N.Y.

8. Walter Dean Burnham has calculated that national turnout in 1864 was 73.8 percent of the eligible electorate, compared to 81.2 percent in 1860. Much of the drop was based on dramatic fall-offs in the border states. In the highly competitive central bloc of states, turnout was 80.9 percent in 1864, compared to 82.7 percent in 1860. See *Historical Statistics of the United States, Colonial Times to 1970* (Washington, D.C., 1975), pp. 1071–72.

"Party Discipline Was Vigorous and Absolute"

The Democrats, of course, had to confront the pervasive structuralism present in the American political culture. The prevailing mood of the times remained, as one Republican put it, one where "party discipline was vigorous and absolute." [9] If a slight majority of the voters favored the Republicans, as they seemed to do in the Northern states after 1860, the Democrats could only hope for victory if they converted some of the enemy or gave some Republican voters cause to sit out the election, thus depressing their opponent's total, as apparently happened in 1862. A status quo in existing voting habits was useless. But the crucial members of the electorate in such cases, the former Whigs and alienated Republicans, were men already deeply suspicious of the Democratic party. They had never voted Democratic in their lives and they contained a fair proportion of people unable "to break away from old names and old associations," or "to overcome old prejudices so far as to allow them to vote the Democratic ticket." [10] In other words, despite the disenchantment with the Republicans that many people felt, they did not, as a consequence, automatically move into the Democratic column.

To convert such voters, in fact to attract even a useful proportion of uncommitted voters to them, the Democrats had, perhaps, one chance. They had to pursue a minority party strategy as the Whigs, for example, had done in 1840 and 1848. Such a strategy was designed to soften the intense party loyalties and prejudices of the electorate by blurring previous partisan distinctions and playing down party labels in the name of a general good. In the 1860s that strategy asked non-Democrats to "say good by to by gones" in favor of the universally agreed upon commitment to conservatism.[11] To do this, Democrats could not allow themselves to appear sectarian, narrow, or par-

9. Henry B. Stanton, *Random Recollections* (New York, 1887), p. 244.

10. John D. Caton, "The Position and Policy of the Democratic party. A Letter to Hon. Horatio Seymour, December 18, 1862," in idem, *Miscellanies* (Boston, 1880), p. 30.

11. *Boston Post,* September 9, 1864.

tisan, for to do so would repel the suspicious, the hostile, and the non-Democrat.

The Democrats, in fact, never really pursued a minority party strategy. They never forsook the label of Democrats, they were not receptive to sharing power or place with conservatives, and they did not play down the principles that distinguished them from the Republicans. The Democrats always made it very clear that they drew the line between what they believed in and advocated and what the Republicans believed in and were doing. Neither Legitimists nor Purists glossed over their conservative stance and their disagreement with administration policies concerning the Negro, finance, tariffs, taxation, or the power of the central government. There was very little, if any, me-tooism, no blurring of the lines, no hiding of their position. This was partly because they believed that their brand of conservative constitutionalism had the support of a majority of the country, including many people who were not members of the Democratic party. In other words, they saw their commitment to the Union and to constitutional conservatism as a broad and general appeal, not a narrow, sectarian one.

At the same time, the Democrats could not pursue a generalized minority party strategy because of their own internal imperatives. The differences within the coalition over how far to advance toward the conservatives were, as we have seen, persistent and bitter. Such a situation is not unusual, nor did the differences among Democratic elites really affect party support among the faithful who would vote Democratic in almost any event, given the hammering of their Civil War experiences. But the internal tensions and the compromises did make it impossible for Democrats to appeal effectively to non-Democratic marginal voters. As most of them saw it, their first need was to prevent the defection of any Democratic voters from the party on election day. Their intense efforts to stay together reinforced their emphasis on the common elements of the Democratic faith: the things that united them and separated them from the Republican enemy. Their stance strengthened loyal Democrats' commitment to their party and may have stirred some other conservatives toward them as well. The cost of their not splitting, however, was an appeal that was narrower and more partisan than was wise in the situation. It failed to disrupt the voting patterns of the 1850s.

There was still another element in the situation as well, perhaps the most important of all. The *substance* and *appearance* of the debate within the Democracy was quite damaging to the party's appeal to marginal, non-Democratic, conservative voters. The Democrats failed to legitimize themselves effectively. In fact, their behavior did the reverse. Even the War Democratic and hostile *New York Herald* admitted that the Democratic candidates in 1863, and especially in 1864, stood upon conservative Union platforms. But the message was lost in the welter of Republican propaganda, lost particularly among just those marginal conservatives and Republicans who had to come over to the Democracy for the party to break through the victory.[12]

Political scientists discriminate between what they call "position" issues and "valence" issues in elections. The first are issues "involving advocacy of different actions or alternative government policies," e.g., should there be a high tariff or not, should habeas corpus be suspended in the interest of national security or not, should slaves be freed by the actions of the federal government or not. The second, while not devoid of issue content, involves "the linking of parties with some condition that is positively or negatively valued by the electorate," is one party the party of the Union, the other the party of separation, for one example.[13] When valence issues become important, they can attract or repel people who might have aligned with a party on the basis of its stand on specific issues. So it was in the case of the Democrats in the Civil War period. There was a valence issue of great impact at work. The Democrats' identification as the party of peace and disunion hurt them badly. The New York *World* once shrewdly noted that "there was, indeed, great previous dissatisfaction with Mr. Lincoln; but men do not change their politics until they see what is proposed to be substituted for the administration they disapprove." [14] The result of the fairly equitable balance of forces

12. *New York Herald,* October 13, 1863, October 26, 1864.
13. Angus Campbell et al., *Elections and the Political Order* (New York, 1966), pp. 170–71.
14. New York *World,* October 13, 1864. On the nature of the Democrats' stance

within the Democracy was an articulation of a position of the war and the Union ambiguous enough to be exploited savagely by the party's opponents. There was a difference, in other words, between what the Democrats believed and what they projected between the reality of their Unionist position and how their position could be made to sound.

The Party of "Dixie, Davis and the Devil"

Unfortunately for their electoral hopes, the Democrats' internal party debates did not occur in a vacuum. They were affected constantly by the changing political situation, particularly the Republican counterattack against the Democratic resurgence. Republicans had not been idle while the Democrats worked out their electoral appeal. Obviously, Republicans bent every will and utilized every weapon and trick, fair and foul, to counter any surge to the Democrats and to maintain the current popular vote distribution in Northern states. The Republican campaigns were designed to activate and reinforce longstanding partisan predispositions so as to prevent any slippage to the Democracy by either Republicans or non-Democratic conservatives. They played down issues, such as emancipation, on which they felt themselves weak.

But, most of all, the Republicans diverted attention from their policies by making the issue the treasonable position of the Peace Democrats. Their message was clear. Indeed, their whole point was to delegitimize the Democratic opposition. They set up elaborate propaganda organizations such as the Loyal Leagues, and these energetically entered the lists. They were hyperactive in arguing against the party of treason and disunion. (One Republican publication during 1864 was entitled "The Coward's Convention.") The complexity of the Democrats' stance, particularly the association of peace with Union, was quickly misted over by the Republicans. They concentrated all attention on the peace portion of the Democrats' message and waved the bloody shirt of Copperhead treason as vigorously as they could in order to discredit their opponents. Horatio Seymour "is in fact a traitor at heart," one had said, setting the tone in 1862, and the

---

on war support policies in Congress, see Leonard Curry, "Congressional Democrats, 1861–1863," *Civil War History* 12 (September 1966): 213–29.

Republicans played on such themes persistently thereafter.[15] "I say Vallandigham is a traitor," one suggested in 1863.

The Democrats' 1864 platform meant "disunion . . . national humiliation, submission to an arrogant and defiant enemy and disgrace to the American flag and name both at home and abroad." The "worst Tory of the Revolution was a patriot and a gentleman compared with a Copperhead of 1864." Republicans laughed at the Democrats' alleged unionism or support for the soldiers or the war as a sham. No, the Democrats had "the smell of treason on their garments." They were the party of "Dixie, Davis, and the devil."[16]

The Democrats did their best to counter this. They tried to "dispel apprehension respecting our position" and to convince Republicans that "resistance" to their "schemes" was "not treason, but war." They railed against "the spell" their opponents had "woven around the hearts of our people, by the cunning use of the words conservatism, patriotism, Union."[17] But the Republican attack was too

15. Isaac Sherman to Francis P. Blair, Sr., September 21, 1862, Blair Family Papers, Library of Congress. On these Republican campaign activities against the Democrats, see Edith Ware, "Committees of Public Information, 1863–1866," *The Historical Outlook* 10 (February 1919): 65–67; George Winston Smith, "Broadsides for Freedom: Civil War Propaganda in New England," *New England Quarterly* 21 (September 1948): 291–312; Frank Freidel, "The Loyal Publication Society: A Pro-Union Propaganda Agency," *Mississippi Valley Historical Review* 26 (December 1939): 359–76.

16. *Proceedings of the Convention of Loyal Leagues Held at Mechanics Hall, Utica, Tuesday, 26 May, 1863* (New York, 1863), p. 32; William Dickson, *Address of William M. Dickson at Greenwood Hall, Cincinnati, September 23, 1863* (Cincinnati, 1863), pp. 30–31; R. G. Corwin to Thomas Ewing, Sr., September 20, 1862, Thomas Ewing Papers, Library of Congress; Rueben Van Pelt, *A Speech Delivered at a Massing Meeting . . . October 29, 1862. . . .* (Yonkers, N.Y., 1862), p. 7; *About the War. Plain Words to Plain People by a Plain Man* (Philadelphia, 1863), p. 15; *A Democratic Peace Offered for the Acceptance of Pennsylvania Voters* (Philadelphia, 1864), pp. 4–6; *Baltimore American*, April 1, 1864, quoted in Jean Baker, *The Politics of Continuity: Maryland Political Parties from 1858 to 1870* (Baltimore, 1973), p. 129; William D. Jones, *Mirror of Modern Democracy: A History of the Democratic Party from its Organization in 1825 to its Last Great Achievement, the Rebellion of 1861* (New York, 1864), p. 245; *Congressional Globe*, 38 Cong., 1 sess., pp. 1502, 1539, 1546, 1771; ibid., 2 sess., p. 861; New York *Evening Post*, September 2, 1864.

17. *Chicago Times*, November 20, 1863; *Congressional Globe*, 38 Cong., 1 sess., p. 2105; S. S. Cox to Manton Marble, September 24, 1863, Clement L. Vallandigham to Marble, October 4, 1863, Marble Papers; *New York Herald*, September 25, November 5, 1864.

strong. The behavior of former Whigs and conservative Republicans demonstrated that quite clearly. Democrats had made some inroads among many old Whig leaders such as John J. Crittenden, Robert Winthrop, and Washington Hunt, since the beginning of the war. They were reluctant to support the Democracy but many of them did. As one wrote, in 1862, "anything is better than the success of these 'architects of ruin' " (the Republicans). As the war progressed, however, support for Democratic candidates from the alienated conservatives grew increasingly harder to come by. More and more of them, though not all, came to talk about the Democrats in unflattering terms and to shun them at the polls. In particular, the conservative Republicans reacted against them vigorously.[18]

The reasons offered for the disaffection provide an insight into the problem of converting voters in this period, given the intensity of the party conflict and the problems of the Democratic image. Former Whigs and conservative Republicans feared Lincoln's deference to the abolitionists but they found themselves in a "choice of evils" situation in 1864. Many thought McClellan himself was respectable and supportable, but they could not "trust the democracy now." Despite their disgust with Republican policies, they had to "act at the coming election according to this principle, namely—not that they hate Mr. Lincoln less but they hate disunion more." After all, the masses of the Republicans were "praying and God fearing men who look[ed] upon Rebels and Copperheads as agents of the Devil and enemies of human progress." In such a mood, Democratic candidates, even of otherwise impeccable quality, became "semi-secessionist." Therefore, disaffected Republicans would "infinitely rather have Mr. Lincoln, with all his tinkering . . . than any man who is sufficiently doubtful to unite in his support the loyal and disloyal components of the opposition party." As one Democratic leader shrewdly wrote to McClellan in September 1864, "the Chicago plat-

18. Washington Hunt to Samuel Ruggles, October 29, 1862, quoted in Mary Patricia Hodnett, "Civil War Issues in New York State Politics" (Ph.D. diss., St. John's University, 1971), p. 81; George B. McClellan to Robert Winthrop, September 20, 22, November 16, 1864, Robert Winthrop Papers, Massachusetts Historical Society, Boston, Mass., Robert C. Winthrop, Jr., *A Memoir of Robert C. Winthrop* (Boston, 1897), p. 235.

form gave all waverers an excuse'' to pull back in horror from their
traditional political enemies.[19]

"I Cannot Think That the Fragmented Opposition Acts Wisely"

The Democrats had been warned, and had warned themselves,
that they had to offer candidates and policies that, as the editor of the
Chicago Times wrote in 1864, appealed "directly and strongly" to the
"absorbing national feeling" of unionism. "The presentation must be
of a fashion which will operate as an injunction upon all cavil and
misrepresentation other than rude, deliberate falsehood."[20] But the
Democrats, as many of them realized, had not done so, certainly not
clearly or strongly enough. The nomination of Vallandigham in Ohio
in 1863 was a case in point. His campaign was intended to bring the
issue of the denial of civil liberties to the forefront of the voter's mind.
It probably also negated any Legitimist pretensions, however. A year
later the pattern repeated itself. At the time of the Democratic national
convention, a friend warned McClellan not to include in his acceptance letter "any word in regard to peace which c[oul]d be tortured by
any[one] into anything like ignoble compromise."[21] McClellan did
not in his letter but his party had in its platform, and the Republicans
proceeded to the torture. Although the ambiguity in the Democratic
stance was not all that great, the crack it opened was enough for the
Republicans to exploit during their counterattack. A conservative

19. B. A. Hill to Thomas Ewing, Sr., September 29, 1864, Orville Browning to
Ewing, September 5, 19, 1864, Thomas Ewing, Jr., to James Legate, July 19, 1864,
John W. Andrews to Thomas Ewing, Sr., September 27, 1864, Ewing Papers; Allan
Nevins and Milton Halsey Thomas, eds., *The Diary of George Templeton Strong,
1835–1875* (New York, 1952), 3: 480–82, 489; John Rees to Horatio Seymour,
September 10, 1864, Seymour Papers; Joel Parker to George B. McClellan, August 27,
1864, T. Jefferson Coolidge to McClellan, September 19, 1864, McClellan Papers;
George Bancroft to Edward Everett, October 24, 1862, Edward Everett Papers, Massachusetts Historical Society, Boston, Mass., Thurlow Weed to John Bigelow, October
19, 1864, Salmon P. Chase to Bigelow, March 18, 1865, in John Bigelow,
Retrospections of an Active Life (New York, 1909), 2: 222, 425; Ransom Balcom to
William H. Seward, March 2, 1866, William H. Seward Papers, University of Rochester, Rochester, N.Y.
20. *Chicago Times,* April 7, 1864.
21. Quoted in Charles R. Wilson, "McClellan's Changing Views of the Peace
Plank of 1864," *American Historical Review* 38 (April 1933): 504.

critic of the Democrats summed this up well in 1863. "I cannot think," he wrote,

that the fragmented opposition acts wisely, nor, as a whole, patriotically, and certainly with but little skill, if they wish to create a successful conservative party. . . . [The Democracy] is so mixed up, that it, as much as anything else, presents the spectacle of a Peace Party.[22]

Thoughout the war, Democrats charged that Republicans were members of a narrow, sectarian party, incapable of reuniting the Union; while the Democracy was the party of the nation—the only one capable of reuniting all sections on traditional constitutional and racial principles. The war, the campaigns, and the internal imperatives of the Democratic coalition had helped the Republicans to counteract and neutralize that idea and to confuse the sectarian image effectively. Elections were about attitudes and issues. But they were also about a party's capacity to govern effectively in the sense of whether it was both an able and a *legitimate* opposition. Support for the Union was a valence issue since everyone thought it was a good idea and supported it. But one party was perceived more favorably in relation to the valence issue than the other party, and that made a difference. In 1864 the Republicans were seen as more supportive of the Union, the Democrats less so. This backfired against the Democracy. Opposition was all right, but not excess. The Democrats could not escape their reputation.

The Legitimists' perception of the reasons for their losses was astute enough. In the aftermath of each defeat they lamented the way their electoral strategy had played into the hands of the Republicans by "making the issue on the War and not in the War policy and conduct," thanks to their rhetoric, platforms, and candidates.[23] But regardless of their ability to perceive the reasons for their electoral problems, the Democrats could do little about them. The dilemma of the Democracy during the war revolved around the conflict between what it had to do

22. T. J. Barnett to S. L. M. Barlow, May 28, 1863, Barlow Papers.

23. S. S. Cox to Manton Marble, March 11, 1863, Marble Papers; S. L. M. Barlow to William B. Reed, October 13, 1864, Barlow Papers; George L. Miller to J. Sterling Morton, October 30, 1864, W. A. Richardson to Morton, May 17, 1865, J. Sterling Morton Papers, Nebraska Historical Society, Lincoln, Neb. (microfilm copy in Cornell Univeristy Library); *Detroit Free Press*, November 23, 1864; James Stokes to George B. McClellan, November 11, 1864, McClellan Papers.

internally in terms of the party and its principles, and how it needed to act externally in the campaigns it waged. In any election year, each party may have to wage two different campaigns with quite different purposes. The first is the campaign for the nomination. Here the emphasis is on party unity, reassuring the faithful, internal compromise, the welding together of a united coalition representing the party's views. The outcome of this campaign is determined by the relative strength and determination of the different elements within the party. But everyone's concentration is on reforging the party community, preventing a party split, and yoking all of the party members together.

But there is a second campaign, this time for the popular vote. Here the elements of partisan purity and internal partisan compromise may not be useful in winning over uncommitted or hesitant voters. In the first instance a candidate must be a good party member, in the second it may be necessary to play down party positions (especially in the case of the minority party) in order to attract the uncommitted. Sometimes the needs of the two campaigns are congruent. They are not necessarily so. This was the Democrats' problem in 1864, as well as at other times during the war. The Democrats' institutional imperatives got in the way of their electoral needs. In 1864 the party acted rationally in terms of its internal organizational imperatives to keep the party functioning together. The peace-Purists, therefore, had a large share of power. But this hurt the party once the campaign got under way, because then it needed more than Democratic votes.

One can coldly look back and evaluate the balance of forces within the Democratic party and see the reasons party leaders did the things they did. One can also see the advocacy of the peace men for what it was, not a peace-at-any-price stance, but something more than that. But cold evaluations after the event, or making subtle distinctions amid the pressures of wartime, are not as relevant as the particular image projected by the party to a certain kind of voter. It has become a truism that parties seek the center of the political spectrum in order to attract the widest possible range of votes. But this, if true, the Democrats never fully did, nor ever *appeared* to do, during the Civil War. Their own ideology and value structure prevented them from moving too far toward the center. The internal complex of party power likewise limited any centrism. The Republicans' effective counter-campaign completed their downfall. In the middle of a particularly bloody and frustrating civil war, Vallandigham's calls for peace and Union coupled with the more extreme assertions by some of his colleagues left him and his party quite vulnerable when the Republicans reacted to the Democratic challenge. All Democrats became Copperheads—all candidates became Vallandigham. As Frederick Stanton wrote, "loyalty to Republicanism was not only accepted as the best evidence of loyalty to the country but of fitness for civil position." Therefore, as S. S. Cox lamented, "I was grossly beaten by a mob of miscreants, for no reason in the world than that I was a Democrat."[24]

Democratic reaction grew increasingly piteous as party members realized the force of the Republican onslaught. In 1862, Allan Thurman told the Ohio state Democratic convention that "never since God made this world has any party been so infamously treated as has the Democratic party since the war began. Though you give your flesh and blood to put down rebellion, if you do not favor abolition you are denounced as a rebel sympathizer." Why keep on "trying to indoctrinate the people with the Austrian idea that the administration is the government"? We may criticize without being disloyal. "There is room for honest difference of opinion between members of the different political organizations." It is obnoxious "to claim for one the possession of all the spirit of patriotism, all the love of country, and to attribute to members of all other political organizations contrary feelings and motives." Yet, despite such pleas, the Republicans seemed able to get away with their campaign successfully. Cannot we convince people that "no traitor blood lurks in my veins"? was the lament of George Woodward. No, they could not. The Republicans rather, were "able to delude and drive" the people into ferocious anti-Democratic attitudes and actions. In the aftermath of the October elections in 1864, a number of Democrats had put their finger on their own central torment. "We are weak in this state," Barlow wrote,

24. Stanton, *Random Recollections,* p. 244; S. S. Cox to George B. McClellan, October 21, 1864, McClellan Papers.

"with a class of men who will not understand Pendleton's real views."[25]

There is another factor as well. No matter how far the Legitimists moved to placate and attract other conservatives on the issues spawned by the war, they had no intention of abandoning Democratic principles to which they were strongly committed. Their stance on a range of traditional economic and other policies was the old stuff, positions that had divided them from Whigs and Republicans for a generation. The articulation of traditional Democratic orthodoxy made it very easy for the Republicans, in response, to draw the lines between the parties sharply and distinctly. The last thing the Democrats wanted to do by their behavior was to rekindle immanent Republican party loyalties, the slumbering anti-Democratic prejudices of former Constitutional Unionists and Whigs, or the fears of patriotic Northern Democrats. But they had. The Democrats seemed to be offering both a narrowly based partisan government, pushing its own sectarian concerns, as well as one dominated by its extremist wing on the war issue. The Democrats reminded the marginal voters of who they were and also suggested worse to follow. Thus, although the Democrats, conservative Republicans, and independent conservatives might share a common attitude at a moment in time, they could not readily overcome the long history of mutual anger and mistrust.

"A Respectable Minority"

In the aftermath of its unhappy defeat in the presidential election of 1864, the Democratic party continued to search for a national electoral majority. Although newspapers hostile to the party liked to claim that the nation was now in a new political era, the Democrats neither thought nor acted so. Quickly disposing of faint-hearted fears for the party's health, party leaders and spokesmen were soon once more articulating their remedies for the end of Radicalism and revolution.

25. Quoted in William F. Zornow, *Lincoln and the Party Divided* (Norman, Okla., 1954), p. 160; *Detroit Free Press,* January 8, 1864; *Congressional Globe,* 38 Cong., 1 sess., p. 103, 1075; George Woodward to Jeremiah S. Black, September 10, 1863, Black Papers; S. L. M. Barlow to Reverdy Johnson, November 14, 1864, Barlow Papers.

Numbers were "no test of truth." Republican policy was wrong and promised nothing but "a repetition of the catastrophes of the four past years." The Democrats would not let that happen. They intended to maintain their organization and continue to pursue a vigorous opposition. They had to keep fighting, for the future under Lincoln promised nothing but "fruitless war, disgraceful peace, & ruinous bankruptcy."[26]

There is an impression that at the end of the war the Democratic party was particularly weak and ineffective. Eric McKitrick has suggested that by 1865 the Republicans had "accumulated a tremendous fund of moral capital" in their role as defenders of the Union, particularly in contrast to the Democrats' pusillanimous conduct in the face of the crisis of the Union.[27] That certainly was true. But there was more to the story. The Democracy had been successful during the Civil War in recovering its stride as a party after its collapse in 1860. Its efforts and accomplishments had been substantial. Democrats had survived their "debacle in 1860," revived, regrouped, articulated a program, and moved once more to battle as a distinct community against the enemy. They succeeded in reinforcing the internal sense of community that gave the party a sense of mission, a commitment to action, and a program to enact.

In fact, their experience during the war had underscored the important role their party still played in American politics due to traditional partisan attachments as well as continued disagreements over public policies. The American people, accepting political parties as the major agencies for determining voting choice and solving particular policy problems, had maintained their partisan predispositions despite all appeals to larger national interests. "Party and party organization," Gideon Welles complained, "rose above country, or duty [during the war]. In fact, party was a substitute for country." People considered public policies "not in terms of good for the country but in terms of good for the needs of the party."[28] Such

26. *New York Herald,* June 8, 1865; New York *World,* November 10, 19, 1864; *Atlas and Argus,* November 10, 1864; Samuel L. M. Barlow to George B. McClellan, November 9, 1864, McClellan Papers.

27. Eric L. McKitrick, *Andrew Johnson and Reconstruction* (Chicago, 1960), p. 47.

28. Howard K. Beale, ed., *Diary of Gideon Welles* (New York, 1960), 2: 427.

persistent partisanship had, of course, aided the Democrats as, with their substantial popular following, they had been able to challenge the Republicans constantly, pose policy alternatives, successfully appeal for votes, and generally perform the functions of a major competitive party within the two-party political system. They continued to win the support of a substantial portion of the electorate, and their habitual vote had remained firm. Whatever fund of moral capital the Republicans had built up in their favor encompassed the support of only a bit more than half the population of the Northern states.

A number of analysts have pinpointed the wartime experiences of the American people as the key element in finally establishing the dominance of the Republican party and the intensification of loyalty to it by thousands of new voters. William Dunning argued more than sixty years ago that during the war thousands of new voters moved into the Republican coalition on the issues of the war.[29] The evidence for this is fragile, however. Rather, the popular voting situation observable during the war had been established in the 1850s and not much shaken thereafter. The war apparently did not create many new Republican or Democratic voters, or else created them in equal numbers or in numbers proportionate to their already existing percentages within the electorate. But the events of the period probably did something else. The intensity of political confrontation during the war reinforced the commitments made during the fifties or earlier. All of the battles over legitimacy and righteousness only reminded people, in the most intense way possible, of the separation between the parties, their own identification and loyalties, and repeatedly forced upon them the necessity to choose between sharply contrasting ideological perspectives as well as the *image* of sharply contrasting perspectives. Perhaps the way to say this is to suggest that the wartime was a period of reinforcement of party loyalties. The Civil War experience hardened the Democrats' perception of their common community and interest and intensified their devotion and loyalty to their party and its principles. They needed no new issues, such as the question of restoration of the South, to restart their energies. They were already angry, united, and committed, especially since they knew in their

29. William A. Dunning, "The Second Birth of the Republican Party," *American Historical Review* 16 (October 1910): 56–63.

bones that the radical onslaught was not going to stop. In short, there was no political vacuum in 1865. There was a strong, functioning, and united Democratic party which had to be taken seriously in the calculus of national politics. They had survived, and survived in strength. They remained, at war's end, in the words of one of their own members, "a respectable minority." Both parties realized this, the Republicans no less than than the Democrats.[30]

But the Civil War Democracy faced the most difficult job of holding their own support *and* winning to its side people not naturally attracted to the party, people who were, in fact, traditionally suspicious of or hostile to anything Democratic. They did not. Disaffected Republicans were caught in the classic situation of the cross-pressured voter, that is, being pulled in opposing directions as election day approached. Their perceptions of the Democrats were complex and involved: some of them were favorable, some of them were not. They, therefore, did not shift. In this kind of situation, of being pulled in opposite directions, why break the anti-Democratic habits of a lifetime? It was easier to remain where they always had been, opposed to the Democratic party and everything it stood for. The Republican party, their accustomed home, for all of its faults remained better than the Democracy.

Thus, given the basic pattern of electoral behavior after the realignment of the 1850s, the Democratic party was left without any sustained hope of victory. The Republican hold on the electorate may have been a fragile thing in terms of percentages but, despite occasional lapses, it was enough to insure victory most of the time. What the Democrats needed, therefore, was some extra element added to the situation which would allow them to shake off their minority position.

30. Thomas Jefferson Coolidge to George B. McClellan, September 19, 1864, McClellan Papers.

8

"The Party of the Future": 1865–1868

THE WAR YEARS HAD been a time of frustration for Democrats despite their party's potential and their own intense efforts. Their hopes had foundered on the rock of Republican control of the Border States, the absence of Southern Democratic votes, and the refusal of conservatives and some Democrats in the North to give the party full support thanks to the psychological pressures of wartime conditions. But all that was now behind them. In mid-1865 there was reason to think that the United States was in a new political era with improved prospects for the Democracy to reassert authority and regain control of the country. Party leaders expected that hesitant Republicans, former Democrats, returning soldiers, and restored Southerners would all swell the party's ranks, because of a significant shift in the issues facing the nation, a shift favorable to the Democracy. Americans had, as Horatio Seymour told a public meeting in late 1865, "closed our lips upon the questions of the past." We have begun "a new political era." The "war issue is dead; the slavery issue is dead and on all living issues the Democratic party are united . . . [and] confident that their policy commands the approval of a large majority of the people." The heterogeneous elements making up the Republican party "were necessarily kept together by the pressure of a great national trial and emergency during the war, but the war once over, what is still to keep them together?"[1]

1. *New York Herald,* July 29, 31, September 5, 6, 8, 1865; Thomas Cook and Thomas W. Knox, comps. *Public Record of Horatio Seymour* (New York, 1868), p. 286 (hereafter, *Record of Seymour*); New York *World,* July 29, August 18, 1865; *Boston Post,* in Albany (N.Y.) *Argus,* August 26, 1865; *Detroit Daily Free*

The signs that the Republicans intended to continue in their Reconstruction policies what Democrats saw as the destruction of the nation's constitutional heritage only heightened expectations. Republicans approached the remaking of the Union, as one of them recalled thirty years later, "in the hotblood of war and the elation of victory." The Democrats, therefore, would now gain "immense accessions from intelligent conservatives everywhere." They belonged now to "the party of the future." As one of them argued, surveying the scene in 1865, "my hope for the Democratic party, and through it for the country, has been founded upon an anticipated reaction in the public mind—a recoil from the extreme revolutionary tendencies which have controlled public events for the past four years. Every other great revolution of modern times has been followed by such a reaction, but in every case the reactionary party has obtained control of the government."[2]

Of course, the most important new factor in the postwar situation was the accession of Andrew Johnson to the presidency. The presence of a renegade War Democrat with generally conservative Republican and former Democratic advisors in the White House instead of the hated Lincoln provided a unique opportunity for the Democrats.

Press, August 31, 1865. Postwar political conditions in the Border states are discussed in Richard O. Curry, ed., *Radicalism, Racism and Party Realignment* (Baltimore, 1969); in the former Confederate states, in E. Merton Coulter, *The South During Reconstruction, 1865–1877* (Baton Rouge, 1947); and John Hope Franklin, *Reconstruction After the Civil War* (Chicago, 1961); and in a number of Northern states in James C. Mohr, ed., *Radical Republicans in the North: State Politics During Reconstruction* (Baltimore, 1976). In addition, there are individual monographs concerning the politics of each Southern state from 1865 onward. They vary in quality and utility but all contain a great deal of information.

The returning soldiers promised additional help for the Democrats. As the Republican New York *Nation* admitted, "soldiers in the field naturally voted as a class, and yielded to the influences prevailing around them. Their sense of patriotic duty was keenly alive, and their sense of party ties very weak." But now they had returned home where they "naturally" returned "into their old habits" to vote "with their friends and neighbors," as they always had before the war. *Nation,* October 18, 1866, p. 311; *New York Herald,* October 6, 1867.

2. Edmund G. Ross, *History of Impeachment of Andrew Johnson* (Santa Fe, N.M., 1896), p. 19; Springfield *Illinois State Register,* October 28, 1865; William D. Shipman to Samuel L. M. Barlow, October 26, 1865, Samuel L. M. Barlow Papers, Henry E. Huntington Library, San Marino, Ca.; New York *World,* June 26, September 9, 1865, February 12, 1866; Albany (N.Y.) *Argus,* March 1, June 27, August 26, 1865.

Johnson was "the right man in the right place" to lead a conservative resurgence. His policies and demeanor were friendly. Democrats gleefully foresaw an inevitable break between Johnson and his Radical Republican colleagues. No compromise was possible. It would be then but a moment for Johnson to come over to the Democrats, for nothing any longer stood in the way. Since "the slavery question is all over . . . [and] new parties must arise," Congressman James Brooks wrote, "I wish the new President would be the leader in creating one of them."[3]

The Democratic propaganda organs and official institutions moved to push this desired outcome as strongly as possible early in 1865. Democratic newspapers constantly repeated their support for the president. At the Maine state convention, the delegates typically resolved that "banishing all minor party considerations, and acting in the spirit of an enlarged and generous patriotism, we will cordially support President Johnson in the policy which he has avowed." Democratic congressmen glowed at Johnson during debates in the House and Senate. As Richard Vaux summed up to the president late in 1865, the Democratic party "will aid and support you in your present trial, encourage you, defend you, sustain you."[4]

This mood soon turned into something stronger: direct contact and then outright negotiations for a formal alliance. The "benign direction" of Johnson's policies led Democratic leaders to the White House. The president's anteroom was described as looking as it would if the Democrats were in power.[5] The story of the subsequent interac-

3. "Every Democrat who has seen Mr. Johnson expresses satisfaction as to the impression he made by his tone and manner." A. J. Glossbrenner to Jeremiah S. Black, June 23, 1865, Jeremiah S. Black Papers, Library of Congress; *Illinois State Register,* July 28, 1865; *Detroit Free Press,* June 10, December 29, 1865; New York *World,* June 21, December 9, 1865; James Brooks to Montgomery Blair, April 19, 1865, Blair Family Papers, Library of Congress.

4. The Maine platform is in *The American Annual Cyclopaedia and Register of Important Events of the Year 1865* (New York, 1865) (hereafter *Appleton's Cyclopaedia*), p. 523. All but one word is the same in the New York resolutions of September 6 and 7, in ibid, p. 614; William D. Shipman to S. L. M. Barlow, September 9, 1865, Barlow Papers; *Congressional Globe,* 39 Cong., 1 sess., p. 3840; Richard Vaux to Andrew Johnson, December 21, 1865, Andrew Johnson Papers, Library of Congress.

5. Charles O'Conor to Jeremiah S. Black, September 25, 1865, A. J. Glossbrenner to Black, June 23, 1865, Black Papers.

tion and its results is a familiar one, well told previously. But it has rarely been surveyed from the point of view of the Democratic party as a whole (as against the perspective of the men around Johnson or of the most actively involved Democratic coalitionists). Nor has the effect of previous Democratic attitudes and circumstances on their postwar experiences been clearly examined.[6]

It should be noted, first, that in line with their own perceptions of themselves, the Democrats were never passive participants, clay to be molded at the whim of the Johnson men. They had their own perspectives and constraints and these were constantly at work. Nor did they approach the president as piteous supplicants. To the men around Johnson, led by Postmaster General Montgomery Blair, anxious to incorporate the Democrats into their plans, the latter may have occasionally appeared to be a shattered, pleading remnant, easily manipulable into doing what was best for the Johnson group. But the Democrats themselves exhibited very little consciousness of weakness. On the contrary, most of the time they approached their opportunity with a sense of strength and optimism which belies the picture sometimes painted of them. To the Democrats the men around Johnson would have to dance to their tune, not vice versa.[7]

Second, there was always a complexity in the Democrats' response. Events had altered political circumstances in mid-1865 but

6. See Eric McKitrick, *Andrew Johnson and Reconstruction* (Chicago, 1960); LaWanda Cox and John Cox, *Politics, Principle and Prejudice, 1865–1866* (New York, 1963); Martin Mantell, *Johnson, Grant and the Politics of Reconstruction* (New York, 1973). None of these are primarily concerned with the internal dynamics of the Democrats nor do any really put Democratic activities, successes, and failures, into a perspective embracing the whole period since 1860. As I have argued throughout this book, the story of the post–Civil War Democracy cannot be fully understood by focusing attention only on what happened to them after the end of the war.

7. I do not subscribe, obviously, to the idea that the Democrats entered the postwar period in a weak or crippled state. The reality and their perception of that reality were more complex than that. That is not to suggest that from the perspective of their opponents or from that of the men around Andrew Johnson the Democrats may have appeared more crippled than they were.

The weakness of the Democrats in the post–Civil War period is usually a given in books about the era. McKitrick, in *Andrew Johnson and Reconstruction,* pp. 67–75, makes a sophisticated and strong case for it. I think, however, that David Montgomery's brief comments about them in *Beyond Equality: Labor and the Radical Republicans* (New York, 1967), pp. 48–58, puts their strength in better perspective.

not the motivating psychology of the Democrats. That psychology was crucial. The Democrats' behavior and approach to politics in the postwar period was a continuation of their wartime stance, not something new developed after April 1865. Of course, there were differences in the situation in the postwar years as the possibility of an actual coalition with conservatives replaced rather vague generalized appeals to them. Nevertheless, despite much less certainty, particularly in 1865 and 1866, as to where given individuals stood, or whether or not they should quickly shift to take advantage of Johnson's position, the central core of wartime differences about how the party should behave remained clearly discernible and importantly operative. As during the war years, a battle erupted between Purists and Legitimists for the soul of the party.[8]

"Minor Points Should Be Yielded"

The Legitimist vision had not changed. Since the party needed more votes than were available from Democratic stalwarts, it could not be impeccably fastidious. Democrats could win "if even a moderate number of the Republicans should reinforce the Democratic army and sustain the President's policy." Therefore, "all true, loyal and patriotic men, whatever their previous party connections," must be called upon to support a conservative counteroffensive against radicalism, even if that support came from "trimmers, time-servers, place hunters and all sorts of foolish men." This meant that the Democrats still had to reach out and broaden themselves. They could not be too demanding. Democrats should not "look to any narrow party advantage." In their policy pronouncements, "minor points should be yielded for the sake of saving the main one." They had to

8. Here, once again, I have made no effort to delineate precisely the numbers in each group or the nature of the socioeconomic and/or psychological elements shaping individual commitment to one group or another. This needs to be done and should be, building through state-level studies toward a national synthesis. Again, however, what is critical for my purposes is that such divisions existed and helped shape the behavior of a minority party seeking to recover control of the political process. Therefore, though the precise components of the various internal groups which were the sources of the shaping is an important matter, in sketching in a general strategic and tactical picture such description becomes somewhat less relevant I believe.

select candidates "who will concentrate all the anti-Radical elements."[9]

But despite the war's end and their hopes for a new political agenda, the Legitimists argued that memories of the war continued to affect their situation and their prospects. The Democracy still had to legitimize itself to win additional support. "The odor of rebellion" would be fatal to their hopes. The obvious way to overcome this, a number of influential Legitimists argued, was in forthright support of the president and a general conservative coalition.[10] They moved vigorously in 1865 to accomplish that. Their position was clearly articulated in a number of state platforms, New York's going the farthest. Democrats there denounced secession and admitted that slavery was dead; thanked the soldiers for restoring the Union; commended Johnson for his correct and constitutional course and ignored all "minor party considersations" in order to support him; and called on all conservatives to join them to defend the Union. That was the basic stance of the Legitimists in New York and elsewhere, and they added little to it in subsequent years. They were also always careful to suggest that the Southern whites who should be restored to power in the South had to be men "who bear true faith to the Constitution and laws."[11]

In addition to platform avowals, they also acted when opportunities presented themselves. Early in 1865, a number of Democratic congressmen voted for the thirteenth amendment to the Constitution, abolishing slavery, despite the bitter opposition of most of the party. The votes in favor apparently were, to a great extent, the product of a

9. C. R. Buckalew to Victor Piolett, April 22, 1866, Victor Piolett Papers, Wyoming Historical and Geological Society, Wilkes Barre, Pa.; James Buchanan to Horatio King, August 29, 1866, in *The Works of James Buchanan*, ed. John Bassett Moore (Philadelphia, 1910), 11: 426; Resolutions, Michigan State Democratic Convention, in *Appleton's Cyclopaedia, 1866*, p. 508; *Detroit Free Press*, June 4, 1866; New York *World*, August 7, September 21, November 14, 1865, October 17, 1866; *Boston Post*, February 21, 1866; James Wall to Andrew Johnson, February 20, 1866, Johnson Papers.

10. William Bogart to Manton Marble, May 16, 1867, Manton Marble Papers, Library of Congress; *Louisville Democrat*, January 25, September 4, 1867. These arguments are effectively detailed in Cox and Cox, *Politics, Principle and Prejudice*.

11. See *Appleton's Cyclopaedia, 1865*, pp. 613–14 for the New York resolutions. The last quote is from the Pennsylvania Democratic platform, ibid., 1866, p. 613.

long series of negotiations and much lobbying by conservative Republicans. The fulcrum of whatever Democratic support there was for the amendment (and it should be noted that only seventeen of seventy-six Democrats voted for it on passage in the House, although eight others abstained) apparently rested on a familiar Legitimist position. "There are powerful reasons of party strategy," Congressman Cox wrote during the debate, for voting for the amendment. He was anxious, he later recalled, "with a view to the upbuilding of the party he cherished, to drive this question, which had become abstract by the death of slavery through powder and ball, from the political arena." Why not, therefore, "strengthen ourselves . . . by throwing off the *proslavery* odium?" Once that had happened and the thirteenth amendment had passed with Democratic support, "then & then only can we hope for Democratic ascendency." The war, after all, had killed slavery and "we must accept the situation. . . . To ask a reconsideration . . . will be to simply announce ourselves a set of impracticables no more fit to deal with practical affairs than the old gentleman in Copperfield. . . . The sooner we realize this the better."[12]

Nor was this the limit of their efforts. In several states in 1865, in what Gideon Welles described as "a coup d'état," they nominated a number of Republican generals as their candidates for various minor state offices. And they actively promoted throughout 1866 a grand union of Democrats, Johnson men, and other conservatives in a National Union party. The party was actually formed at Philadelphia in June 1866. When these tactics proved ineffective, some of the Legitimists went a step farther and argued that the Democrats had to accept black suffrage, and the various acts to reconstruct the Union promulgated by the Republicans in Congress. They pled with their Southern brethren to do so as well, all in order to sweep the slate clean and prepare for future elections. In other words, they argued against narrowness and bitter partisanship and in favor of a general acceptance

12. S. S. Cox to Manton Marble, January 13, 26, February 13, 1865, Marble Papers; Samuel S. Cox, *Three Decades of Federal Legislation* (Providence, 1885), p. 327. The best description of this episode is in Cox and Cox, *Politics, Principle and Prejudice*, pp. 1–30. See also Dean Richmond to Manton Marble, January 23, 1865, Marble Papers.

of what seemed to be the minimal demands of the South by the Northern people.[13]

The Legitimists certainly held the initiative in the party immediately after the war. Even the most extreme of the wartime Purists showed a different face in the first flush of Johnson's accession. "The time has come," Clement Vallandigham wrote to Horace Greeley, of all people, shortly after Johnson's assumption of office in April 1865, "not for giving up party, but for new associations of men upon the new questions just arising. . . . We *must* lay aside, for a time, both past and future differences, and associate upon the pressing questions of the moment. . . . The man who cannot get out of old ruts now, had better not attempt to travel." A year later he continued in a similar vein: *"The past must be forgotten, antecedents ignored, and the great issues of the hour be made the sole test of present fellowship and cooperation."*[14]

"It Is Not True That 'Old Political Issues . . . Are Dead' "

Even so, at every step of the way the Legitimists had to look back over their shoulders. As during the war, they spoke for only one thread

13. Howard K. Beale, ed., *Diary of Gideon Welles* (New York, 1960), 2: 372–73; Samuel L. M. Barlow to George B. McClellan, February 26, 1867, George B. McClellan Papers, Library of Congress; J. Glancy Jones to Alexander H. Stephens, April 2, 1867, Alexander H. Stephens Papers, Library of Congress; Allen Pierce to Andrew Johnson, November 21, 1866, J. W. Taylor to James L. Orr, January 26, 1867, Johnson Papers; B. S. Hedrick to Jonathan Worth, February 28, 1867, in *The Correspondence of Jonathan Worth*, ed. J. G. de Roulhac Hamilton (Raleigh, 1909), 2: 903; William Jordan to A. H. Stephens, March 20, 1867, Herschel V. Johnson to Stephens, March 29, 1867, Stephens Papers; *Louisville Democrat*, January 23, May 16, 1867. The story of the Philadelphia convention is well told in Thomas Wagstaff, "The Arm-In-Arm Convention," *Civil War History* 14 (June 1968): 101–19; and in his dissertation, "Andrew Johnson and the National Union Movement, 1865–1866" (Ph.D. diss., University of Wisconsin, 1967).

The Democrats also worked hard to influence returning soldiers. They dominated, if not organized, a number of "conservative soldiers' and sailors' conventions" in the early postwar period, which were intended to demonstrate the widespread Legitimist support they received.

14. Clement L. Vallandigham to Horace Greeley, April 20, 1865, in Charles H. Coleman, "Three Vallandigham Letters," *Ohio Archaeological and Historical Society Quarterly* 43 (October 1934): 464; Vallandigham to George W. Morgan, December 11, 1866, in Frank L. Klement, *The Limits of Dissent: Clement L. Vallandigham and the Civil War* (Lexington, Ky., 1970), p. 304. See also Fernando Wood to Andrew Johnson, February 24, 1866, George Pendleton to Johnson, January 28, 1866, Johnson Papers.

in the web that was the Democratic party. Any hint of a coalitionist policy infuriated those Democrats who preferred to maintain party doctrines in their purest form, without change or apology. "It is not true," the *Detroit Free Press* argued, "that 'old political issues and dogmas are dead.' They survive in even greater force than ever before on all subjects." So what then should be the policy of the Democratic party? James Buchanan had a familiar answer to that: "I have never known any good coming to the Democratic party from hiding or suppressing their principles for the sake of expediency. A bold avowal & maintenance of them can alone ensure its triumph." Therefore, he continued, the submergence of Democratic identity in some grand conservative coalition was wrong. "Drop the principles and the name of Democracy and our cause would be hopeless." It was far better to be "an honest minority than a dishonest majority," it was far better to be "a small party of convictions than a large party of accidents." If the conservative men of the country wished to rally together, Democrats should insist it be done under the leadership of their own organization. Any other course would be "treason to the party."[15]

Hostility toward the Republicans and the War Democrats only intensified the Purist vision. Johnson and his fellow War Democrats had spent the past few years assailing those who, while adhering to the Union, had chosen to maintain their party organization and to oppose what they saw as the outrageous policies of the Lincoln administration. The War Democrat's treachery to the party was not forgotten. As Horatio Seymour said in 1867, "We who have held to the cause of constitutional liberty have not always agreed in our views. At times there may have been irritation. But surely past trials have made a ground work of an attachment and confidence which cannot be felt towards those who turned against us or who shrank away in our times of trouble." Furthermore, for thirty years Republicans such as William Seward had used all of their considerable skills to defeat the Democratic party. To work with them now, despite their anti-Radicalism, was too much for many Democrats. Johnson's loyalty to Seward and other conservative Republicans fouled the relationship

15. *Detroit Free Press,* February 20, 1865, July 24, 1866; James Buchanan to George Lieper, November 30, 1866, in *Works of Buchanan,* ed. Moore, 11: 429; New York *World,* April 10, 1866; William Cassidy to Horatio Seymour, October 27, 1866, Horatio Seymour Papers, New York State Library, Albany, N.Y.

constantly. "Seward and Stanton, Weed and Raymond," the president's advisor, Francis P. Blair, admitted in mid-1866, "are extremely ticklish support to lead over the chasm that must be passed by conservatives of either side to unite all those who must come together to crush the Radicals."[16]

Bitterness between the different groups in the party also continued to show up throughout the period as it had earlier. One Connecticut Purist set the tone for his group when he celebrated the electoral defeat of a Legitimist candidate in his state. "As between a *negro* and a *mulatto* I have no choice. . . . I fairly blushed . . . to witness the eagerness to win back a few renegades, and to get a few republicans of supposed easy political virtue without thought of the true and honest democrats they might be driving from the polls." The editor of the *Dayton Ledger* attacked those "who counsel with pale lips how we may give least offense to our adversaries, instead of boldly advancing to right the wrongs we have suffered. . . . No success is worth the effort unless it secures the ascendancy of Democratic principles. Better a thousand times, defeat in an open, honest struggle for principle, than success, if it brings only mere personal triumphs, the demoralizing spoils of office and the gains of legislative blunderings."[17] Legitimist behavior since 1864 only confirmed the charges of the Purists that the line could not be held once party principles were compromised. In order to legitimate themselves the former had had to continue to move further and further toward the Republicans. They had lost too much as a result. The party might, one wrote, "have saved the country had it been true to principle." Instead, the "contrivers and tricksters who make politics a trade" had destroyed whatever chances

16. Horatio Seymour to Samuel J. Tilden, December 13, 1867, in *Letters and Literary Memorial of Samuel Jones Tilden*, ed. John Bigelow (New York, 1908), 1: 214–15; Francis P. Blair, Sr., to Francis P. Blair, Jr., June 25, 1866, Blair Family Papers. See also William Reed to Manton Marble, May 27, 1866, Marble Papers; George W. Morgan to Andrew Johnson, July 7, 1866, Johnson Papers; S. L. M. Barlow to Richard Taylor, December 9, 1865, Barlow Papers.

17. C. C. Burr to Thomas H. Seymour, April 3, 1866, C. M. Ingersoll to Seymour, n.d., 1867, Thomas H. Seymour Papers, Connecticut Historical Society, Hartford, Conn.; *Dayton Ledger*, February 15, 1868, clipping in Manton Marble papers, University of London Library.

the party had through their manipulations.[18] The anger of the Legitimists toward the Purists was equally savage and equally repetitive of past themes. "God knows I hate Vallandigham & those fellows as cordially as I do Greeley & that is saying a good deal," was the summarizing comment of the chairman of the Democratic National Committee.[19]

As a result of these internal conflicts, the Democratic reaction to their conservative opportunity was always mixed. While most of the party during the last part of 1865 and in the spring and summer of 1866 moved toward coalition with Johnson and other conservatives, the tugs from the others prevented this from being a clear-cut, or ultimately acceptable, policy engaged in by the party as a whole. As early as 1865, Democratic platforms articulated a number of policy positions which could be considered either neutral or anti-Legitimist in their tone and direction. Among the neutral-sounding declarations were calls that there only be rigorous adherence to the Constitution; that loyal white men should run the South; that there should not be Negro suffrage; and that there should be the subordination of military to civilian rule. At the same time a number of Purist positions were also expressed: that the war was caused when the principles advocated by the Democratic party were ignored, and that, with the war over, the South and Southerners were entitled to full representation in Congress and the right to vote.[20]

But neither faction entirely dominated the situation. Each was aware of the other's strength; each had to be taken seriously and deferred to by the other. Even the Legistimists felt that they could not

18. Columbus (Ohio) *Crisis,* January 25, 1865; James A. Bayard to Thomas F. Bayard, February 7, 1865, Thomas F. Bayard Papers, Library of Congress; Clement L. Vallandigham to James Wall, November 26, 1865, in Coleman, "Three Vallandigham Letters, pp. 462–63.

19. August Belmont to Manton Marble, July 17, 1866, Marble Papers. See also S. L. M. Barlow to G. B. McClellan, August 14, 1866, McClellan Papers; *Boston Post,* August 15, 1866.

20. These state resolutions are reprinted or reported in various editions of *Appleton's Cyclopaedia,* under each state's entry. Samuel L. M. Barlow to Samuel J. Tilden, August 31, 1865, in *Letters and Literary Memorial,* ed. Bigelow, p. 197; Barlow to Richard Taylor, December 9, 1865, Barlow papers. See also Montgomery Blair to Jeremiah S. Black, August 31, 1865, Black Papers.

sacrifice too much for an alliance with Johnson. The Democrats' position became that they would work with Johnson when appropriate, but without either giving up their party organization or soliciting non-Democratic or former Democratic elements too warmly. They never moved toward Johnson as much as the president or his advisors desired. The party kept "aloof from all entangling alliances." It supported Johnson when he was "right, freely and generously." But it had "no responsibility," and would "take none," for his administration. In 1866 and 1867, therefore, Democrats and Union party people continued to work together in many places, but out of a community of shared ideas rather than through formal institutional arrangements, as Johnson and his friends had wished. Nor was it an easy relationship. It could not be, given the different perspectives about how the conservative alliance was to work. Tension increased between the Democrats and non-Democrats. By 1867, parts of the Democratic press were referring to Johnson's "maladroit, unstatesmanlike, unpopular administration."[21]

There was, to repeat, little new in all of this. The Democrats' postures and attitudes in the postwar years differed little from those developed during the war. There was more flexibility in their response, to be sure, and more confusion. Occasionally Purists seemed to agree to some form of coalition, and often Legitimists drew back from Johnson in disgust. The diffusion of Democratic attitudes and uncertainties as to the correct course to follow sometimes echoed the 1861–1862 period. But opportunities were present that had not been before. There was good and sufficient evidence that the Republican hegemony was crumbling, that Johnson was open to Democratic influence, that they had a chance of a major breakthrough, all things that were not present in the past. Given that, even the most extreme Purist might be induced to think why not explore contacts with the non-Democrats. After all, the game to be won was the very biggest. It was this increased opportunity that occasionally fuzzes the line between Purist and Legitimists, especially in 1865 and 1866.

Nevertheless, the two traditional strands were still present. And,

21. *Detroit Free Press,* September 15, 1865, April 18, 1866; New York *World* February 28, April 10, 1866, September 12, 1867.

in the last analysis, the crucial partisan imperative also remained present and operative. The line drawn by adherence to that imperative could not be readily or permanently crossed. "The courageous tenacity of the Democratic party" remained both a strength and a limitation. It prevented an alliance with Johnson on Johnson's terms or under his lead. Despite the opportunities presented by the presence of a large number of conservative Republicans, ex-Democrats, and former Whigs in the postwar political situation, cooperation between Democrats and other groups could never be easily accomplished. The Democrats had their own perspectives and influences affecting their behavior. The imperatives of continuity and of a traditional political structure continued to limit the maneuverability of Democrats searching for an electoral majority.[22]

"The Innovative Spirit Has Broken Loose and Runs Wild"

While party councils resounded to arguments over how best to take advantage of changed political circumstances, Democrats were never unsure or ambivalent about the basic core of principles on which they stood, or what their policy goals were in seeking to regain power. The Democratic critique of Republican policies reaffirmed the same conservative stance that the party had set forth so extensively during the war. As before, the Democracy's twin themes were opposition to reckless radical destructiveness, as embodied in Republican principles, and a commitment to the static constitutionalism of a white-man's nation. Democrats believed that the Republicans learned nothing and forgot nothing. They were intent on continuing their rampaging, revolutionary radicalism. Only a political overturn could forestall this.

The battleground had moved from the Northern states alone to the defeated South as well. But to the Democrats, the fact of Republican madness, constitutional perversion, and individual repression remained a constant. The Republican party continued "in revolution against the Constitution," determined to "cut loose from all Constitutional restraints." They "hate" the Constitution and as a result were

22. New York *World*, May 6, 1867.

"revolutionizing our government." Their Southern policy "outstrips in wicked despotism the worst Parliaments of England." They continued to be ruled by "pernicious passion" and "vengeful hate." As a result, the country was forced to live in "a period in which the innovating spirit has broken loose and runs wild."[23]

The Democrats bitterly opposed the specific plans of the Republicans to reconstruct the South, as divisive, unconstitutional, and destructive of the peace of the Union. The South had given up the fight. All opposition had ended. Restoration was the only proper policy now. Democrats, therefore, avowed their continued support for mild reconstruction policies, for speedy restoration of the Southern states, amnesty for most Confederate officials, and the full return of civil rights to the white men in the conquered ex-slave states. The time had come for the North to spread over the South "a Broad mantle of mercy." But the Republicans refused to accept this. In the South, "radicalism now holds high carnival among the rights of men." Their "absolute despotism" over the South relies, "like an eastern prince" upon "the power of armed janizaries" to maintain their control.[24]

The most unacceptable face of Republicanism was revealed, as before, in its policy concerning blacks. The Democrats expended more energy on condemning in the fiercest terms the "malignant efforts to degrade the white inhabitants of the Southern states and place them at the mercy of an inferior race" than on anything else. The whole gamut of Republican policies, from granting civil rights to blacks to extending the suffrage to them, was an "effort to place the African on a level with the Caucasian" by first corrupting and degrading elections, then granting special legislative favors, then allowing them to dominate and control the electoral process. None of this Africanization policy could be tolerated. As one Democrat told An-

23. A Democratic congressman asserted that he thought, as he watched the Republicans at work, that he was "in the midst of a revolutionary tribunal." *Congressional Globe,* 39 Cong., 1 sess., p. 388; James A. Bayard to Thomas F. Bayard, November 25, 1866, Bayard Papers; "Speech of George Pendleton, Milwaukee Wisconsin, November 2, 1867," printed pamphlet in Marble Papers, London; *Argus,* February 22, 1868; *Congressional Globe,* 39 Cong., 1 sess., p. 87; ibid., 40 Cong., 2 sess., pp. 479, 112; New York *World,* April 18, 1868.

24. New York *World,* May 11, 1865; *Congressional Globe,* 40 Cong., 2 sess., p. 580; ibid., 39 Cong., 1 sess., p. 152; ibid., 2 sess., p. 1171.

drew Johnson, "I did not seek to uphold the American flag that ignorant Negroes may rule over white men." The crucial point was that this was "the country of the white race, given by the Almighty on which to build a great white nation. There is not and must not be any Negro, Indian, Mongolian mixtures in it." In short, "no more nigger!"[25]

Other familiar issues were debated in the postwar period as well. Once more the tariff, finance, and social policy attracted attention and much rhetoric. Republicans were raising the tariff, meddling in financial matters, imposing their values on other people, and expanding the power of the federal government to accomplish these things. They were once again reviving restrictive legislation against immigrants. The Democrats reacted to all of this as before, seeing each element as part of a puritan-Republican drive to control and determine individual behavior through the power of government. "Talk as we may," Horatio Seymour said in 1867, "about the rise and fall of parties, there are sentiments in the minds of our people, which will always make one party favor centralization and meddling. It may in the future, as in the past, change its name and pretext, as the result of its policy makes it odious. It has filled our land with bloodshed and strife. It has loaded us down with debt and taxation. It has put back religion, temperence, and virtue by dragging them into political strife, and by the passage of laws which tend to make them odious in the minds of the people. It is ever on the lookout for some pretext to meddle with the rights of the people."[26]

As before, also, the Democrats' description of the intent of Republican policy was presented in the most lurid and extravagant terms possible. Negroes, for example, were barbarians. They were "not naturally bloodthirsty. Rape was their peculiar crime." But the war had "transformed their natures and many of them would do an

25. R. Baber to Andrew Johnson, June 28, 1866, Johnson Papers; Charles Mason to Jeremiah S. Black, June 14, 1865, Black Papers; *Congressional Globe,* 39 Cong., 1 sess., p. 83; Moses Bates to Andrew Johnson, December 14, 1867, Johnson Papers; *Louisville Democrat,* November 20, 1867; *Illinois State Register,* April 4, 1866; Forrest Wood, *Black Scare, The Racist Response to Emancipation and Reconstruction* (Berkeley and Los Angeles, 1968).

26. *Record of Seymour,* p. 309.

assassin's work.'' Democrats therefore had to ''oppose the commingling of what God and nature have so unmistakable intended to preserve separate and distinct.'' Otherwise, attempts to impose ''Negro domination'' on the South ''votes for the inauguration of the most cruel, merciless and devastating of all wars,'' one between the races.[27]

Beneath their extravagance, however, was the same commitment to fundamental limited constitutionalism the Democrats had always articulated. There was, they believed, a reasoned, peaceful, and constitutional alternative to Radical extremism. ''The Democratic party springs naturally out of the very essence of the Federal Constitution.'' No ''modern rush-lights'' attracted them. Democrats were ''a staid people . . . a conservative people . . . [who] wish to preserve the Constitution of our country as it was handed down . . . by our fathers.'' They did not want ''the old house torn down and a new house built up by modern architects.'' Against the specific policies of ''centralization and meddling'' Democrats ''oppose the doctrine'' that government be ''made strong by leaving states and individuals as much as we can to their own action; that minding your own business and letting your neighbor's business alone, is good statesmanship in public and good morals in private life.'' Democrats, therefore, would ''have no Negro suffrage''; they would ''oppose protective tariffs''; they would ''permit no infringement of state rights''; they would ''oppose the dangerous concentration in the hands of the federal legislature''; they would, in sum, ''make war against all centralization of power.''[28]

The Democrats still believed these were winning issues and the means to overturn the Radical domination. When they argued in favor of ''the old Democratic doctrine . . . to permit the town to do nothing

27. *Detroit Free Press,* July 3, 1865, November 15, 1867; L. G. Dupre to William Seward, July 15, 1867, Johnson Papers; *Louisville Democrat,* June 9, 1865; speech of George W. Morgan, Democratic gubernatorial candidate in Ohio, 1865, quoted in Edgar A. Topping, ''Negro Emancipation in Historic Retrospect: Ohio,'' *Journal of Human Relations* 11 (Winter 1963): 238.

28. James Bush to Asa Packer et al., March 23, 1867, in *Works of Buchanan,* ed. Moore, 11: 441; *Congressional Globe,* 39 Cong., 1 sess., p. 114; ibid., 40 Cong., 2 sess., pp. 597, 598; *Illinois State Register,* November 22, 1866; *Record of Seymour,* p. 309.

which the school district could do as well, the state nothing which the county or city could do, and the federal government nothing the state could as completely and safely accomplish,'' they thought they were striking a most potent chord among millions of Americans. They firmly believed electoral victory would follow the perception by the electorate of the reality of the threat facing them unbefogged by false scents, distorted claims, and outrageous deceptions. Their leaders urged each other to play on these matters; their newspapers never stopped drumming the threats and dangers the country faced from blacks, a repressed South, and a rampaging, imperialistic New England. They knew that the Republicans were divided, particularly on the black issue, and showed signs of retreating in the face of the political disasters looming in front of them. As one conservative Republican, Edgar Cowan, said, expressing a feeling more and more were coming to have, ''any party with an abolition head and a nigger tail will soon find itself with nothing left but the head and the tail.''[29]

Through all of the debates and rhetoric, the Democrats demonstrated, despite their tactical differences, both a unity and a inflexibility of commitment typical of the ideologically engaged. In the mountains of Democratic rhetoric after 1865, despite an occasional change in emphasis, there really was remarkably little deviation from a core of basic values. The language of their platforms and addresses, drafted at each annual or biennial state party convention and intended as guides for the campaign and as exhortations to the voters, not unexpectedly, was very similar. Often the same words were used from state to state. As Democratic spokesmen expressed similar beliefs concerning the crisis facing the country, Democrats throughout the Union knew

29. New York *World,* March 7, 1865; William Brock, ''The United States,'' in *New Cambridge Modern History* (Cambridge, 1962), 11: 488ff; Ira Brown, ''Pennsylvania and the Rights of the Negro, 1865–1887,'' *Pennsylvania History* 28 (January 1961): 51; Thomas Hendricks to Franklin Pierce, January 27, 1866, Franklin Pierce Papers, Library of Congress; George Ticknor Curtis to Manton Marble, November 7, 1867, Marble Papers; Thomas F. Bayard to James A. Bayard, February 23, 1868, Bayard Papers.

It was a conservative Republican who commented privately that Radical attempts in favor of black suffrage were ''a species of fanaticism, zeal without discretion.'' *Diary of Welles,* ed. Beale, 2: 374. The issue gave ''the reactionary elements every possible advantage.'' Aaron Perry to J. D. Cox, July 28, 1865, quoted in Felice Bonadio, *North of Reconstruction: Ohio Politics, 1865–1870* (New York, 1970), p. 48.

exactly where they stood in terms of their principles and hawked them vigorously, regardless of any tactical disagreements. The Democrats continued to be ideologically one on the danger facing the Union and the only way the country could be saved.

In their public behavior they repeatedly demonstrated their community of interest. In Congress in the years after Appomattox, the Democrats displayed a consistently high degree of unity in opposition to the Republicans. They did this both in speech and, more tellingly, in their voting behavior over the whole range of legislation dealing with reconstruction. Their unity was clear-cut and persistent in both Houses, except for a brief separation into two blocs in 1865–1866 in the House of Representatives. Often they were joined by Johnsonian Unionists and Border state conservatives. More often, particularly in the early years, they separated from the conservatives in their own isolated party positions. In all of these years they clearly voted differently even from those whom Michael Benedict has labelled "extreme Conservative Republican."[30] Because of this, neither party faction would, in the last analysis, give up its Democratic loyalties, the party itself, or its principles. Most people in both factions wanted "to prevent the disintegration or demoralization of the Democratic organization." For the sake of the country, Barlow said, he was willing to forgo all questions "which concern the party only." Nevertheless, the country's future depended upon its affairs being run "by the democratic party proper."[31]

There were occasional specific areas of disagreement despite this essential unity. A critical one stemmed from differences over an ancient Democratic belief, favoring hard money. Some Democrats in the postwar period, beset as they were by economic hard times, favored an inflationary monetary policy, particularly the continued

30. On Democratic behavior in Congress, see Michael Les Benedict, *A Compromise of Principle: Congressional Republicans and Reconstruction, 1863–1869* (New York, 1974), particularly the appendices.

31. John Lynch to Israel Washburn, February 21, 1866, in Gaillard Hunt, *Israel Elihu and Cadwallader Washburn* (New York, 1925), p. 119; Manton Marble to Joseph Warren, August, n.d., 1866, Marble Papers; S. L. M. Barlow to George B. McClellan, October 12, 1865, Barlow Papers. See also Samuel S. Cox to S. L. M. Barlow, August 13, 1865, Barlow Papers; Washington Hunt to Manton Marble, March 13, 1866, Marble Papers.

use of greenback currency. They condemned any return to prewar hard-moneyism as inappropriate in current conditions. There was much disagreement and anger among Democrats about this, and some crippling confrontations within the party. The bitterness was exacerbated because the main center of inflationary sentiment was among Western Purists such as George Pendleton and his Ohio cronies.[32] Without denigrating its importance, however, even this disagreement has to be placed alongside the basic core of agreement among party members. Democratic communalism still held as something distinct from other groups in the political arena. They were different, they said so, and they acted so. This underlying commitment to keeping the party together against Republican policies was seen vividly in the campaigns and election activity the Democrats engaged in each year after the war.

To *"Break Radicalism All to Pieces"*

At first, the Democrats did poorly, losing in both 1865 and 1866. But the results of state and local elections in 1867 were better than anything that had happened to them since the heady days of 1862. They not only increased their proportion of the vote sizably, cutting Republican majorities down almost to the vanishing point in some places, but they also took a number of critical and indicative major statewide races in New York, Pennsylvania, California, and Connecticut. "We are getting used to chronicling radical losses," was the *New York Herald*'s sardonic comment.[33]

Democrats were jubilant. The Republicans had clearly suffered a major setback and were in great disarray as a result. "We have

32. There was, however, pro-greenback sentiment expressed by Eastern state conventions as well. As with Purism, it was not exclusively a sectional phenomenon. Irwin Unger, *The Greenback Era, A Social and Political History of American Finance, 1865–1879* (Princeton, 1964), and Robert Sharkey, *Money, Class and Party, An Economic Study of Civil War and Reconstruction* (Baltimore, 1959), are excellent introductions to the politics of currency expansion. On Democratic differences over the issue, see Mantell, *Johnson, Grant and Politics of Reconstruction*, pp. 104–12.

33. *New York Herald*, October 9, 1867. In some of these states they received their greatest share of the vote since before 1860. See below, chapter nine. On these elections, generally, see Michael Les Benedict, "The Rout of Radicalism: Republicans and The Elections of 1867," *Civil War History* 18 (November 1972): 334–44.

scotched the radical hydra." The "reaction which we have been waiting for for so long seems to have commenced at last." The future seemed bright indeed. For one thing, conservatives and marginal Republicans were proving friendlier than they had in some time. "We do not claim these as Democratic victories," Congressman Ross of Illinois said. "By no means. It is the Union loving Republicans coming to the rescue and standing side by side and shoulder to shoulder with the patriotic Democracy that have assisted in gaining these great victories." Republicans "of *strong party* ties cast their ballots for our candidates for Congress openly avowing that Congress was going too far." Many of these men remained quite reluctant and hesitant about what they were doing, but reconciled themselves to the necessity of it. "I would be unwilling to see the . . . unmitigated Democracy restored to power," the elder Ewing wrote, "and nothing but the utter abandonment of principles by the Republican Congress and their contempt of constitution and law could have induced [me] to aid the Democracy. . . ." But "against this revolting programme of negro rule and white enslavement in the South," his son continued, "I would even stand on George Francis Train's platform—'women suffrage, repudiation, and hellfire.' "[34]

The aftermath of the elections of 1867 saw another reason for Democratic optimism. Since the war the role of the south in contributing to Democratic strength had been all but nil. Not only did the political conditions imposed on the South by Congress limit any anti-Republican political life, but many Southerners were themselves lying low. Some had been barred from political life. Others refused to get involved. Others proved hesitant about supporting the Democracy. This latter situation was partly because of persistent partisan

34. *Congressional Globe,* 40 Cong., 2 sess., p. 72; A. E. Burn to Gideon Welles, April 5, 1867, Gideon Welles Papers, Library of Congress; Thomas Ewing, Sr., to Ellen Sherman, January 27, 1868, Ewing Papers.

Writing to his father from New Hampshire just before the election, Thomas Ewing, Jr., reported that "there are a great many non-committed men—but among them none who went with the Democracy a year ago. The undercurrent, whatever there is of it, is with the Democracy." Thomas Ewing, Jr., to Thomas Ewing, Sr., March 5, 1868, Ewing Family Papers, Library of Congress. The best the Republican New York *Nation* could say was that "the Democratic party is evidently going to be strong enough next year to make it worthwhile beating them." New York *Nation,* November 7, 1867.

tensions and divisions in the South. In the antebellum South, there had been a sustained two-party tradition with a strong anti-Democratic group which had never been completely reconciled to pressures promoting Southern unity against the Northern threat. These political divisions, rooted in prewar conditions, continued to be a factor in Southern political life both during the war and afterward. As the *Hinds County* (Mississippi) *Gazette* said in mid-1866, "It would be quite as hard for the old Democrats to become latter day Whigs as it would for us old Whigs to become Democrats."[35]

At the same time, Northern Democrats looking South in the postwar period found much anger against themselves due to their pro-war stance after 1861. The Democratic party, one Southerner wrote, "for present profit, sacrificed the South and the fundamental principles which we thought controled [*sic!*] Democrats." Therefore, "all parties" in the North "are unsound as far as we are concerned." One result of all of this was that, as Southern politics revived in 1865 and 1866, hostile Southerners preferred to work through non-Democratic organizations. They called themselves conservatives locally, and seemed bent on erecting a new system of politics in the South free from all old associations. There was much Southern support for the Philadelphia convention and National Union movement of 1866 and "Conservative" parties appeared in many Southern states to contest the Republicans. Therefore, although the Democrats never really stopped trying to rebuild their old contacts in the South, exhorting and

35. Although party organizations and institutions had disappeared during the war, partisan tensions with traditional roots in old conflicts between Whigs and Democrats had remained. There had been a persistent "party idiom" in Confederate political debates. Thomas B. Alexander and Richard Beringer, *The Anatomy of the Confederate Congress* (Nashville, 1972). See also Richard Beringer, "The Unconscious 'Spirit of Party' in the Confederate Congress," *Civil War History* 18 (December 1972): 312–13.

In 1866, a visitor to North Carolina commented that "I discover with proper amazement, that the old parties are both alive and neither of them a whit older or less pugilistic than it was twenty years ago. . . . In private conversation half the delegates had no measuring rule for a man but the fact that he is either a Whig or a Democrat, and no judgment for a measure but that it originate with one of these parties." Sidney Andrews, *The South Since the War* (Boston, 1866), pp. 135–36. In 1868, the New York *Nation* noted that much of the South's white Republicanism was "due to the hearty hatred which the old Whigs still bear to the old Democrats." New York *Nation,* October 1, 1868. See also B. S. Hedrick to Jonathan Worth, September 16, 1866, in *Correspondence of Worth,* ed. Hamilton, 2: 784.

encouraging political rebirth, they were never really sure how much there was to be gained in electoral terms from the Southern states torn both by radical control and internal political complexity.[36]

In the aftermath of the elections of 1867, however, there was clearly a different tempo in the South. The Democrats' great success against the Radicals seemed to reinvigorate Southern Democrats and to attract many Southern Whigs. Suddenly there were moves toward Democratic organization, the shucking of hesitancies, and a turning away from apathy and from acquiescence in non-Democratic movements. Even Whigs came to agree with Howell Cobb's statement that "the Democratic organization presents the opportunity for concentrating all conservative and constitutional elements in the coming struggle for constitutional liberty." They admitted that "we now find the only consistent advocates of the Constitution and the union act under the name of the Democrats." Therefore, the editor of a Mississippi Whig paper concluded, "the Whigs of the South cannot do otherwise than vote with the Democrats, though they do so under protest." The problem of Radical control and the counting of Southern votes still remained. But the political complexities and turmoil in the South began to settle down more and more into support of both the program and the institution of the Democratic party.[37]

36. "You cannot have failed to have observed in your Southern exchanges of late, expressions of distrust of our Northern Democracy." Marcellus Emery to Manton Marble, June 1, 1867, Marble Papers; D. Stewart Hessey to Thomas F. Bayard, November 19, 1867, Bayard Papers; Benjamin Hill to Mrs. Madison Cody, October 30, 1868, in "Some Benjamin Harvey Hill Letters, Part I," ed. Katherine M. Chapman, *Georgia Historical Quarterly* 47 (September 1963): 312.

"What we want, therefore, is a new party, made up of the true men from the old parties." A. O. P. Nicholson to Andrew Johnson, February 27, 1866, Johnson Papers; Michael Perman, *Reunion without Compromise, The South and Reconstruction, 1865–1868* (Cambridge, 1973), pp. 195–97. Two examples of their difficulty are reported in John Forsyth to Manton Marble, October 13, 1866, December 19, 1867, Marble Papers. Forsyth was editor of the *Mobile Register*.

37. Howell Cobb to J. D. Hoover, January 4, 1868, in *The Correspondence of Howell Cobb, Robert Toombs and Alexander H. Stephens, Annual Report of the American Historical Association For the Year 1911*, ed. Ulrich B. Phillips (Washington, D.C., 1913), pp. 693–94; Jonathan Worth to William Clark, October 26, 1867, in *Correspondence of Worth*, ed. Hamilton, 2: 1064; Thomas B. Alexander, "Persistent Whiggery in Mississippi Reconstruction: The *Hinds County Gazette*," *Journal of Mississippi History* 23 (April 1961): 76.

Such movements gave the Democrats a confidence they had only occasionally expressed earlier. They were in their best condition for many years. It was just in time. Republican licentiousness continued unabated. During the middle months of 1868 their attempt to impeach the president confirmed the worst.[38] The Constitution was indeed in the greatest danger it had ever been. The upcoming presidential election was to be, therefore, of "vital importance to the preservation of our Republican institutions." Fortunately, the Democrats were ready. The issues were clear enough to them. They were, in the words of the *New York World,* "1. Opposition to Congressional usurpation. 2. Opposition to Negro supremacy. 3. Immediate restoration of the unity and peace of the nation." The United States had been ruled long enough by "an irresponsible oligarchy upheld by a standing army and negro votes."[39]

Of course, as one Democrat reminded his party colleagues early in 1868, their basic problem still remained that "with our own strength merely we cannot win." But every Democrat seemed "very desirous," in August Belmont's words, "that an earnest appeal should be made to the conservative element throughout the Union which has not heretofore acted with the Democratic party."[40] But what did that mean? What price were Democrats willing to pay to attract the conservative element? As before, the answer to that question provoked deep disagreements within the party. The Legitimists, remem-

See the discussion of this revival in George B. Dickson to Thomas F. Bayard, October 10, 1867, Bayard Papers; James S. Rollins To Alexander H. Stephens, November 8, 1867, Stephens Papers; circular from Democratic party of Louisiana to Francis P. Blair, Jr., January 22, 1868, Blair Papers; William Montague Browne to S. L. M. Barlow, January 26, 1868, Barlow Papers; Henry S. Fitch to Andrew Johnson, February 8, 1868, Johnson Papers.

38. Democrats saw in this action nothing really new or unexpected. It was an extension of tendencies toward radical destruction in keeping with all that had been going on. Democratic reaction and activities during the impeachment fill the pages of the *Congressional Globe* and their newspapers.

39. *Detroit Free Press,* November 7, 1867; New York *World,* April 14, 1868.

40. August Belmont to Samuel J. Tilden, February 1, 1868, Samuel J. Tilden Papers, New York Public Library; *Argus,* February 22, 1868; John D. Van Buren to Horatio Seymour, May 1, 1868, Seymour Papers. See also the resolutions passed early in the year by state Democratic conventions in *Appleton's Cyclopaedia, 1868,* pp. 203, 377, 385, 505, 603, 605–06, 619.

bering their lost opportunity of 1864, were, if anything, more insistent than ever that the party make no missteps. While there was general dissatisfaction with the conduct and policy of the Republican organization, the prejudices engendered by the war still lingered in the minds of great numbers who wished for "a change in the conduct of public affairs." Therefore, they had to be attracted to the Democratic cause in a way preventing false issues or other memories from blotting out the frightening danger of the Radical menace. Some Democrats argued for a clear public endorsement of all of the reconstruction amendments to indicate the party's acceptance of the consequences of Southern defeat. Further, Legitimists did not want any provocations from Southern whites which would inflame Northern sensibilities. "Blood and thunder," or any violent course, Herschel V. Johnson warned his fellow Southerners, "will lose us the conservative Republican vote." Not "impudent speeches," but acceptances of the results of the war had to be the South's course during the campaign.[41]

As before, also, the Legitimists concentrated on the presidential nominee. They had to select as presidential candidate someone who was "neither rebel nor Radical," and who would not put the party on the defensive. Andrew Johnson's clumsy efforts to win the Democratic nomination were quickly rejected as provocative. Nor should the nominee be "a mere party man." It would also help if he were a military man. As Robert J. Walker pointed out, about one-third of the North's voters were veterans of the war and the Democratic party had not heretofore paid sufficient attention to them. Furthermore, Grant's candidacy promised a Republican "bloody shirt" campaign which the

41. Horatio Seymour to James Schuckers, September 12, 1873, in James Schuckers, *The Life and Public Services of Salmon Portland Chase* (New York, 1874), p. 570; Herschel V. Johnson to Alexander H. Stephens, August 5, 1868, J. A. Stewart to Stephens, July 27, 1868, J. Barrett Cohen to Stephens, May 25, 1868, Stephens Papers.

The organizers in the South were very careful to nominate candidates and to take stances on war-related and reconstruction issues that would not embarrass the national Democratic party and feed on the "bloody shirt" appeal of the Northern Radicals. Benjamin Perry even felt that the South should not publicly support their choice for the Democratic presidential nomination, George Pendleton of Ohio, because of the latter's antiwar stance which probably would hurt him and the party in the North. Unless we use a little "common sense," the editor of the *Louisville Democrat* wrote in early 1867, "we will annihilate the Democratic party of the North." That remained the Southerners' position thereafter. *Louisville Democrat,* February 21, 1867.

nomination of a soldier could effectively short-circuit.[42]

The thrust of these suggestions was clear: only by running men "who in the late Civil War were active and unqualified supporters of the government" could the Democrats win the election. Legitimists vehemently opposed the candidacy of George Pendleton, the leading candidate of the Purist wing of the Democracy. Pendleton, one of the staunchest upholders of Democratic principles during the war, "has and deserves the entire confidence of the party." But, "he will not do." His nomination would "be fatal to the conservative cause" because, as an ultra peace man, he was "obnoxious to all moderate Democrats and detestable to all conservative Republicans."[43]

The Legitimists, unfortunately, did not have a primary candidate of their own behind whom they could rally as effectively as they had done four years before. A few generals were suggested: Winfield Scott Hancock, McClellan, even William T. Sherman. Some safe civilian candidates—Thomas Hendricks of Indiana; the War Democrat and former general John A. Dix; the conservative Republican Charles Francis Adams—were also listed. Some clearly were frivolous suggestions; none had the clear and substantial attractiveness or the support McClellan had had in 1864.

Many came to see success in the nomination of Chief Justice Salmon P. Chase. As S. L. M. Barlow wrote, the idea flowed directly out of their "earnest desire for success."[44] Chase, once a Democrat, then, successively, a Free Soil senator, Radical Republican secretary of the Treasury, and finally, Chief Justice under Abraham Lincoln, had several attractive qualities. He had grown increasingly disenchanted with the direction the Republican party had taken in recent

42. Robert J. Walker to Samuel J. Tilden, May 30, 1868, Tilden Papers; John B. Gordon to S. L. M. Barlow, April 6, 1868, Barlow Papers; George L. Miller to James Sterling Morton, December 26, 1867, J. Sterling Morton Papers, Nebraska Historical Society, Lincoln, Neb. (microfilm copy, Cornell University Library).

43. John A. Dix to Samuel J. Tilden, May 15, 1868, Tilden Papers; W. C. Patterson to Alexander H. Stephens, June 6, 1868, Stephens Papers; Samuel S. Cox to Manton Marble, November 11, 1867, Marble papers; S. M. Johnson to S. L. M. Barlow, May 5, 1868, Barlow Papers; James S. Rollins to Francis P. Blair, March 6, 1868, Blair Papers; William M. Browne to Howell Cobb, May 12, 1868, in *Correspondence,* ed. Phillips, p. 696.

44. S. L. M. Barlow to George B. McClellan, June 30, May 28, 1868, McClellan Papers.

years and his demeanor during the president's impeachment trial had attracted conservatives to him. Chase's nomination would be a prime indication of the Democrats' eminent respectability and unionism, and would bring to them many of the conservatives and Whigs whose presence was an absolute necessity for victory. Or, as one enthusiast asserted vigorously, *"We cannot elect any other man than Chase —we can elect him."* His nomination "will break Radicalism all to pieces." As a result, there was a vigorous and persistent Chase campaign carried on within the party.[45]

"They Prefer to Lose as 'Life-Long Democrats' "

As was to be expected, the Legitimist stance met great opposition from within party ranks. The Purists still refused to accept the basic tenets of the Legitimists' argument. They remained suspicious of any entangling collusion with the conservatives and the Republicans surrounding the president. They argued that the party did not need to nominate conservatives or safe candidates in order to win; but probably, as things now stood, the party "can elect any man whom it will nominate." Their convincing victory in 1867 was "a great Democratic triumph" won on "Democratic" issues. The party did not need, therefore, "to go astray after strange Gods" or "dishonorable proposals." Nor did it have to adopt expedient stances on reconstruction by accepting any of the "monstrous" measures of the past few years. Rather, the Democrats would win if they pursued a straight-out, pure Democratic stance because of "the great reactionary spirit of the

45. James Dixon to Manton Marble, May 30, 1868, Marble papers; F. A. Ken to S. S. Cox, June 22, 1868, Samuel S. Cox Papers, Brown University Library, Providence, R.I. Even Vallandigham supported Chase at this juncture. He continued to take a fairly Legitimist position as he frequently had since 1865. James L. Vallandigham, *A Life of Clement L. Vallandigham* (Baltimore, 1872), p. 424; Clement L. Vallandigham to Montgomery Blair, June 13, 1868, Blair Papers. Chase himself maintained that he still believed in Democratic policies and the Democratic faith on which he had been nurtured. He apparently was prepared to accept a Democratic nomination if the party accepted, in its turn, as the new departure men were prepared to do, the idea of Negro suffrage. Other than that he made no demands of the party. Salmon P. Chase to Manton Marble, May 30, 1868, Marble Papers; Salmon P. Chase to A. I. M. Duganne, September 21, 1868, Salmon P. Chase Papers, Library of Congress.

masses—and the question of race entering into it."[46]

To the Purists, the idea of nominating Chase was particularly repulsive. It would "involve the abandonment of all principles." No supporter of abolitionism, Lincoln, and congressional reconstruction could be an acceptable Democratic candidate. "Chase is out of the question," a leading Democrat told Samuel J. Tilden. "He is the weakest man we could have. We will use him well, but must not think of nominating him." The whole idea was "too preposterous to admit of discussion." As the Purist James A. Bayard summed up, "as I can perceive no other reason for the selection of the founder of the republican party than his supposed availability, I should deeply regret such a nomination by the Democracy."[47]

The Purists demanded, instead, the nomination of a representative of the party's traditional principles. "Let the convention give us a consistent and pronounced democrat; no outsider, no cheese, no renegade radical, and the triumph of the ticket will be complete and overwhelming. Principles first, men afterwards." To them Pendleton had unimpeachable credentials. "Pendleton is the man," one Democrat wrote, for whom the "democracy would work . . . with a zeal that had never been equalled since the days of Jackson." He "occupies a larger place in the hearts of the people than ever did Douglas." Most of all, he was free of all *"mongrel* associations."[48]

There were, as before, many strains and continuous tension fostered by these differences. New disagreements, such as the vigorous debate over financial policy, only intensified the existing strains. The confrontation over the "Pendleton Plan" to inflate the currency was

46. Amos Layman to Andrew Johnson, October 12, 1867, Johnson Papers; *Detroit Free Press,* June 21, 1868; Thomas F. Bayard to James A. Bayard, June 10, 1868, Bayard Papers.

47. Sanford E. Church to Samuel J. Tilden, June 10, 1868, in *Letters and Literary Memorial,* ed. Bigelow, p. 229; Thomas F. Bayard to James A. Bayard, May 31, 1868, Bayard papers; James A. Bayard to S. L. M. Barlow, May 31, 1868, Barlow Papers. See also, John Bigelow to —— Huntington, June 17, 1868, in Bigelow, *Retrospections,* 2: 187.

48. *Illinois State Register,* July 8, 1868; John L. Dawson to Jeremiah S. Black, June 14, 1868, Black Papers; Allen Thurman to John White Stevenson, June 3, 1868, Stevenson Papers; Washington McLean to S. L. M. Barlow, October 11, 1867, Barlow Papers; George Cass to Samuel J. Tilden, June 18, 1868, Marble Papers.

particularly intense, and often searing throughout 1868. But, to reiterate an earlier point, sharp disagreements within the party over priorities of issues or tactics to be followed, or even over candidates, no matter how bitter, did not necessarily mean that party disintegration followed. The Democrats continued to remain cognizant of the many things that united them, from similarity of outlook and heritage to the sheer political necessity of staying together. They shared too much in common not to recognize each other's needs and qualities and not to try to find a way to stay together with all members turning out to do their best."[49]

The meaning of this was clear. "While throwing open wide the doors of the party to everyone who seeks or claims entrance," one editor wrote, "we do not for a moment propose to venture upon any experiment that would endanger the unity of the party. We intend to go with the men who for the past eight years have travelled with us, the rough and dangerous paths of adversity. They are our brothers." As in 1864, this meant recognizing each other's claims to a share of the power. The New York *World* underscored their commitment. "When parties nominate their candidates for a Presidential contest, the majority determine who shall have the first place on the ticket, and the minority are conciliated by giving the second place to a man acceptable to them or fitted to win over votes from the opposition."[50]

As the tenth Democratic National Convention convened in the newly erected Hall of the Tammany Society in New York City on July 4, 1868, the party's course was still unclear. But the Purists proved to have the initiative. They held tight to their candidate while the Legitimists, once they backed away from Chase, had no agreed-on alternative. One observer commented that "the delegates, *except the Pendleton men,* are at sea and hardly know what to do," a judgment confirmed by the Legitimists themselves. "I fear that we are to be embarrassed by the want of a candidate to oppose Mr. Pen-

49. There were warnings that the Chase movement had so angered so many good Democrats that the "violence of the Pendleton men" could create an uproar at the national convention. Frederick Aitken to Andrew Johnson, June 27, 1868, Johnson Papers; L. O. Washington to Howell Cobb, June 21, 1868, Cobb Papers, p. 392. The demands for party union were redoubled. *Illinois State Register,* April 22, 1868.

50. *Argus,* June 26, 1868; New York *World,* May 17, 1868.

dleton. . . . Is it possible at this late day to unite upon a man with whom we can head off Pendleton?"[51] They could not and did not. But thanks to the two-thirds rule they did block Pendleton. The Ohioans' support was never enough to reach the necessary plateau of delegate votes. The result was deadlock. Only after several frustrating ballots did a break occur. The delegates from Pendleton's home state changed their votes to the former governor of New York, Horatio Seymour, the convention's presiding officer. Other states followed suit and the nomination was swiftly accomplished.

It has been suggested that Seymour's support came from people desirous of blocking the nomination of General Hancock or Senator Hendricks, both of whom had significant support among the delegates, to make way eventually for Chase.[52] (Seymour himself had been both a Chase supporter and a hard-money man.) Perhaps a number of the delegates and kingmakers did feel that way. But there had been some preconvention sentiment for Seymour. He was, after all, a well-known, respected, and often successful vote-getter in the largest state in the Union. But he was more than that. He was someone the Purists could support although he was not one of them. His major claim to fame was his strong opposition to the Lincoln administration despite his support for the war effort. He had tussled publicly with the president during the war, and had played a significant role in delaying and limiting the draft in his state. He had come quickly to Vallandigham's support when the Ohioan had been arrested in 1863. There is evidence that this record made him attractive to the Purists as a presidential candidate once Pendleton's chances collapsed. "Governor Seymour's course during the war was so nobly sound and Democratic that he attained a very strong hold upon the confidence and affections of the democracy of this and of all Northern and Western States," one Purist wrote Tilden. "His name will, I assure you, develop a hearty enthusiasm among Democrats that can be drawn out by no other." Furthermore, his strong, almost mystical commit-

51. A. E. Burr to Gideon Welles, July 4, 1868, Welles Papers; W. F. Allen to Samuel J. Tilden, May 25, 1868, in *Letters and Literary Memorial,* ed. Bigelow, 1: 231.

52. Klement, *Limits of Dissent,* p. 307. The convention proceedings are recorded in *Official Proceedings of the National Democratic Convention, 1868* (Boston, 1868).

ment to the Democratic party was well known. He was recognized as
"a Democrat of Democrats" whose "general political orthodoxy"
could not be "disputed." His nomination was, in short, a straight-out
party one, a fact particularly pleasing to Purists.[53]

Francis P. Blair, Jr., once a Democrat, more recently a conservative Republican and close associate of President Johnson, won the
vice-presidential nomination. He, too, was more acceptable to the
Purists than to the Legitimists, among whom he was a controversial
figure. Just before the convention he had, apparently in a bid for
Southern support, written a letter arguing that Southern whites could
escape from their thralldom by overtly resisting the reconstruction
acts.[54]

The Democratic platform was a mixed bag. It contained a great
deal of Legitimist sentiment recognizing that slavery and secession
were dead issues, "never to be renewed or reagitated"; praising the
Union soldiers and sailors who had carried the American nation to
victory "against a most gallant and determined foe"; and calling on
every conservative patriot, forgetting all past differences of opinion,
"to unite with us in the present great struggle for the liberties of the
People." But it had a strong Purist aura as well. There were violent
attacks on the excesses of Republican financial and tax policies, a
sentiment not likely to attract conservative non-Democrats without
complications. Nor did the platform give any quarter on reconstruction policies. Black suffrage was condemned and Radical reconstruction, the platform makers wrote, "had subjected ten States in time of
profound peace, to military despotism and negro supremacy." These
policies were a "usurpation, and unconstitiutional, revolutionary, and

53. A. Loomis to Samuel J. Tilden, June 8, 1868, in *Letters and Literary Memorial*, ed. Bigelow, 1: 229; Andrew D. White, *The Autobiography of Andrew D. White*
(New York, 1905), 1: 105; *Cincinnati Enquirer*, July 10, 1868. Seymour was described
as "powerful all through the west," second only to Pendleton. George L. Miller to
William Cassidy, January 4, 1868, Seymour Papers. It was also claimed that he was the
man whom Pendleton had "desired to win" at the convention. *Cincinnati Enquirer*,
July 10, 1868.

54. There were fears expressed that Blair's nomination roused "*violent
denunciations*" that ultimately "will damage us north." Sam Ryan, Jr., to Horatio
Seymour, July 14, 1868, Seymour Papers; Thomas Ewing, Jr., to Thomas Ewing, Sr.,
July 12, 1868, Ewing Papers.

void.'' To cap the Purist part of the document, the platform also included the inflationary greenback plank demanded by Pendleton's supporters and anathema to many conservatives and Legitimist Democrats too.[55]

The Democratic convention of 1868 capped the decade-long battle between Purists and Legitimists. Generally, the Democrats opted in their convention more for party regularity and policy purity than anything else. Partly this was because the Purists had outmaneuvered the Legitimists. They did not get everything their own way. But they were able to dominate most areas, partly because of their strength, partly because they had, unlike the Legitimists, fall-back positions, particularly as to the candidates. But the essential point was that, given the partisan pulls of the age, it was not surprising that some sort of Purist policy at last resulted, despite the hopes and plans of some leaders for a more clear-cut opening to conservative non-Democrats. The Democrats had gone much farther toward purism than they had in 1864 when the war still raged. The difference in the Democrats' situation between the two presidential years probably caused the change. Given the power of an individual Democrat's devotion to his party and its principles, commitment to traditional party stances and appeals primarily to the elect always had great appeal among the party faithful. But in 1864, in the aftermath of the shattering defeats of 1863, the Legitimist appeal for vote maximization made sense to many of the Democrats at Chicago. But now, in the aftermath of the elections of 1867, with Republican policies rejected, secession and the war fading in memory, and the Republicans apparently divided, the Legitimist arguments did not seem as compelling as once they had. Many Democrats, believing that they did not have to bow down to the sensibilities of others outside of their party, could opt for continuity and tradition and policy purism.[56]

55. The platform is reprinted in Kirk H. Porter and Donald Johnson, *National Party Platforms, 1840–1972*, 5th ed. (Urbana, Ill., 1973), pp. 37–39.

56. *New York Herald*, March 14, 1868. There were indications that the Legitimists would go along. Before the convention the New York *World* said that Democratic unity was assured because of "the general willingness to accept the judgment of the convention on platforms and candidates. . . . There is not the slightest danger that any portion of the Democratic party will fail to sustain the action of the Convention." New York *World*, June 9, July 1, 1868.

At the same time, however, the convention delegates had not gone as far out of their way to repel non-Democrats nor to insult the Legitimists beyond an acceptable point as they might have done. But they had succeeded in giving the party more of a Purist focus than the Legitimists thought wise. There were, as was to be expected therefore, recriminations against the convention's decisions. The feeling was strong in some quarters that the nominations had destroyed "the hope of a present conservative reaction." The party had sacrificed "the country on the altar of party," and threw away "the chance to redeem" the country from the Radicals. As one observer subsequently noted, "our organization has been imbued with the spirit of 'Peace Democracy' & has been made up of men who have no idea of progress. They will not see that we must get accessions to our ranks in order to win. They prefer to lose as 'life-long Democrats' rather than win as a fresh and vigorous party."[57] Still, many of the Purists believed they could win the way they had chosen to go. They counted on the pull of party devotion on the Legitimist Democrats, and the fears of radicalism in conservative ranks, to keep both in support of the party.

"The Party of Hate"

The Democrats pulled out all emotional stops in a bitter and vicious campaign designed to frighten conservatives to their side. Their position was well set forth by August Belmont in his opening speech to the national convention. The Republicans, he told his audience, *"intend congressional usurpation of all the branches and functions of the Government, to be enforced by the bayonets of a military despotism. . . .* Austria did not dare to fasten upon vanquished Hungary, nor Russia to impose upon conquered Poland, the ruthless tyranny now inflicted by Congress upon the Southern states. Military satraps are invested with dictatorial power. . . ." The people "must see that the conservative and national principles of a liberal

57. The ticket "will poll the entire democratic vote, but whether it will take much from the dissatisfied portion of the Republican party may well be doubted." William D. Shipman to S. L. M. Barlow, July 11, 1868, Barlow Papers; C. S. Bradley to Manton Marble, July 14, 1868, Marble Papers; M. Bradbury to Thomas Ewing, Jr., September 15, 1868, Ewing Papers.

and progressive Democracy are the only safeguards of the Republic.'' Only they could ''stay this tide of *disorganization, violence, and despotism.''* Nor was the black issue forgotten. ''To my mind,'' wrote S. L. M. Barlow, ''the most effective campaign document that can possibly be circulated'' in Pennsylvania, New York, and Ohio, was ''the series of portraits of the negroes who now govern L[ouisian]a.'' The keystone of their campaign was, as the *Louisville Democrat* indicated, first ''promulgated by Douglas ten years ago, a government by white men, of white men, for white men.'' Over all was the sense that the Republicans were ''the party of hate,'' and that the Democrats were in a contest between ''directly opposite conceptions of government.''[58]

At the same time, they legitimized themselves constantly by defending their record and their bona fides. ''The passions and prejudices generated during the war have been stimulated into a new life,'' one Democrat wrote, by the Republicans ''so as to affect the result'' of the election without regard for the real issues: the reconstruction policies of the past three years and the attempted disruption of the constitutional system itself as manifested in the impeachment of the president. But ''the distress, exhaustion, and disgust of the nation to-day are not to be appeased by singing songs over the events of 1865.'' Much attention was paid to courting and attracting army veterans to support the Democrats as a loyal party. The Democrats, the nation was told, ''have been true to the Union, the Constitution and the enforcement of the laws at all times.'' No one could point to any actions of the Democratic party that gave ''encouragement to the rebels while in arms against the Constitution and the Union.''[59]

58. *Official Proceedings,* pp. 4–5 (italics in original); *Congressional Globe,* 40 Cong., 2 sess., pp. 2722, 2929, 4033, *Appendix,* p. 213; *Argus,* June 8, 1868; *Louisville Democrat,* July 30, 1868; *Illinois State Register,* June 4, October 29, 1868; New York *World,* October 31, 1868; *Boston Post,* September 14, 1868; George B. McClellan to Douglas Taylor et al., October 2, 1868, McClellan Papers; S. L. M. Barlow to Samuel J. Tilden, September 21, 1868, Tilden Papers; *Louisville Democrat,* July 6, 1868; *Boston Post,* September 14, 1868.

59. David G. Croly, *Seymour and Blair, Their Lives and Service* (New York, 1868), p. 4; *Louisville Democrat,* August 27, 1868; New York *World,* July 20, 1868; *Congressional Globe,* 40 Cong., 2 sess., p. 3978.

They also talked about some of the traditional economic issues that had always

Despite difficulties, the Democrats ran a clear, crisp, and united campaign echoing their past. Certain conditions had changed since 1865, and opportunities not present before were now open to the party. But the party leaders followed a predictable pattern already well laid out over a decade of opposition, repeated familiar themes, and moved in well-worn grooves. There were differences in their emphases perhaps, differences in some of their priorities certainly, but no differences in the main thrust of their behavior and their principles. Democratic behavior in the post war years sharply underscored the continuity of their conception of the issues and the nature of the ideological conflict. Their postwar behavior also revealed a continuation of internal themes within the party as to how to deal with the political situation in which they were caught. In 1868, as in the whole period since 1865, there had only been a slight turning into a new political era. But it still remained to be determined if the third leg of party experience—voting support—showed the same patterns of continuity as well.

---

separated Democrats and their opponents. Republican financial policy, their taxation schemes, their commitment to the few of monied capital rather than to the mass of labor, had made many, including Republicans, "ripe for revolt." Their high tariff was "destroying our commerce." The Radicals did not "intend to relieve taxpayers." The Democrats "must spoil the programme of the money kings, or we are their slaves." George Schmidt to Horatio Seymour, July 14, 1868, Seymour Papers; John A. Dix to Samuel J. Tilden, May 15, 1868, in *Letters and Literary Memorial,* ed. Bigelow, 1: 226; *Illinois State Register,* June 18, July 10, November 2, 1868.

9

"The Popular Element . . . Is Pretty Stable and Fixed": Party Competition, 1865–1868

∽∽∽∽∽∽∽∽∽∽∽∽∽∽∽∽∽∽∽∽∽∽∽∽∽∽∽∽∽∽∽∽

THE DEMOCRATS WORKED hard in postwar election campaigns. Their enthusiasm and commitment were intense, their organizational activities "unprecedented" in scope and vigor.[1] Money, pamphlets, and newspapers were lavishly distributed throughout the nation. Local partisans compiled lists of voters; clubs and committees were organized everywhere.[2] Horatio Seymour, himself, canvassed extensively in 1868. But it was all in vain. Election outcomes for the party after the war proved to be the same combination of infrequent victory, close but serious defeats, and ultimate frustration that had characterized the Civil War years. The Democrats could never translate their

1. As one wrote to Horatio Seymour in 1868, "the disposition of the masses is in our favor," but it still required "considerable means and energy to make them move in the right direction." Magnus Gross to Horatio Seymour, July 22, 1868, Horatio Seymour Papers, New York State Library, Albany, N.Y.

2. Allen C. Beach of the New York Democratic state committee described one such organization to Seymour in late July:

"I have a perfect canvass of Jefferson County, names, politics & post office of every voter, and all doubtful voters and moderate republicans noted; there are about twelve hundred of these, & I have arranged with the World to send each of them the Campaign World until after the election. The canvass will be revised before [the] election &, by its aid, all our votes can be polled. I know of nothing that can be more effective. Other counties have also completed their canvass." By a state meeting on August 13 we will be able to report a situation "relative to organization that will be surprising and unprecedented." Allen C. Beach to Horatio Seymour, July 27, 1868, Seymour Papers. The Seymour Papers are filled with such details of the organizing effort.

occasional "splendid victories," as in 1867, into any sort of "permanent strength."[3]

"So Small a Majority"

At the beginning of the postwar era a number of state elections offered the Democrats their first opportunity to rebound from their wartime defeats. Twelve Northern and Western states elected governors and four others held elections for other statewide offices in the spring and fall of 1865. In addition, there were congressional elections in two New England states and Nevada, and a delegate election in Colorado. Nationally, turnout fell from the year before. The Democrats won none of the races contested, even losing the two congressional seats they held in New Hampshire and Connecticut. In two states, Michigan and Rhode Island, their share of the vote fell precipitously (although they did not mount fully organized independent efforts in either state). The only positive result so far as party members were concerned was the defeat of Republican-inspired black suffrage referenda in Connecticut, Wisconsin, and the District of Columbia.[4]

Of course, as before, the record of wins and losses only partially indicated the state of the Democracy in 1865. They averaged 37.9 percent of the popular vote in the statewide contests, hardly a distinguished showing, although their low totals in a number of one-sided anti-Democratic states distorted the national mean. More to the point, the Democratic situation had not changed all that much from the year before. There were a few wild swings in their share of the vote in such marginal (and small) states as Rhode Island, Kansas, and Oregon, but in most states percentage shifts were slight. In the three Middle Atlantic states, New York, New Jersey, and Pennsylvania, for example, the Democracy lost only 2.1 percent from its totals of the previous year, as turnout at the polls fell for both parties. In the Middle West, except for Michigan, the Democrats actually improved their showing by 3 percent over 1864 and just over 5 percent from their lowpoints in

3. Joseph Warren to Manton Marble, November 9, 1867, Manton Marble Papers, Library of Congress.
4. In the analysis that follows I am still concentrating, with a few exceptions, on the non-Border, nonslave states. The actual percentages in the state office races are listed in Table 9.1, below.

the statewide races in 1863. This apparently was due to patterns of differential turnout in these states. In Ohio, for example, the Democrats received over 190,000 votes, a very slight increase over their wartime totals there, but the Republican total vote dropped by over 60,000 from their triumphant race in 1863. Across the nation as a whole, however, popular voting behavior and the Democratic record in 1865 were not very much different from recent state and national elections. Unfortunately, that was hardly cheering news for party leaders in their efforts to regain control of the national government.

In the spring of 1866, however, the Democrats won ''a great moral victory'' in the Connecticut state elections, reducing the Republican majority in a year from 11,000 to 500, and gaining a striking 7 percent in the popular vote over the year before.[5] (This was due to a voter surge to the Democrats. They received over 12,000 more votes than they had the year before, while the Republican vote increased only slightly.) Democratic hopes revived dramatically. It was 1862 all over again. Their attack on Republican reconstruction policy seemed to be paying dividends. The revolt of President Johnson and his allies against the congressional Republicans and his alliance with the Democrats promised additional strength for the party. And if the Democrats were ever to make a significant move it would be in the congressional elections of 1866. Their opportunity to change the direction of national policy was, short of a presidential election, unparalleled. In addition to an array of statewide races, all but a few seats in the House of Representatives would be contested.

But in the fall, the Democrats' ''evil days'' continued.[6] Their hopes for a backlash against Republican policies were dashed. Turnout increased across the country but that did not help the Democracy. They won governorships in the Border states of Missouri and Delaware and in the South. But they lost badly everywhere else. They lost governorship races in New York, Pennsylvania, New England, and several Western states. They fared no better in a number of other statewide races. They lost three congressional seats in Pennsylvania

5. James English et al., to Samuel S. Cox, April, n.d., 1866, Samuel S. Cox Papers, Brown University Library, Providence, R.I.

6. Eric L. McKitrick, *Andrew Johnson and Reconstruction* (Chicago, 1960), p. 460.

and New Jersey, won one more than they had in 1864 in Illinois and Ohio. But thanks to Republican gains in the South and Border, the new Congress would not only be controlled by the Radicals but would be apparently veto-proof. Nor was there any Democratic holder of a major office who could serve as a rallying point for the faithful and a base on which to build for the future.[7]

Nevertheless, the shock of Democratic losses in 1866 obscured the by now customary situation in which, in percentage terms at least, nothing much had changed. The results were actually much more encouraging for the Democracy, in comparative terms, than Kenneth Stampp's description of an "astonishing" margin of victory for the Republicans.[8] The Democrats' total popular vote in statewide races averaged just under 40 percent and 43 percent in the congressional races, very bad indeed, but little changed from the most recent similar races in the same states. In fact, in 1866, by and large the Democrats did better than they had done the year before, albeit only slightly. Their national percentage was up over 2 percent from the year before, although down slightly from their amount in the presidential race in the same states two years before. They actually gained somewhat in almost every one of the large states. In both New York and Pennsylvania, for example, they increased by 1 percent over their totals there the year before, and in both lost less than 1 percent from their vote in the presidential race of 1864.[9] Their total popular vote in New York was over 352,000, up 80,000 from the year before, and almost to their 1864 total. In Pennsylvania they picked up 75,000 votes from the year before. But in both states the Republicans increased their popular vote total by almost as much.

Similarly, there was only a slight movement in the percentages registered for each party in the congressional races. Turnout increased in many of these races as well but, again, for both parties proportionately. In most states the Democrats lost about 3 percent from their total

7. For some Democratic reactions to their situation, see *Chicago Times,* November 12, 1866; William B. Reed to Andrew Johnson, November 11, 1866, Andrew Johnson Papers, Library of Congress.

8. Kenneth Stampp, *The Era of Reconstruction, 1865–1877* (New York, 1965), p. 117.

9. See Table 9.1.

vote for these same seats two years before. They actually gained a little in Pennsylvania, Ohio, and Indiana. In short, what had occurred was a relatively small shift in vote totals in a few districts. Unfortunately for the Democrats, that shift had been predominantly in their opponents' favor. The Republicans gained a few more votes than did the Democracy. In a situation where there were narrow margins between the parties, a landslide in terms of seats won had resulted. There continued to be truth in the New York *World*'s comment that the Republicans held control "on so small a majority that it will take but a slight change to place them in a minority." The problem was that the vote remained static enough so that no matter what the Democrats did they could not break up the settled, slightly Republican majority.[10]

These conditions continued into the next year as well. In contrast to 1866, however, the elections of 1867 turned out to be a great Democratic triumph. For the first time in this period, the Democracy increased its share of the vote in every state where there had been contests in 1866. In some states—New York, Massachusetts, Connecticut, and New Jersey—the party received its greatest proportion of the vote since before 1860. Overall, the Democrats won 44 percent of the national vote, a gain of almost 5 percent from the year before and back very close to their totals in 1864. As early as April 1867, they had seen the tide turned and a "return to reason on the part of the people" with the Connecticut local elections.[11] They won the governorship there for the first time since 1856, with 50.5 percent of the vote. In the fall they won the California governorship, and major statewide races in New York and Pennsylvania as well. They picked up three congressional seats in Connecticut, two in California, and supported an Independent Republican conservative who won in an Ohio district. Even more startling, perhaps, they came within 3,000 votes of taking the Ohio governorship against Rutherford B. Hayes, with 49.7 percent of the vote. They also ran very close races in Wisconsin and New Hampshire. Their capture of the Ohio state legislature insured the election of a Democratic United States senator. The Republicans were also defeated badly in a number of black suffrage referenda, support

10. New York *World*, November 26, 1866.
11. Edmund Cooper to Andrew Johnson, April 5, 1867, Johnson Papers.

for black voting falling well below the Republican vote.

The elections of 1867, like those of five years before, seemed a bright beacon for the Democracy breaking through a persistent, dense fog. Republican radicalism had at last been found out by the American people. Differential turnout hurt the Republicans. Their total popular vote fell off substantially from 1866 while the Democrats' totals did not. The latter's vote in 1867 was 111 percent of their previous year's total; the Republicans received only about 92 percent of their earlier total. Apparently, many Republican voters refused to support black suffrage, or did not vote at all out of hostility to the turn that Republican policy was taking in the Northern states. Certainly, many of the observers at the moment believed that the Democrats' use of the race issue had materially affected the outcome of these local elections. The electorate, a Californian wrote Johnson, felt the "deepest indignation" at the Republican attempt to place "the negro and the Chinaman upon an equal footing . . . with the white man." Even the Republicans were convinced that they had been hurt by the issue. "The nigger whipped us," Senator Ben Wade of Ohio reportedly said, while George Templeton Strong somewhat more elegantly noted that "our party leaders have been going a little too fast for the masses." As a result, "from Maine to California the Democracy are rising."[12]

But, of course, behind the actual returns there was a fragility to the Democrats' triumph in the persistence of a generally static voting universe. The Democrats had gained less than 1 percent in Connecticut from the year before, just over that in New Hampshire and Pennsylvania, and only 4 percent in New York and Ohio. A very large gain (and a temporary one) of better than 19 percent in Massachusetts, because of an alliance of the Democrats with the conservative Republicans there, made the party's overall figures look larger

12. Ben Truman to Andrew Johnson, September 7, 1867, Johnson Papers; Fawn Brodie, *Thaddeus Stevens, Scourge of the South* (New York, 1959), p. 317; Allan Nevins and Milton Halsey, eds., *The Diary of George Templeton Strong, 1835–1875* (New York, 1952), 4: 160–61. If the issue of black suffrage had been submitted unfettered by appeals to party loyalty and the resultant disciplinary pressures, another correspondent wrote, Ohio would have defeated the measure by 150,000 votes instead of 38,000. Lewis D. Campbell to Andrew Johnson, October 12, 1867, Johnson Papers. For support of this view, see Phyllis F. Field, "The Struggle for Black Suffrage in New York State, 1846–1869" (Ph.D. diss., Cornell University, 1974).

than they were. Democrats did pick up over 8 percent in their vote in the congressional races in Connecticut and more than 3.5 percent in New Hampshire. Again, differential turnout was the cause. Both the actual totals and the percentage swing toward them in some states provided hope for the Democrats, and rightly so. But the stay-at-home vote had given only ephemeral help in the past and there was no evidence that major shifts in voter choice were as yet going on in any kind of sustained way. The elections of 1867 were an occasion for rejoicing, but would the promise last?

The elections of 1868 completed this postwar sequence of Democratic attempts to regain national power. Once more, there was only a two-party national race, with the Democrats, unlike 1864, coming off a very good electoral year. Their momentum continued in the spring state races. Both parties gained votes over the year before, the Democrats slightly more. They took the Connecticut governorship and came even closer than the year before in New Hampshire. In the fall they picked up twelve congressional seats in the Northern states while losing three, won back the governorships in New York and New Jersey, received 49.9 percent of the vote for governor in Indiana, and came within two percentage points of victory in Pennsylvania. It was one of their best moments in the 1860s.

In the presidential election of 1868, turnout nationally was 78.1 percent, an increase of more than 4 percent over 1864 (although not quite back to where it had been in 1860). More spectacularly, turnout in some of the large competitive states, New York, New Jersey, and Ohio, for example, was around the 90 percent mark. But this did not mean victory for the Democracy. Both parties got their voters to the polls and the Republicans won a very close victory. They won twenty-five states with 214 electors to the Democrats' eight states and eighty electoral votes. The Democrats received just over 47 percent of the national popular vote, a slight gain over 1864 and their best national average since before the war. They did very well in the central belt of states, continuing to maintain a very close position there. Democrats won in New York for the first time since 1852, and in New Jersey, and came within two percentage points of a majority in Connecticut and Indiana. They were also close to a winning margin in Pennsylvania and only slightly less so in Ohio. In the critical eight states of the central core with their 127 electoral votes, the Democrats won two, and averaged 47.7 percent of the total vote, about the same as in 1864. They also made a strong showing in a number of Border and Southern states.

In the congressional races, the Democrats won seventy-seven seats nationally, a gain of forty-two over 1866 (thanks to substantial improvement for them in the Border). Still, the Democrats' position had not improved very much at all in their total vote in these races. In elections to the House of Representatives in New York, for one example, they gained two seats but lost one other that they had won in 1866, and wound up with just three more seats than in 1864. They averaged 50.1 percent of the vote in New York's congressional races as against 47.5 percent in 1866 and 50.5 percent in 1864. In Indiana their percentages were 50.1 percent in 1868 as against 48.0 percent in 1866; in Pennsylvania, 49.4 percent as against 49.0 percent. The Democrats made much hay based on a slight swing in the vote and the apparent return to political normality in a number of the Border states.

Electorally, the election of 1868 revealed the same potential in regard to Democratic fortunes as had most elections since 1860. Their margins in 1867 and 1868 suggested also that the Democrats may have been settling into a new popular vote plateau, above the 45-percent mark for the first time since 1862. And the Democrats were better off than their 47 percent of the national vote indicates. Much of the depression in their overall totals was due, as always, to one-sided conditions favoring the Republicans in states such as Vermont, Massachusetts, Rhode Island, Kansas, and Nebraska, where the Democrats won only 35 percent of the vote or less, or in the still controlled South and Border. The states in which the Democracy was strong could determine the outcome of future presidential elections and control of Congress. Even the stalwartly Republican New York *Nation* referred to "the comparative smallness of the majority by which the fate of the campaign has been decided."[13] The Democrats remained very close to their opponents and continued to pose a significant threat. They had much to be hopeful about.

13. New York *Nation*, October 22, 1868, p. 324.

"An Enormous Actual Resident Strength"

Some Republican commentators were startled by the closeness of the presidential election of 1868 which tended, in James Blaine's words, "to qualify the sense of gratulation and triumph on the part of those who give serious study to the progress and results of partisan contests." With a "bad candidate and bad platform," the Democracy still "polled an enormous vote." They were "a living thing after all."[14] In reality, however, the Democrats remained, at best, at the threshold of power, still unable to break through to victory. As during the war and postwar years, they continued to win some races, lost many key ones, could not make significant breakthroughs in a consistent manner, and lost the biggest race of all, the presidency.

Furthermore, closer analysis confirms that there had been little shift in the electoral status of the party from its situation during the war. Computing the index of competition for each Northern and Western state indicates that there were, between 1865 and 1868, no "safe" Democratic states. But five states with eighty-two electoral votes were intensely competitive between the parties; four others with thirty-seven electoral votes were in the moderately competitive category. (See Table 9.1.) The rest of the non-Southern states, with eighty electors, were either safe or dominant Republican. (See Table 9.2.) In wartime elections, in contrast, there had been two intensely competitive states—Pennsylvania and Connecticut, with thirty-two electoral votes—and six moderately competitive states, all in the central core, with eighty-two electoral votes. The Democrats in the postwar years, in terms of their competitive potential, remained about the same in the Northern states as they had during wartime. (There were now five additional electors in the competitive categories.) The former slave states still did not contribute much to the Democrats. Seymour, for example, won only in Delaware, Maryland, Kentucky, Louisiana, and Georgia. The situation in these states, particularly those in the former Confederacy, was at best uncertain and could not be readily

14. James G. Blaine, *Twenty Years of Congress: Lincoln to Garfield* (Norwich, Conn., 1893), 2: 407; William Schouler to Israel Washburn, October 26, 1868, quoted in Gallaird Hunt, *Elihu, Israel and Cadwallader Washburn* (New York, 1925), p. 124; W. H. Bogart to Manton Marble, November 5, 1868, Marble Papers.

Table 9.1
Democratic Popular Vote Percentages
and
Index of Competition, 1865–1868

STATE	PERCENTAGE									INDEX OF COMPETITION
	STATE 1865	CONG. 1865	STATE 1866	CONG. 1866	STATE 1867	CONG. 1867	PRES. 1868	STATE 1868	CONG. 1868	
Maine	36.8	—	37.5	37.9	44.4	—	37.6	42.3	43.3	79.9
Vermont	24.3	—	24.9	24.7	26.6	—	21.4	26.4	25.9	49.8
New Hampshire	45.0	44.2	46.5	—	47.6	47.8	45.0	48.4	—	92.7
Connecticut	42.5	42.4	49.7	—	50.5	49.3	48.5	50.9	—	94.6
Rhode Island	7.0	13.6	25.2	—	30.1	18.5	33.5	35.8	—	46.8
Massachusetts	23.3	—	22.5	23.7	41.7	—	30.3	32.9	31.0	58.4
New York	47.6	—	49.0	47.5	53.4	—	50.6	51.6	49.9	96.7
New Jersey	49.0	—	—	49.4	—	—	50.9	51.4	48.9	97.8
Pennsylvania	47.5	—	48.6	49.0	50.1	—	47.8	49.3	48.4	97.7
Ohio	46.4	—	45.5	45.3	49.7	—	46.0	48.3	48.7	94.3
Indiana	—	—	47.8	48.0	—	—	48.6	49.9	49.9	97.7
Illinois	—	—	—	42.2	—	—	44.3	—	44.8	87.5
Michigan	25.7	—	41.2	40.9	42.0	—	43.0	43.1	44.0	80.0
Wisconsin	45.3	—	—	41.1	48.3	—	43.8	—	44.3	89.1
Iowa	43.3	—	37.9	38.3	39.3	—	38.1	—	39.3	78.7
Minnesota	44.5	—	—	37.8	45.9	—	39.2	—	39.3	82.7
Kansas	—	—	29.5	29.7	—	—	31.1	34.0	32.3	62.6
Nebraska	—	—	49.1	45.6	—	—	35.9	41.6	40.7	85.2
Nevada	—	—	—	37.0	—	—	44.6	—	46.2	85.3
California	44.1	—	—	—	54.0	47.9	49.8	—	—	93.9
Oregon	—	—	49.2	48.6	—	—	50.4	—	47.3	97.4

Table 9.2
States Listed by Competitiveness Categories,
(With Number of Electoral Votes)
1865–1868

SAFE REPUBLICAN		DOMINANT REPUBLICAN		MODERATELY COMPETITIVE		INTENSELY COMPETITIVE	
Minnesota	4	Wisconsin	8	Connecticut	8	New Jersey	7
Michigan	8	Illinois	16	Ohio	21	Indiana	13
Maine	7	Nevada	2	California	5	Pennsylvania	26
Iowa	8	Nebraska	3	New Hampshire	3	New York	33
Kansas	3		29		37	Oregon	3
Massachusetts	12						82
Vermont	5						
Rhode Island	4						
	51						

counted on.[15] But the Democrats enjoyed "an enormous actual resident strength" among the voters elsewhere, remained quite competitive in enough states to give them place and hope, but were not as well situated as were the Republicans in terms of their vote expectations.[16]

In individual congressional races, too, little had changed for the Democracy in the postwar years. In fact, the party was slightly worse off. A majority of the House of Representatives was 117 seats in 1868. Of the 158 seats outside the Confederacy and Border, the Democrats held ten safe seats (six in New York, three in Pennsylvania, and the twelfth Ohio), and were dominant in six others. Thirty more were intensely competitive, thirty-seven were moderately so, a total of eighty-three in which the Democrats could hope to complete effectively with their opponents. (See Table 9.3.) In contrast, the Republicans held fifty-seven safe seats, and were dominant in fifteen others. In the Northern states, the Democrats remained very close and could win control of a substantial bloc of seats in the House from that region so long as everything went right for them; but, generally, the Republicans started to better advantage. As with the presidential vote, of course, so far as ultimate control of the legislative branch was concerned much depended on the uncertain situation in the South.[17]

This stability of voting patterns at the state and national levels was not produced artificially by equal cross-cutting movements by the voters between parties. It is true that both parties had added voters to their rolls during the 1860s. In New York, for example, the total

15. They did receive more than 45 percent of the popular vote in 1868 in Alabama, Arkansas, and North Carolina, less elsewhere.

16. W. H. Bogart to Manton Marble, November 5, 1868, Marble Papers.

17. The figures in wartime had been nineteen safe Democratic seats, three in which the Democrats had been dominant, twenty-seven intensely competitive seats, and thirty-six moderately competitive ones. See above, chapter six. Another way of evaluating the Democrats' fortunes in 1868 is by comparing their totals to their "normal" or expected vote. In most states, for example, their margins in the presidential election of 1868 hovered around their average of the popular vote over the four preceding elections (their "normal" or expected vote). In New York, the Democrats had averaged 49.9 percent of the vote in the four preceding elections, including the presidential race in 1864; now they improved themselves by 0.7 percent. In Pennsylvania, they lost 0.8 percent in 1868 over their normal average; in Ohio, they lost 0.3 percent; in Connecticut, they gained 1.0 percent. The "normal" vote is derived by computing the mean of the party's percentage in the four preceding elections.

Table 9.3
Congressional Districts Listed by Competitiveness
Categories, 1865–1868

SAFE DEMOCRATIC
New York: 2,4,5,6,7,8
Pennsylvania: 1,8,11
Ohio: 12

INTENSELY COMPETITIVE
New York: 11,12,14
New Jersey: 2,4,5
Pennsylvania: 3,5,10,13,16,21
Ohio: 1,3,6,7,9,10,13,16
Indiana: 1,3,4,6,7,8,9
Illinois: 13
California: 3
Oregon: 1

SAFE REPUBLICAN
Maine: 2,3,4,5
Vermont: 1,2,3
Rhode Island: 1,2
Massachusetts: 1,2,3,4,5,6,7,8,9,10
Connecticut: 3
New York: 17,22,23,24,25,26,27,31
Pennsylvania: 7,9,22,23
Ohio: 17,18,19
Indiana: 5
Illinois: 1,2,3,5,6
Iowa: 1,2,3,4,5,6
Wisconsin: 2,3,5,6
Minnesota: 1,2
Michigan: 2,4
Kansas: 1
Nevada: 2

DOMINANT DEMOCRATIC
New York: 9
New Jersey: 3
Pennsylvania: 15
Ohio: 5
Indiana: 2
California: 1

MODERATELY COMPETITIVE
New Hampshire: 1,2,3
Connecticut: 1,2,4
New York: 1,3,13,18,21,28,30
Pennsylvania: 4,6,12,14,17,18,
19,20,24
Ohio: 2,4,8,14,15
Indiana: 10,11
Illinois: 4,9,10,11,12
Wisconsin: 1
Michigan: 1,5

DOMINANT REPUBLICAN
Maine: 1
New York: 15,16,19,20,29
New Jersey: 1
Pennsylvania: 2
Ohio: 11
Illinois: 7,A–L
Michigan: 3,6
California: 2
Nebraska: 1

number of Democratic voters increased by 117,000 between the presidential elections of 1860 and 1868, while the Republicans added 57,000 voters to their rolls. In Indiana, both parties picked up just under 40,000 voters; in Connecticut, the Democrats about 14,000, a few thousand more than their opponents. But these additional voters fit themselves into existing grooves of political sentiment in their communities. Inter-election correlation coefficients remained remarkably high in the postwar period, again suggesting, as during the war, a pervasive continuity in mass voting behavior. In the states of the central core, the mean correlation figure for postwar elections varied from .99 in Indiana and .98 in Ohio and Pennsylvania, to .94 in New Jersey. New Jersey's figure was the lowest in the central bloc. In these states, the average of all postwar election correlations was the very high figure of .97. (See Table 9.4.)

The war and postwar stability is also dramatically indicated by two other calculations. Correlating the presidential election of 1864 with the presidential election four years later (Column *b* in Table 9.4) produces a mean coefficient of .95 for the eight critical central states, with no correlation falling below Connecticut's .92. Similarly, comparing the statewide elections in 1862, when the Democrats had regained their competitive stride after the confusion engendered by the war's outbreak, with the last election in the sequence, the presidential

Table 9.4
Inter-election Correlations, Eight States, 1862–1868

	a. MEAN CORRELATION, ALL ELECTIONS 1865–1868	b. CORRELATION, PRESIDENTIAL ELECTION OF 1864 WITH 1868	c. CORRELATION, ELECTION OF 1862 WITH 1868
Connecticut	.96	.92	.96
New Hampshire	.97	.94	.97
New York	.97	.97	.97
New Jersey	.94	.94	.94
Pennsylvania	.98	.98	.98
Ohio	.98	.97	.96
Illinois	.98	.93	.89
Indiana	.99	.95	.92

election of 1868, again demonstrates very stable voting behavior. For these two points, the eight-state central core mean is again .95, with only Illinois falling below .90 and then only slightly. This phenomenon continued to be unaffected by races for different offices of off- or on-year situations. Despite an amalgam of federal, and major and minor state offices, inter-election correlations between successive years and over several years were strikingly high. A glance at two states indicates the high relationship between successive elections, no matter what the office or particular electoral situation happened to be. (See Table 9.5.)

Table 9.5
Inter-election Correlations,
Ohio, Pennsylvania
1866–1868

	OHIO				PENNSYLVANIA		
	SS–'66	G–'67	President 1868		G–'66	J–'67	President 1868
Governor, 1865	98	97	98	Atty General, 1865	98	97	98
Sec State, 1866	—	98	99	Governor, 1866	—	99	99
Governor, 1867		—	98	Justice, 1867		—	99

The pattern revealed in the correlation figures is confirmed by another set of electoral comparisons. The high correlation figures do not mask surges to one party or another all across the board. The average of all county changes in each party's percentage of the vote in five central states between 1867 and 1868, for one example, was 2.6 percent. In New York, the average shift was 2.8 percent in the era; in Pennsylvania, 2.0 percent; in Connecticut, 3.6 percent; in Ohio, 3.2 percent. The largest shift in all of these states was 6.8 percent in Connecticut, between 1865 and 1866. Most of the time, the sum total of all county-level shifts between two elections hovered around 2 percent, a very much smaller amount than during the war.

Obviously, once again there was some variability in voting patterns. Not every state acted exactly the same way and there were no perfect correlations. Some of the correlations were lower in the postwar years than they had been earlier; some were higher. Individual variations caused by unique factors in any given election were present. Turnout occasionally varied between the two parties. As before, some party voters stayed home on every election day. Occasionally, because of the rejection of a particular party's policies the number of stay-at-homes was disproportionately high among the members of one party, and therefore favored the other. Occasionally, too, one party benefited from a surge of voters to them due to some immediate attractiveness, while their opponents in the same race did not. In a closely divided electorate these movements could have profound temporary effects in the number of seats won or lost, particularly in off-year elections.

But, as before, none of this changes the main point. The outstanding characteristic of Northern voter behavior in the post–Civil War years was that the voters had remained in their accustomed grooves as established in the aftermath of the realignment of the mid-fifties and reinforced by wartime experiences. The Democratic party's support had not been transformed. The social base of its electorate remained similar to what it had been in 1860. The geography of its popular vote coincided with its postrealignment pattern. That pattern remained hard and unshaken. Since 1860 the party had maintained its position, role, and general level of support, despite all difficulties. It teetered on the brink of victory often and occasionally tumbled over into it. But what stood out starkly and plainly overall was that the Democrats had not been able, despite all of their apparent opportunities, as one Democratic editor succinctly put it, to "translate" their occasional "splendid victories into permanent strength."[18] Despite their strength and vigor, the Democrats had been unable to overcome the inertia of public voting habits. As the New York *Nation* sardonically commented in 1866, the New York *World* "has demonstrated, to its own

18. Joseph Warren to Manton Marble, November 9, 1867, Marble Papers. See also Charles R. Buckalew to Victor Piolett, November 5, 1868, Victor Piolett Papers, Wyoming Historical and Geological Society, Wilkes Barre, Pa. Once again, the work of Peyton McCrary, from a different perspective confirms the stability argument offered here. See his "The Civil War Party System, 1854–1876: Toward a New Behavioral Synthesis?" (paper presented before the Annual Meeting of the Southern Historical Association, Atlanta, Georgia, 1976). Needless to say, Professor McCrary is not responsible for the conclusions I have drawn.

entire satisfaction, after every election for four years past, that the party of slavery was growing and gaining; yet it has been regularly defeated every year.''[19] The Democrats remained locked into a minority party position, albeit a strong and competitive one.

"The Canvass . . . Is Substantially Between the Government and the Rebellion"

There was nothing mysterious about the Democracy's continued failure to build a popular voting majority after 1865. Some party observers blamed transient things: for example, Republican control of the South and their manipulation of the black vote. Each, perhaps, was part of the truth. But neither explained the Democracy's failure to do better in the Northern states. There, the problem of voter conversion still badly frustrated the party. While it continued to attract the support of its own constituency readily and enthusiastically, the party remained unable to convince non-Democrats to support it consistently, if at all. Democrats expected to. Over and over, Democratic commentators argued that ''men must either stand with the Democratic party or with the radicals.'' There could be no ''half way house between them.''[20] But very few unhappy Republicans or conservatives readily supported the Democracy. Effective cross-pressures, some created by the Democrats' own actions, others created by Republican propaganda, negated any attractiveness that the Democrats offered to conservative nonparty members. Their image continued to plague them. The war continued to affect them. The intensity of traditional party loyalties and the depth of prejudice against an opposing party continued to hinder them.

The Republicans never underestimated the Democratic threat to their hegemony. Despite their own internal differences therefore, Republican leaders worked actively from 1865 on to maintain and reinforce traditional commitments to them. They countered the Democratic attack in a most potent way. They realized that a party could only be attractive to those not normally committed to it if it were free from any hint of extremism, unacceptable behavior, or commit-

19. *Nation,* October 18, 1866, p. 311.
20. *Detroit Free Press,* May 9, 1867.

ment to a narrowly partisan policy. They took every opportunity from 1865 on, therefore, to remind everyone that they were fighting "the pestilent Copperheads of the North" and the "southern fiends incarnate." No matter how disguised, the issue before the country had only two sides to it: "the unrepentant rebel and the loyal." The Democrats' position was clear. The party, Oliver Morton suggested in 1866, could be described as "a common sewer and loathsome receptable into which is emptied every element of treason North and South, and every element of inhumanity and barbarism which had dishonored the age." The Democrats supported "rebels whose hands have been stained with the blood of our Union soldiers." They were willing to clasp these bloodstained hands and receive the rebel soldier "with open arms and call him brother." But people in the loyal states would prefer another war to admitting the Confederates to an equal share of the government "before we have some adequate security for their future good conduct." It was the Republican mission, therefore, to "save the country from the control of the democratic demagogues who organized rebellion and declared against the supremacy of the Constitution." In sum, they argued, "an opposition which in a rebellion, takes sides with insurgents, forfeits for the future all claims upon public confidence."[21] Republican efforts reached a crescendo, of course, during the presidential election of 1868 when their danger was greatest. They seized every opportunity provided by the failure of the Democratic Legitimists to dominate their party to make their points. When Rutherford B. Hayes became governor of Ohio early in 1868, he exulted that his Democratic-controlled legislature was "foolish enough to be repealing Ohio's assent to the Fourteenth Amendment."

21. Joseph Medill to Hugh McCulloch, June 23, 1865, Hugh McCulloch Papers, Library of Congress; John Sherman to William T. Sherman, August 29, 1865, July 2, 1866, in Rachel Sherman Thorndike, *The Sherman Letters* (New York, 1894), pp. 255, 271; Henry C. Lea, *The Record of the Democratic Party, 1860–1865* (n.p., n.d.), p. 39; Emma Lou Thornbrough, *Indiana in the Civil War Era, 1850–1880*, volume 3 in *The History of Indiana* (Indianapolis, 1865), p. 235; *Congressional Globe*, 39 Cong., 1 sess., pp. 1616, 2089; ibid., 40 Cong., 2 sess., pp. 933, 3975; *Record of Hiester Clymer* . . . (Philadelphia, 1866), p. 8; John Bingham to Thomas Ewing, Sr., November 14, 1867, Thomas Ewing Family Papers, Library of Congress; *Nation*, June 25, 1868; William P. Fessenden to Hugh McCulloch, September 11, 1866, McCulloch Papers.

Similarly, the New Jersey Democrats' attempts to repeal that state's ratification of the thirteenth amendment, and the vigor and activity of Southerners on behalf of the Democracy, provided plenty of ammunition for the Republicans as the election loomed.[22]

They were particularly "jubilant" over the nomination of Seymour and Blair. Seymour's speech to antidraft rioters in New York City in 1863, Blair's preconvention letter arguing that a Democratic president could "declare these [reconstruction] acts null and void, compel the Army to undo its usurpations at the South, disperse the carpet-bag State Governments, allow the white people to reorganize their own governments and elect Senators and Representatives," all provided particular opportunities. Campaign pamphlets: "Seymour, Vallandigham and the Riots of 1863," "Horatio Seymour, The War Record of a Peace Democrat," and "Who Nominated Seymour and Blair? [the South]," for example, along with congressional and stump speeches and newspaper editorials, hammered the point home.[23]

The Republicans even shrewdly reversed the Democratic charge that the Radicals were engaged in perpetual revolution. Democratic victory, they argued, would unsettle everything in order to reraise all the old issues, and uplift the enemy. "The Democratic party has declared for war, continuous, unending war, except upon the condition of the success of the principles of the rebellion." They want "revolution" to turn the clock back. To allow the Democrats into office now "would be to continue, perhaps to increase, the lamentable political excitement." The issue, therefore, was between "Blair & revolution & Grant & Peace."[24]

The Democrats fought back as best they could. "Last year, the

22. C. M. Ingersoll to Thomas Hart Seymour, August 23, 1866, Thomas Hart Seymour Papers, Connecticut Historical Society, Hartford, Conn.; Charles Williams, ed., *Diary and Letters of Rutherford B. Hayes* (Columbus, Ohio, 1924), p. 50.

23. Samuel Ward to S. L. M. Barlow, July 16, 1868, Samuel L. M. Barlow Papers, Henry E. Huntington Library, San Marino, Ca.; *Congressional Globe,* 40 Cong., 2 sess., p. 4137; William C. Dryer to Horatio Seymour, July 18, 1868, Magnus Gross to Seymour, July 22, 1868, Horatio Seymour Papers. There are copies of the campaign pamphlets in the Manton Marble Collection, University of London Library.

24. *Congressional Globe,* 40 Cong., 2 sess., pp. 3911, 4143; Frederick W. Seward, *Seward at Washington, 1861–1872* (New York, 1891), p. 386; S. P. Chase to John D. Van Buren, October 21, 1868, Salmon P. Chase Papers, Library of Congress.

Republicans carried most of the elections by inflammatory appeals based on the then recent New Orleans riots," the New York *World* warned in 1867. Democratic leaders did not want such an opportunity to occur again. They pled against any provocative actions by the South or the president or their own colleagues. They repeatedly defended their bona fides as Unionists and defenders of the war. The majority of their party were not Copperheads; the Democratic enlistment record was fine. The bones of party members "lie bleaching on a thousand battle fields." Nor are the Democrats "half so ferocious as the Radicals allege."[25]

Despite all of their efforts, however, the question of Democratic legitimacy was fully before the country throughout all election campaigns in the postwar years. The Republican rhetoric was extreme, nasty, often hysterical, but very effective in once more raising a valence issue in terms positive for the Republicans. It was a shrewd maneuver for a majority party, for its aim was to prevent defections and reinforce determination to support one's normal party. The Republicans successfully created a cross-pressure against any existing anti-Radical tendencies among Republicans. "It is in vain," the editor of the New York *World* wrote in 1868, "that our Republican contemporaries endeavor to revive the passions and prejudices of the war."[26] But it was not. Republicans, even those unhappy with the trend of Radical policy, saw no real choice in the situation except to continue opposing Democrats. The reinforcing campaign of the party leaders only confirmed their existing inclination to remain loyal Republicans. "I confess misgivings about Negro suffrage," George Strong wrote in his diary in 1867, "but I don't want A. Johnson to be encouraged in his execrable courses by anything he can construe into a popular endorsement." A year later the feeling was even stronger. "We believe," the New York *Nation* said, "that the Republican party, as represented by its legislators, has done many unwise, and some invalid acts; but we more firmly believe that if the positions of the Democratic party be adopted, the war for nationality will have

25. New York *World*, August 22, 1867; *Congressional Globe*, 39 Cong., 1 sess., p. 2411; ibid., *Appendix*, 289; *Illinois State Register*, October 2, 1868; *Boston Post*, August 11, 1868.
26. New York *World*, July 13, 1868.

been turned into a farce." In short, "what was won by the bayonet must not be surrendered at the ballot."[27]

But the Republican counterattack was even more successful than merely holding their own people to them in the critical elections. The reactions of the men around Johnson, that amalgam of former Democrats, wistful Whigs, and renegade Republicans, well indicated the potency of the Republican offensive and the problems of conversion the Democrats faced. The Johnsonian conservatives clearly perceived the danger the nation was in from the extension and growth of Radical policies in the years after the war. The Republicans, James Dixon argued, "seem to be tormented like the infernal furies with an insatiate thirst for human blood." To Thomas Ewing, the "Radicals in the two Houses are acting like madmen." Indeed these conservatives made their mark in opposing them. They and the Democrats were no different from one another on that score. Therefore, many of them proved willing to forget old associations and work for any Democratic candidate "without regard to his antecedents."[28]

At the same time, however, many conservatives held back. Like the staunchest Republicans, they accepted what was suggested about the Democrats. To win conservative support, they warned, the Democrats had to "repudiate their war record, declare the Chicago platform a mistake, and agree to behave in the future." But the Democrats did not. Gideon Welles argued that the Democrats' great mistake was in believing that Republican policies "were so atrocious that the people would accept and vote for almost any man even those who were on the opposite extreme." But, although our people do not want Radical policies to prevail they "have a horror of Copperheads." They "shrink from contact" with such as Vallandigham or his associates. As the War Democrat, John A. Dix summed up, "it has been my

27. *Diary of Strong,* ed. Nevens and Halsey, 2: 150; *Nation,* June 25, 1868; Gustavus Vasa Fox to Gideon Welles, October 26, 1868, Gideon Welles Papers, Library of Congress; John Sherman to William E. Chandler, October 4, 1868, in Leon B. Richardson, *William E. Chandler, Republican* (New York, 1940), p. 92.

28. James Dixon to Horace Greeley, November 12, 1866, Horace Greeley Papers, Library of Congress; Thomas Ewing, Sr., to Ellen Sherman, January 27, 1868, Ewing Papers; John A. Dix to ?, August 28, 1866, John A. Dix Papers, Syracuse University Library, Syracuse, N.Y.

earnest desire to see the Democratic party reorganized & reinstated in the public confidence. With such leaders as the Vallandighams and the Seymours all hope of such a result must be abandoned."[29]

In short, the Republicans had been able to retain the initiative, particularly in setting the atmosphere in which elections after the war were fought. The Democrats played into their hands by the kinds of selections they made and the campaigns they fought. That is, they provided enough targets for the Republicans to shoot at regardless of the amount of legitimizing strictures the Democrats also offered. There were "multitudes who do not believe and cannot be made to believe that he [Grant] will favor ultra measures of government, under whatever auspices he may be elevated to power." And Horatio Seymour shrewdly noted, in 1867 we "looked to settling questions. Our platform in 1868 looked to unsettling them—at least so the public thought." Most of all, "it was unwise to nominate Blair. The Southern Democrats made an injudicious choice of delegates to the nominating Convention—the men who have been conspicuous in the rebellion should not have been chosen, and if chosen, should not have consented to come." They could not even get full mileage out of the issue of race with which they tarred the Republicans. The Republicans were always very adept at ignoring, confusing, and cross-pressuring so effectively as to prevent any clear referendum's ever taking place on the one issue that probably would have helped the Democrats.[30] There was so much noise of various kinds in the electoral atmosphere that it once again placed a premium on most Republicans' and conservatives' not making the extensive effort in their minds and hearts that would have been necessary for them to move into the Democratic column.

29. James T. Pratt to Gideon Welles, July 19, 1866, Welles Papers; Joseph H. Geiger to Andrew Johnson, August 2, 1866, Edwin C. Wilson to Johnson, October 11, 1866, Johnson Papers; *Diary of Gideon Welles,* ed. Howard K. Beale (New York, 1960), 3: 400; John A. Dix to Nahum Capen, October 2, 1868, Dix Papers.

30. John A. Dix to Samuel J. Tilden, May 15, 1868, in *Letters and Literary Memorials of Samuel J. Tilden,* ed. John Bigelow (New York, 1908), 1: 226–27; Horatio Seymour to George L. Miller, December 20, 1869, Horatio Seymour Papers, New York Historical Society, New York, N.Y.; Hiram Ketchum to Samuel J. Tilden, November 12, 1868, Samuel J. Tilden Papers, New York Public Library, New York, N.Y.

"The Unmitigated Democracy"

But there was more than just the war and reconstruction, more than just Vallandigham or Blair or Confederate brigadiers in Congress or New Orleans riots at work limiting the Democracy. Conservative hesitancy and Republican revulsion also fed on the intense and deep mixture of traditional prejudices and suspicions between the parties that went back more than a generation. Even legitimated Democrats prompted strong and negative reactions. Democrats, after all, remained Democrats. As always, that meant that they carried a heavy load so far as non-Democrats were concerned. The latter were always uneasy. When Democrats praised Johnson it made "the masses of the Union party feel as members of a Christian Church do when Sabbath breakers, whoremasters and gamblers praise their preacher." Therefore, the elder Ewing revealingly wrote, "I would be unwilling to see . . . the unmitigated Democracy restored to power, and nothing but the utter abandonment of principles by the Republican Congress and their contempt of constitution and law would have induced [me] to aid the Democracy." He hoped that Democratic success could be effectively limited so that they would "retain just power enough to enable them to *prevent* and not to do mischief." Throughout their relationship there was much similar uneasiness, tension, and suspicion on the part of the conservatives against the Democrats. There were constant expressions of hostility and fears of being overwhelmed by the Democrats, as well as complaints against that party's selfish and narrow partisanship.[31]

Despite agreement on some basic principles of reconstruction policy, what Manton Marble called "differences of attitudes and prejudices" about policies, people, and public life, spanning a generation of division and anger between two groups of deeply committed men, one Democratic, the other not, continued to run through the postwar political culture as it had during the war. Men in both groups

31. Ransom Balcom to Andrew Johnson, January 2, 1866, Johnson Papers; Thomas Ewing, Sr., to Ellen Sherman, October 17, 1868, Ewing Papers; Francis P. Blair, Sr., to Francis P. Blair, Jr., November 2, 1867, Blair Family Papers, Library of Congress. The Ewing Papers and Welles diary in particular are revealing about this conservative uneasiness.

were conservative in ideology. But their ideological commitment was always tied to their party loyalties. Former Whigs and Republicans and Democrats were simply not comfortable together. The former, after all, were men who had rejected everything Democratic. George B. McClellan put his finger on the problem most clearly when he said of the conservatives that *"talk* as they may they are pretty certain to find some trivial excuse for acting with the radicals." Trivial or not, there was a basic truth there that did not alter over these years of postwar political warefare: that non-Democrats did not really want to join their traditional enemies.[32]

The Democrats felt the same. Despite a situation calling for them to pursue a minority party strategy, blurring divisions and playing down old battles, they demonstrated that in ideological and organizational terms they were willing to give very little to their opponents. Their platforms, campaigns, and candidates, which often contained much symbolic deferring to the Legitimist and non-Democratic sensibilities of the conservatives, were always also built on a basic bedrock of devotion to their own fundamental party principles. They still resisted the power of the central government and the puritan interventionism they believed inherent in Whig and Republican thought. Conservatives complained about how Democrats "conducted the campaign [in 1868] so as to *win no accessions from independent conservatives.*" Democrats recognized the identity of interests they had with conservatives and were willing to point these out and stress them. But, at the same time, their actions and activities were shot through with narrow, non-Legitimist or partisan Democratic commitments.[33]

What the Democrats, in their advocacy and behavior, said was that they were traditional party loyalists and therefore strongly anti-Republican and anti-Radical, in favor of normal politics in the South and would neither apologize for their previous policy commitments

---

32. Manton Marble to Joseph Warren, August, n.d., 1866, Marble Papers; George B. McClellan to Samuel L. M. Barlow, December 14, 1866, George B. McClellan Papers, Library of Congress.

33. Clipping quoting New York *Journal of Commerce,* n.d., 1868, in Marble Collection, London.

nor their wartime positions nor would they abandon those Democrats whom other parties did not fully like or deem respectable. They never presented, in short, a clear Legitimist call, or a clear nonpartisan call, that could not be challenged by reference to other parts of their platforms or other of their actions.

Democratic behavior was not deliberately provocative. Party members could not be nonpartisan nor completely open, given the imperatives of partisanship in this period. In the post-1865 years the Democrats, after all, had not done much rethinking of their basic principles, but rather had focused on how best to take advantage of Republican disarray. They were still Democrats, first of all, as well as conservatives. Because of that they never provided a channel to unite all of the disparate anti-Radical groups. Or, to repeat the lament of a disgusted conservative, apparently they still preferred "to lose as 'life-long Democrats' rather than win as a fresh & vigorous party." Some conservatives could overcome their prejudices; others obviously could not, especially in the face of the Republican counteroffensive. The result was confusion. "The conservatives," Thomas Ewing had noted in 1867, "dissatisfied with the party in power and fearing mischief from the Democracy, divided in their vote."[34] They had done so before; they continued to do so subsequently.

Even when there appeared to be good reason to be more open and forthcoming, the Democrats were unable to and wound up looking foolish and unsure of themselves with a bitter internal party fight on their hands. The October state elections in 1868, the ones most Democrats believed had to be won for any chance in November, were lost. A number of leading party members then lost their nerve and called upon Seymour and Blair to resign from the national ticket in favor of Chase. This would allow them to "reap the entire fruits" of a conservative strategy. It would "utterly demoralize the Repub[lican]s," keep thousands from voting at all, gain many thousand votes and win by a *"coup d' état"* that they would "be proud of." In the three weeks remaining they would not only win but "lay

34. A. M. Bradbury to Thomas Ewing, Jr., September 15, 1868, Thomas Ewing, Sr., to Hugh Ewing, October 16, 1867, Ewing Papers.

the foundation of a great party, broad & deep, & do our whole country a lasting service.''[35] But, as was to be expected, there was a quick, angry, and revealing reaction. The ''infamy'' and the ''treachery'' of the idea was bitterly assailed. The Democrats would not let ''a handful of treacherous politicians'' destroy them. They were not downhearted. ''The *people* here feel determined. There is no backing out—no despair—no 'giving up.' We fight on.'' Nothing came of the idea. The partisan imperative continued to work. The Democrats would fight on as straight-out party members behind Seymour and Blair.[36]

James Blaine saw the closeness of the election of 1868 as ''unaccountable.'' The Democrats saw it as frustrating and yet hopeful. But the essential point is that the postwar elections had continued the static quality of their wartime predecessors. ''The popular element,'' Gideon Welles lamented, ''is pretty stable and fixed. People do not easily change their party relations.''[37] The intense Democratic partisanship, the Republican campaign, and the normal pull of loyalties repeatedly drew sharp party lines in postwar elections rather than blurring them into a generalized radical-conservative dichotomy which some Democrats and most conservatives saw as the only basis for victory. What the Republicans and the Democrats both had done was to reinvigorate the memory of these party relations, and this had aided the Republicans. As a result, the Democrats remained a substantial force, but a minority one, in the popular vote of the American people.

35. On the necessity of winning the October state elections, see A. E. Burr to Gideon Welles, September 4, 1868, Gideon Welles Papers, Library of Congress; *Louisville Democrat,* September 19, 1878. The argument in favor of dropping Seymour and Blair is articulated in S. L. M. Barlow to Francis Kernan, October 14, 1868, Francis Kernan Papers, Cornell University Library, Ithaca, N.Y. See also Barlow to S. J. Tilden, October 14, 1868, Tilden Papers; and the New York *World,* October 15 et seq., 1868.

36. Unidentified newspaper clipping in Marble Collection, London; *Address of the County Committee of Erie County Democrats,* October 19, 1868, in ibid.; A. E. Burr to Gideon Welles, October 27, 1868, Welles Papers.

37. Blaine, *Twenty Years,* 2: 408; *Diary of Welles,* ed. Beale, 3: 309.

10

"They Live and Die in the Faith of Their Fathers": The Democratic Party, 1860–1868

IN THE AFTERMATH of Seymour's defeat, the Democrats once more went through the depressing ritual of examining the reasons for their loss. They had little new to say. Their confidence had been misplaced. The behavior of the voters perplexed them. They were bitter, particularly that "so long as war passions survive or can be lashed into animation," so long did the Republicans have the "advantage over their opponents."[1] It was not the best of times. Nevertheless, in the years that followed, Democratic commitment and energy never flagged. Radicalism remained rampant and Democrats continued to fight Republican iniquity. They planned for each election enthusiastically, weighed the outcome of the polls carefully, and always sought some advantage that would reverse the current tenor of national politics.

The period after 1868 did contain a share of surprises. Clement Vallandigham embraced legitimacy forcefully in 1871, arguing that since the thirteenth, fourteenth, and fifteenth amendments had become the law of the land, "contention about them would be vain and useless." Democrats, therefore, should not "waste time and strength in a fruitless enterprise." And, as party leaders optimistically sniffed the odor of victory as 1872 approached, they engaged in what veteran party Congressman Michael Kerr called "the most surprising event in American politics." They coalesced with the Liberal Republicans in a straight-out, Legitimist approach behind, of all people, Horace

1. Albany (N.Y.) *Argus,* November 11, 1868.

Greeley, once described by Daniel Voorhees as "that political harlot." There was much soul-searching, heart-burning, and bitter recrimination in the Democratic ranks over this shift in strategy. But most Democratic leaders finally agreed to "make this sacrifice of party pride" because, as one put it, Greeley "stinks but Grant stinks more."[2]

But underneath the vibrations of these dramatic events there was, of course, nothing new in any of this. New personalities, new events, and new issues did arise; Republicans and Democrats fought bitter battles over new landscapes for the rest of the nineteenth century. Exciting and revealing in their own terms as many of these battles were, until the nineties they continued to be rooted in a set of traditional and relatively unchanging political arrangements and textures. Party operations after the sixties echoed familiar rhythms: the grooves in which both Democrats and Republicans ran were well marked. The Democrats continued to be trapped in an era they had entered fifteen years before, an era solidified and confirmed by the confrontation of the Civil War and its aftermath. Ideological opposition to the Republicans, and Legitimist versus Purist debates over party strategy, echoed much of what had gone on during the previous decade. Even Greeley's defeat, although of landslide proportions, reflected little that was new, for it apparently resulted from traditional partisan constraints working to keep some Democrats home on election day and many Republicans and conservatives away from a Democratic candidate. Events in the early seventies confirmed that the Democrats were firmly settled into a hard structure of assumptions, operations, and support. In the years that followed, although they occasionally made some significant breakthroughs, these were usually due either to some slight shifting of

2. James L. Vallandigham, *A Life of Clement L. Vallandigham* (Baltimore, 1871), p. 449; Michael C. Kerr to David Wells, June 14, 1872, David Wells Papers, Library of Congress; *Speeches of Daniel W. Voorhees of Indiana* . . . comp., Charles Voorhees (Cincinnati, 1875), p. 116; Samuel S. Cox, *Grant or Greeley?* (New York, 1872), p. 8; James M. Smith to John I. Hall, April 22, 1872, quoted in Judson C. Ward, Jr., "Georgia Under the Boubon Democrats, 1872–1890" (Ph.D. diss., University of North Carolina, 1947), 1: 59.

There was a separate "pure" Democratic ticket in 1872 which nominated Charles O'Conor, a New York lawyer, to run for the presidency. It received 29,000 votes of almost six and a half million cast.

voters toward them in response to the flashing of an intense and immediate issue, or because of the increasing normalization of Southern politics from the seventies on. These later events and Democratic advantages were always built, however, on top of the edifice created in the Northern states, at least, in the fifties, and little changed thereafter.[3]

"A United and Consolidated Party"

The Democratic party demonstrated all of the qualities of an active, prosperous, and effectively functioning party during and after the Civil War. It was a well-defined community of ideas, support, and constraints. The Democracy had made a remarkable comeback from the defeats and disaster of 1854–1860. Its leaders had regained their stride after the debacle that opened the decade; they had reorganized and, after a period of confusion, successfully reestablished the party in its major competitive role against the dominant Republicans. The Democracy had maintained its position thereafter despite the problems and pressures of its wartime role, the Republican manipulation of issues, and the latter's control of the electoral process in the Border and Southern states. The Democrats overcame problems of internal dissent and stayed together. They confirmed once again, throughout the 1860s, that they were a "united party, full of vitality, and holding points of vantage for the future."[4]

Of course, the Democracy was never free from problems. Internally, War Democrats, Purists, and Legitimists all had distinctly different attitudes about what role the party should play in wartime and how it should play it. They violently disagreed over tactics at every national convention, and at state and local meetings as well. Personal attacks on one another were common; speculation concerning the

3. For insights into the stability of this electoral system into the seventies and eighties, see Paul Kleppner, *The Cross of Culture, A Social Analysis of Midwestern Politics, 1850–1900* (New York, 1970); Richard Jensen, *The Winning of the Midwest: Social and Political Conflict, 1885–1896* (Chicago, 1971); and Samuel T. McSeveney, *The Politics of Depression: Voting Behavior in the Northeast, 1893–1896* (New York, 1972).

4. Springfield *Illinois State Register,* November 7, 1868; *Detroit Free Press,* November 4, 1868; William Shouler to Israel Washburn, October 26, 1868, quoted in Gaillard Hunt, *Israel, Elihu and Cadwallader Washburn* (New York, 1925), p. 124.

sanity, good sense, or intelligence of each other was frequent. Threats were plentiful. The potential for party warfare and ripping apart reminiscent of the years 1857–1860 was always there. But, unlike the earlier era, the internal disagreements never led to disastrous party splits. True, the War Democrats departed in 1861 and 1862, when the bulk of the Democracy moved into strong opposition to the Lincoln administration. But their numbers and importance for the party's continued operation were never great. More important, those who stayed behind found the means to stand together. Despite all of their hassling and anger with one another, the visions of party leaders contained many common elements, particularly a commitment to militant constitutionalism and a determination to remain in the organization of their fathers and make that organization triumphant again. Whatever their potential for separation, their ideas and partisan commitment overcame differences over strategy, tactics, approaches, and perception of the electorate.[5]

The catalyst in the situation prompting the Democrats' vitality and strength was, of course, the importance of the partisan imperative. That imperative, the commitment to a party growing out of a pattern of human and communal relationships in which one's party was a crucial force as guide, teacher, and church, and independent force of ideas and loyalties, did more to shape the behavior of the Democracy (and the Republicans) and the outcome of elections, and, therefore, of national policy, than any single event, no matter how dramatic.

This partisan imperative was not new in the 1860s. Years before, for many reasons, a large number of voters commited themselves to the Democratic party. Their commitment remained strong through the intervening years despite the fading of the original reasons for their association, and was transmitted in full strength to their sons. Some, an electorally decisive share, had left the party in the 1850s. But the vast majority remained Democrats and their loyalty to the cause became a deeply imbedded traditionalism guaranteeing the party a great deal of support in every election. The loyalty went beyond a rational weighing of specific or material rewards. There was also a

5. The phrase is Philip Paludan's in *A Covenant With Death: The Constitution, Law and Equality in the Civil War Era* (Urbana, Ill., 1975), p. 91.

psychological factor at work. As the *Baltimore American* put it in 1866, "the children of a Protestant or Roman Catholic usually attach themselves to the churches of their parents and think all other denominations on the road to perdition. So it is with the Democrats. They live and die in the faith of their fathers and are not easily drawn to any new organizations."[6] They would never vote Republican.

"Principles That Are Dear to Them"

The partisan imperative, however, also limited the ability of the Democrats to change the outcomes of successive elections in the 1860s. The party's story in this decade was one of continued frustration. Democrats were not numerous enough, by themselves, to win a major national victory, either in presidential races or in the battle for control of Congress. The 1850s had established a pro-Republican majority in the politically decisive loyal Northern states. The Civil War provided the Republicans with means of protecting their majority, not by adding significant numbers of new voters to their cause, but by intensifying the existing commitment to the party.

Yet the situation was never entirely static. There was some room for maneuver. There was occasional variability in electoral behavior. The race issue showed frequent pro-Democratic potency and became the most stressed of all Democratic themes. War weariness, too, occasionally was a shaker of electoral commitments, as was the anger engendered by war-induced limitations on civil liberties. The job of the Democratic leaders was to find the combination of issues and appeals which would bring to their support enough defectors, new voters, or traditional Republicans, to give them the necessary leg up toward political dominance. Many of these leaders calculated their chances of victory shrewdly and always sought to maximize them by what Michael Hurst has referred to as "mixing the idealistic and the machiavellian in proportions well adapted to the pursuit of enlightened statecraft"—or, in this case, enlightened party management and electioneering.[7] But they could never find the key to detach enough

6. October 15, 1866, quoted in Jean Baker, *The Politics of Continuity: Maryland, Political Parties, 1858–1870* (Baltimore, 1973), p. 157.

7. London *Times Literary Supplement*, October 24, 1975, p. 1261.

marginal Republicans and conservatives and bring them to their side. They placed a great deal of faith in their conservative appeal, believing that the ideological commitments of many Americans would be stronger than the psychological tugs of party loyalty, at least for Republicans and former Whigs. But they were wrong.

The constraints on the Democrats were, first, organizational and ideological, and, second, the way the public viewed them. It is a conventional truism of political analysis that parties, in choosing their candidates and selecting their issues, "drive toward the center" of the political spectrum.[8] But it was not that easy during the Civil War era. If patronage, the spoils of office, and other selfish concerns, were all there really was to party politics, someone such as Chase would have been nominated by the Democrats in 1868 without a second thought. He was "right" on most of the questions of the day, and, most important of all, he could bring additional support to the ticket. Similarly, why choose someone such as Seymour or Blair whose very careers would allow the Republicans to raise the "bloody shirt" in full panoply? But the Democratic leaders could not operate only in terms of simple vote maximization. They always had to shape their tactics within communal norms. Gideon Welles complained in 1868 of Democratic "arrogance" which had not been "softened, chastened, and corrected" by their adversity. They, therefore, had "endangered and probably sacrificed a good cause by not being more [generous and] forebearing." They have, he concluded, "not learned to humble themselves in order to be exalted."[9]

The point, of course, was that the Democrats could not do any such thing. Their own principles and commitments would not let them take the easy road, to be completely coalitionist and legitimist. Their faith in their party and its principles, their devotion and loyalty once more circumscribed the way the Democrats could and would respond to the problems confronting them. Party elites and party followers constantly interacted with each other. Pamphlets, speeches, and

8. Richard Scammon and Benjamin Wattenberg, *The Real Majority* (New York, 1970), p. 279.

9. Howard K. Beale, ed., *The Diary of Gideon Welles* (New York, 1960), 3: 446.

newspaper editorials were part of a dialogue between leader and led (as well as with outsiders). Different leaders could try to stretch the Democratic community's boundaries in this dialogue, but could not go beyond them without a severe and crippling backlash from within the community. They sought respectability and made overtures to the conservative non-Democrats only so far as not to weaken in any way their commitments and ideological positions which were the primary *raisons d'être* for the Democratic party. As the editor of the *Detroit Free Press* wrote during the campaign of 1868, those who chided the Democrats for continuing to fight in a hopeless manner for a hopeless cause "cannot appreciate the fact that the Democracy are conscious they are contending for principles that are dear to them and essential to the well-being of the people and the perpetuation of free institutions."[10] Therefore, the party had to, and would, put its organization, its name, its community, and principles first, and wait for the good sense of the American people to return it to its rightful control of the American government.

Nor were the Republicans supine. They played on those themes that best kept alive the anti-Democratic attitudes of many potentially volatile conservatives in their own ranks and among conservatives outside of either party. From the first, they saw the war as their major opportunity, eagerly chastising the Democrats as the most craven and seditious opponents of the Union, reducing the complexities of the Democratic position to the simple epithet "Copperheads," stressing that the Republican was the party of the Union. Their appeal proved potent. Their counterstrategy won the day by limiting defections from their ranks. People who had casually gone to war in 1861 were learning to hate passionately both their enemies and anyone in their own ranks who seemed to support their enemies. As one Republican later recalled, "there was something unthinkable to me about being a Democrat [in this era]—Democrats, Cooperheads, and atheists were

10. *Detroit Free Press*, October 25, 1868. After the election the editor wrote that "come weal or come woe—the Democracy of the nation have but one duty before them, and that is to fight ever for the success of their principles through which alone can the people find happiness and their liberties protected.' " Ibid., November 4, 1868.

persons whom one did not know socially. As a boy I did not play with their children.''[11]

By 1868, therefore, the Democratic situation had been firmly established. There was a continuity in their behavior, in their ideology, in their voting support, and in the role and function of their party after 1860. The importance and necessity of their organization had been established in the 1830s. Their ideals had been honed throughout the antebellum years. The social alignment of the voters had been set in the 1850s. War was a reinforcing, not a disrupting, factor in the life of each of these elements. The party community had not been transformed during the war. Its commitments, support, and ideology had changed very little. And the postwar period was a continuation of the earlier years. Of course, there were changes in day-to-day possibilities. But basically the Democratic party's strength flowed out of a historically determined complex structure of voting behavior and the imperatives of partisanship.

The voting cycle in which they were caught was clear and recognized. They were the minority party, if competitive. But their devotion to their principles and their community made it impossible to overcome their disadvantage. Campaigns reminded people of the differences between the parties. The Democrats were proud of those differences and accepted them. But they provoked grave problems for the party. Nor could the Democrats pursue a different strategy from the one they did. They partisan imperative would not let them. Thus, they could make gains, particularly in off-year elections, but then could not cast off their minority shackles. In presidential races, where the full force of appeals to traditional political ideas and labels was unleashed by both sides, the Republicans could always maintain themselves.

"A Respectable Minority"

We Democrats remain, Jefferson Coolidge wrote to George McClellan in 1864, "a respectable minority," able to garner signifi-

11. Quoted in William E. Leuchtenburg, "The Pattern of Modern American National Politics," in *Institutions in Modern America, Innovation in Structure and Process,* ed. Stephen E. Ambrose (Baltimore, 1967), p. 42.

cant numbers of votes in any election.[12] That was certainly true. But they remained respectable in other ways as well. They were respectable in what they advocated, in terms of the times in which they lived, despite the Republican claims to the contrary. Copperheadism had never dominated the party as much as their opponents suggested. Once the Republican prism is removed it is clear that the Democratic stance consisted of a complex amalgam rooted in primitive constitutionalism and devotion to a particular vision of the Union. The party never took a peace-at-any-price stance. Its members wanted the Union restored to its former dimensions with as little social and constitutional change as possible. They were, perhaps, wrongheaded. They were certainly not congenial either to their Republican contemporaries or to late-twentieth-century tastes. But their ideology was congruent with many of the political and social rhythms of their day. Certainly, the Democrats provided a reference point, a focus, for a significant number of Americans. It was the party's particular misfortune, given the way its supporters saw the world, that the existing political structure ran against them. Their own deep commitment, their party's ambiguous aura among potential Republican defectors and independents, the Republican majoritarianism in the Northern states, the abnormal political situation in the Border states during the war and in the Confederacy afterward, all led in one direction, to defeat. But this never lessened the Democratic party's central importance to many Americans. Because of that, the party remained a potent institution in the life of the nation's politics in the Civil War era.

12. T. Jefferson Coolidge to George B. McClellan, September 19, 1864, George B. McClellan Papers, Library of Congress.

Bibliographic Note

THE SECONDARY LITERATURE on the politics of the 1860s is extensive and important for understanding what happened and why. My dependence on both older and more recent works is evident in the footnotes. They cannot all be mentioned here, nor is there any need to since bibliographies about the 1860s are readily available. See, especially, the one in James G. Randall and David Donald, *The Civil War and Reconstruction,* 2nd ed., rev. (Lexington, Mass., 1969).

Several good essays in William N. Chambers and Walter Dean Burnham, *The American Party Systems: Stages of Political Development,* 2nd ed. (New York, 1976), provide powerful insights into the nineteenth-century political structure. See, particularly, those by Richard McCormack, Eric L. McKitrick, Frank Sorauf, William N. Chambers, and Walter Dean Burnham. The role of political parties in American political culture can be better understood after consulting Frank Sorauf, *Party Politics in America,* 2nd ed. (Boston, 1972). Several studies of contemporary voting behavior also enrich understanding of the past including Angus Campbell et al., *The American Voter* (New York, 1960); their *Elections and the Political Order* (New York, 1966); Walter Dean Burnham, *Critical Elections and the Mainsprings of American Politics* (New York, 1970); and James L. Sundquist, *Dynamics of the Party System: Alignment and Realignment of Political Parties in the United States* (Washington, D.C., 1973).

Among the most representative, most suggestive, and most useful general studies of the Civil War period, Allan Nevins's massive analysis, *The War for the Union,* 4 vols. (New York, 1959–1971), stands alone for both its great amount of detail and its many insights into the politics of wartime. Nevins is, it should be noted, not sympathetic to the Democratic opposition. Similarly, James Garfield Randall, *Lincoln the President,* 4 vols. (New York, 1945–1955; vol.

4 co-authored by Richard N. Current), includes a detailed overview of the political climate during the war.

Kenneth Stampp, *And the War Came: The North and the Secession Crisis, 1860–1861* (Baton Rouge, 1950); and David Potter, *Lincoln and His Party in the Secession Crisis* (New Haven, 1942), are excellent analyses of politics and other matters in the winter of 1860–1861. William B. Hesseltine, *Lincoln and the War Governors* (New York, 1948); William Frank Zornow, *Lincoln and the Party Divided* (Norman, Okla., 1954) on the 1864 campaign; and T. Harry Williams, *Lincoln and the Radicals* (Madison, Wis., 1941), also provide much information on Civil War politics, usually focusing, as is clear from their titles, on the party in power. James A. Rawley, *Turning Points in the Civil War* (Lincoln, Neb., 1966); Harold Hyman, *Era of the Oath: Northern Loyalty Tests During the Civil War and Reconstruction* (Philadelphia, 1954); and his *A More Perfect Union: The Impact of the Civil War and Reconstruction on the Constitution* (New York, 1973); Philip Paludan, *A Covenant With Death: The Constitution, Law and Equality in the Civil War Era* (Urbana, Ill., 1975), are all very good on areas impinging on political confrontation. Rawley's *The Politics of Union: Northern Politics During the Civil War* (Hinsdale, Ill., 1974) is a brief survey of wartime politics.

On Congress during the war, see Leonard P. Curry, *Blueprint for Modern America: Nonmilitary Legislation of the First Civil War Congress* (Nashville, 1968). Michael L. Benedict, *A Compromise of Principle: Congressional Republicans and Reconstruction, 1863–1869* (New York, 1974), picks up aspects of the story in midwar. Allan G. Bogue's articles on the Senate during the war, "Bloc and Party in the United States Senate, 1861–1863," *Civil War History* 13 (September 1967): 221–41; "The Radical Voting Dimension in the U.S. Senate During the Civil War," *Journal of Interdisciplinary History* 3 (Winter 1973): 449–74; "Some Dimensions of Power in the Thirty-Seventh Congress," in *The Dimensions of Quantitative Research in History,* ed. William O. Aydelotte, Allan G. Bogue and Robert W. Fogel (Princeton, 1972), pp. 285–318, suggest some new directions for our thinking about voting blocs in wartime, as do David Donald, *The Politics of Reconstruction, 1863–1867* (Baton Rouge, 1965), and Glenn Linden, " 'Radicals' and Economic Policies: The House of Representatives, 1861–1873," *Civil War History* 13 (March 1967): 51–65. They, too, focus primarily on the Republicans. An excellent unpublished study is John L. McCarthy, "Reconstruction Legislation and Voting Alignments in the House of Representatives, 1863–1869" (Ph.D. diss., Yale University, 1970).

Josiah Benton, *Voting in the Field* (Boston, 1915), covers the process of soldier voting in wartime elections. It should be used in conjunction with T. Harry Williams, "Voters in Blue: The Citizen Soldiers of the Civil War," *Mississippi Valley Historical Review* 31 (September 1944): 37–47, and Oscar Osburn Winther, "The Soldier Vote in the Election of 1864," *New York History* 25 (October 1944): 440–58.

Five good biographies of Republican and conservative politicians were very helpful on the framework of wartime and postwar politics: Glyndon G. Van Deusen, *William Henry Seward* (New York, 1967); Benjamin P. Thomas and Harold Hyman, *Stanton: The Life and Times of Lincoln's Secretary of War* (New York, 1962); Albert Kirwan, *John J. Crittenden; The Struggle for the Union* (Lexington, Ky., 1962); William E. Smith, *The Francis Preston Blair Family in Politics,* 2 vols., (New York, 1933); and John C. Niven, *Gideon Welles* (New York, 1973).

There is a great deal of general literature on the postwar period. Kenneth Stampp, *The Era of Reconstruction, 1865–1877* (New York, 1965), a wide-ranging study; David Montgomery, *Beyond Equality: Labor and the Radical Republicans 1862–1872* (New York, 1967), which contains some sharp insights on the political situation just after the war; Eric McKitrick, *Andrew Johnson and Reconstruction* (Chicago, 1960); LaWanda Cox and John H. Cox, *Politics, Principle and Prejudice, 1865–1866* (New York, 1963); Hans Trefousse, *The Radical Republicans: Lincoln's Vanguard for Racial Justice* (New York, 1969); Harold H. Hyman, *The Radical Republicans and Reconstruction, 1861–1870* (Indianapolis, 1967); Hyman, *New Frontiers of the American Reconstruction* (Urbana, Ill., 1966); Harold Beale, *The Critical Year: A Study of Andrew Johnson and Reconstruction* (New York, 1930); W. R. Brock, *An American Crisis:*

Congress and Reconstruction, 1865–1867 (London, 1963); Irwin Unger, *The Greenback Era, A Social and Political History of American Finance, 1865–1879* (Princeton, 1964); Martin Mantell, *Johnson, Grant and the Politics of Reconstruction* (New York, 1973); Michael L. Benedict, *The Impeachment and Trial of Andrew Johnson* (New York, 1973); William Gillette, *The Right to Vote: Politics and the Passage of the Fifteenth Amendment* (Baltimore, 1965), are all indispensable for understanding the political arena after 1865 even if I often think some of them do not fully appreciate the Democrats' situation and behavior.

Thomas P. Alexander and Richard Beringer, *The Anatomy of the Confederate Congress* (Nashville, 1972), provides background on the political situation in the South. A very useful introduction to the postwar South is Michael Pearman, *Reunion Without Compromise, The South and Reconstruction 1865–1868* (Cambridge, 1973). On certain aspects of Southern politics, see Thomas B. Alexander, ''Persistent Whiggery in the Confederate South, 1860–1877,'' *Journal of Southern History* 27 (August 1961): 305–29; and John V. Mering, ''Persistent Whiggery in the Confederate South: A Reconsideration,'' *South Atlantic Quarterly* 69 (Winter 1970): 124–43. On the National Union movement of 1866, see Thomas Wagstaff, ''Andrew Johnson and the National Union Movement, 1865–1866'' (Ph.D. diss., University of Wisconsin, 1967).

The experience of the blacks and their role as a political issue can begin to be followed in James M. McPherson, *The Struggle for Equality* (Princeton, 1964); Forrest Wood, *Black Scare: The Racist Response to Emancipation and Reconstruction* (Berkeley and Los Angeles, 1968); V. Jacque Voegeli, *Free But Not Equal: The Midwest and the Negro During the Civil War* (Chicago, 1967); and in a number of articles: Ira V. Brown, ''Pennsylvania and the Rights of the Negro, 1865–1887,'' *Pennsylvania History* 28 (January 1961): 45–57; John H. Cox and LaWanda Cox, ''Negro Suffrage and Republican Politics: The Problem of Motivation in Reconstruction Historiography,'' *Journal of Southern History* 33 (August 1967): 303–30; Phyllis F. Field, ''Republicans and Black Suffrage in New York State: The Grass Roots Response,'' *Civil War History* 21 (June 1975): 136–47, and her unpublished dissertation, ''The Struggle for

Black Suffrage in New York State, 1846–1869'' (Cornell University, 1974); Leslie Fishel, "Northern Prejudice and Negro Suffrage, 1865–1870," *Journal of Negro History* 39 (January 1954): 8–26; Edgar A. Toppin, "Negro Emancipation in Historic Retrospect: Ohio—The Negro Suffrage Issue in Post Bellum Ohio Politics," *Journal of Human Relations* 11 (Winter 1963): 232–46; Forrest G. Wood, "On Revising Reconstruction History: Negro Suffrage, White Disenfranchisement, and Common Sense," *Journal of Negro History* 51 (April 1966): 98–113; C. Vann Woodward, "Seeds of Failure in Radical Race Policy," *Publications of the American Philosophical Society,* no. 110 (February 18, 1966), pp. 1–9. On the state level, three especially good studies are Charles Lewis Wagandt, *The Mighty Revolution: Negro Emancipation in Maryland, 1862–1864* (Baltimore, 1964); Vernon Lane Wharton, *The Negro in Mississippi, 1865–1890* (Chapel Hill, N.C., 1947); and Joel Williamson, *After Slavery: The Negro in South Carolina During Reconstruction, 1861–1877* (Chapel Hill, N.C., 1965).

A number of state- and local-level studies, even some very old ones, were quite good in supplying elusive details on politics below the national level. On the central bloc, see Sidney D. Brummer, *Political History of New York State During the Period of the Civil War* (New York, 1911); Homer Stebbins, *A Political History of the State of New York, 1865–1869* (New York, 1913); John Niven, *Connecticut For the Union* (New Haven, 1965); Joanna Cowden, "Civil War and Reconstruction Politics in Connecticut, 1863–1868" (Ph.D. diss., University of Connecticut, 1974); Charles Knapp, *New Jersey Politics During the Period of the Civil War and Reconstruction* (Geneva, N.Y., 1924); Stanton L. Lewis, *Pennsylvania Politics, 1860–1863* (Cleveland, 1935); William Dusinberre, *Civil War Issues in Philadelphia, 1856–1865* (Philadelphia, 1965); George H. Porter, *Ohio Politics During the Civil War Period* (New York, 1911); Eugene H. Roseboom, *The Civil War Era, 1850–1873* (Columbus, Ohio, 1944); Felice Bonadio, *North of Reconstruction, Ohio Politics, 1865–1870* (New York, 1970); and Kenneth Stampp, *Indiana Politics During the Civil War* (Indianapolis, 1949), an unusually good state study. Richard N. Current, *The Civil War Era, 1848–1873*

(Madison, Wis., 1976), vol. 2, *The History of Wisconsin,* is a superb recent addition to such works. James C. Mohr, *Radical Republicans in the North: State Politics During Reconstruction* (Baltimore, 1976), has essays on a number of Northern states. On the Border states, three excellent introductions are Richard O. Curry, *A House Divided: Statehood Politics and the Copperhead Movement in West Virginia* (Pittsburgh, 1964); Richard O. Curry, ed., *Radicalism, Racism and Party Realignment: The Border States During Reconstruction* (Baltimore, 1969), which contains individual essays on each of the Border states and a number of articles on larger political themes there as well; and Jean H. Baker, *The Politics of Continuity: Maryland Political Parties from 1858 to 1870* (Baltimore, 1973).

The Democrats Themselves

The secondary literature on the Democrats in the Civil War era remains minute alongside that of the Republican party. It is also highly fragmented in its coverage. Nevertheless, what does exist provides major building blocks for many of the insights contained in this essay. Two studies stand out on the party on the eve of the war: Roy F. Nichols, *The Disruption of the American Democracy* (New York, 1947); and Robert Johannsen, *Stephen A. Douglas* (New York, 1973). The voter realignment of the 1850s is discussed in Michael F. Holt, *Forging a Majority: The Formation of the Republican Party in Pittsburgh, 1848–1860* (New Haven, 1969), which, despite its subtitle, has much to say about the Democratic decline; and Ronald P. Formisano, *The Birth of Mass Political Parties, Michigan, 1827–1861* (Princeton, 1971). The party's actions in the secession crisis are touched on in Robert Johannsen, "The Douglas Democracy and the Crisis of Disunion," *Civil War History* 9 (September 1963): 229–47; and John T. Hubbell, "The Northern Democracy and the Crisis of Disunion, 1860–1861" (Ph.D. diss., University of Illinois, 1969).

There is no overview study of the Democracy as a whole during the war or afterward. There is, however, much detail about the party's history in George McJimsey, *Genteel Partisan: Manton Marble,*

1834–1917 (Ames, Iowa, 1971); Frank L. Klement, *The Limits of Dissent: Clement L. Vallandigham and the Civil War* (Lexington, Ky., 1970); and Irving Katz, *August Belmont, A Political Biography* (New York, 1968). A number of articles by Richard Curry place the advocacy of the Democracy into a perspective different from the Republican image of their treason. See "The Union as It was: A Critique of Recent Interpretations of the Copperheads," *Civil War History* 13 (March 1967): 25–39; and "Copperheadism and Ideological Continuity: Anatomy of a Stereotype," *Journal of Negro History* 57 (1972): 29–36. See also William G. Carleton, "Civil War Dissidence in the North: The Perspective of a Century," *South Atlantic Quarterly* 65 (Summer 1966): 390–402; and Robert Rutland, "The Copperheads of Iowa: A Re-Examination," *Iowa Journal of History* 52 (January 1954): 1–30. Leonard P. Curry, "Congressional Democrats: 1861–1863," *Civil War History* 12 (September 1966): 213–29, is alone on its subject. An attempt to describe Democratic ideological positions is Van M. Davis, "Individualism on Trial: The Ideology of the Northern Democracy During the Civil War and Reconstruction" (Ph.D. diss., University of Virginia, 1972).

Internal party conflict during the war is covered primarily in a number of biographies. On the Legitimists see, in addition to the McJimsey and Katz volumes already noted, David Lindsey, *"Sunset" Cox, Irrepressible Democrat* (Detroit, 1959); Stewart Mitchell, *Horatio Seymour of New York* (Cambridge, Mass., 1938); Alexander C. Flick, *Samuel Jones Tilden* (New York, 1939); and William Starr Myers, *General George Brinton McClellan* (New York, 1934). There is, unfortunately, no biography of Samuel L. M. Barlow.

Klement's biography of Vallandigham is superb on the leading Purist of them all. See also his *The Copperheads in the Middle West* (Chicago, 1960). Wood Gray, *The Hidden Civil War: The Story of the Copperheads* (New York, 1942), remains useful although caught up in old prejudices toward the peace movement. James L. Vallandigham, *A Life of Clement L. Vallandigham* (Baltimore, 1872), contains much material on his brother. James C. Olsen, *J. Sterling Morton* (Lincoln, 1942); Arnold Schankman, "William B. Reed and

The Civil War,'' *Pennsylvania History* 39 (October 1972): 455–69; Jerome Mushkat, ''Ben Wood's 'Fort Lafayette': A Source for Studying the Peace Democrats,'' *Civil War History* 21 (June 1975): 160–71; and H. H. Wubben, ''Dennis Mahoney and the Dubuque *Herald*, 1860–1863,'' *Iowa Journal of History* 56 (October 1958): 289–320, provide insight on other Purist spokesmen. Fernando Wood has received no adequate attention, and Thomas Seymour none at all.

There is not very much on the War Democrats specifically. Christopher Dell, *Lincoln and the War Democrats* (Madison, N.J., 1975), tries to cover the subject, often in a heavy-handed manner. Martin Lichterman, ''John Adams Dix, 1798–1879'' (Ph.D. diss., Columbia University, 1952), is quite informative. There are a number of other worthy (but less useful) biographies of some others in this group, but none about the important Daniel Dickinson.

Among local studies of the party, G. R. Tredway, *Democratic Opposition to the Lincoln Adminstration in Indiana* (Indianapolis, 1973); and Arnold Shankman, ''Conflict in the Old Keystone: Antiwar Sentiment in Pennsylvania, 1860–1865'' (Ph.D. diss., Emory University, 1972), reveal something of the kinds of studies available and do provide much useful detail. Two leading Democratic newspapers (both Purist) are analyzed in Charles Ray Wilson, ''The *Cincinnati Daily Enquirer* and Civil War Politics: A Study in 'Copperhead' Opinion'' (Ph.D. diss., University of Chicago, 1934); and Mrs. L. E. Ellis, ''The *Chicago Times* During the Civil War,'' *Illinois State Historical Society Transactions of the Year 1932* (Springfield, Ill., 1932): 135–81. Insight into wartime elections is provided in Winfred A. Harbison, ''The Elections of 1862 as a Vote of Want of Confidence in President Lincoln,'' *Michigan Academy of Science, Arts, and Letters* 14 (1930): 499–514; William F. Zornow, ''McClellan and Seymour in the Chicago Convention of 1864,'' *Journal of the Illinois State Historical Society* 43 (Winter 1950): 282–95; Charles R. Wilson, ''McClellan's Changing View of the Peace Plank of 1864,'' *American Historical Review* 38 (April 1933): 498–505; and Paul G. Hubbard, ''The Lincoln-McClellan Presidential Election in Illinois'' (Ph.D. diss., University of Illinois, 1949).

Edward L. Gambill, ''Northern Democrats and Reconstruction,

1865–1868'' (Ph.D. diss., University of Iowa, 1969), introduces the postwar Democrats. Martin Mantell, ''New York and the Elections of 1866 (Master's thesis, Columbia University, 1962), and especially Charles Coleman, *The Election of 1868, The Democratic Effort to Regain Control* (New York, 1933), cover their activities in the crucial postwar contests. The studies of the presidential elections of 1860 (by Elting Morison), 1864 (by Harold Hyman), and 1868 (by John Hope Franklin) in *History of American Presidential Elections 1789–1968,* ed. Arthur M. Schlesinger (New York, 1971), all in volume two, add a great deal to our knowledge (even when I frequently disagree with their emphases or interpretations).

Contemporary Source Materials

Much of the basic source materials surviving from the 1860s —letters, newspapers, pamphlets, official documents, and election returns—is fragmentary and unbalanced. More remains of the Legitimist perspective than that of their party rivals. And as in the case of the secondary literature, Republican materials outnumber those of the Democrats by a wide margin. Nevertheless, what there is is rich in insight and detail concerning the matters covered here.

The most extensive surviving manuscript collections of Democratic leaders are the voluminous Manton Marble Papers in the Library of Congress, and the many boxes and letterbooks of Samuel L. M. Barlow in the Henry E. Huntington Library, San Marino, California. Marble's scrapbooks of newspaper clippings and odd items are in the University of London Library. Among the many other collections revealing the Legitimist perspective, the most valuable were the relatively small but meaty group of Samuel S. Cox Papers in the Brown University Library; the George B. McClellan Papers (a very large collection) in the Library of Congress; and the two smaller collections of Horatio Seymour Papers in the New York Historical Society and in the New York State Library, Albany. The Samuel J. Tilden Papers in the New York Public Library were also very useful. There are also small collections of August Belmont Papers in the

Library of Congress, the New York Historical Society, and the New York Public Library.

The largest manuscript collections of Purist leaders were those of Thomas F. Bayard in the Library of Congress; Thomas Hart Seymour in the Connecticut Historical Society, Hartford; and the James Sterling Morton Papers, Nebraska Historical Society (available on microfilm). Very few Vallandigham letters have survived. There is a small collection of Fernando Wood letters in the New York Public Library, with very little of value in them for this study. There are also some other collections of some of the less prominent Purists scattered around the country.

Other useful manuscript collections of Democratic politicians include the William Allen, Jeremiah S. Black, Edmund Burke, Franklin Pierce, Alexander H. Stephens, John White Stevenson, Henry Watterson, and David A. Wells Papers, all in the Library of Congress; the James Buchanan Papers in the Historical Society of Pennsylvania; and some miscellaneous (and very small) collections at the New York Historical Society. The Stephen A. Douglas Papers in the University of Chicago Library are very good for the years 1860–1861.

The papers of the War Democrats were few and scattered. The best collections are the John A. Dix Papers in the Columbia University Library; the George Bancroft Papers in the Massachusetts Historical Society; and the John McClernand Papers in the Illinois State Historical Society Library. As in the case of the other party blocs, there are also small collections of less major figures in various state archives and libraries.

Among the politicians who worked with or were wooed by the Democrats, the most useful collections were those of the Blair Family, Salmon P. Chase, John Jordan Crittenden, James R. Doolittle, the Ewing Family, Andrew Johnson, Reverdy Johnson, Hugh McCulloch, and Thurlow Weed, all in the Library of Congress; and the Robert Winthrop Papers in the Massachusetts Historical Society. The attitudes and behavior of the Democrats' enemies are revealed in the papers of Horace Greeley, Joseph Holt, Edwin McMaster Stanton, and Lyman Trumbull, all in the Library of Congress. The Abraham

Lincoln Papers have been microfilmed and contain much antagonistic comment about the Democratic party.

Surviving manuscript collections must be supplemented with published collections of letters and speeches as well as autobiographies and reminiscences of the involved politicians. Among the most valuable were John Bigelow, ed., *Letters and Literary Memorials of Samuel J. Tilden,* 2 vols. (New York, 1908); Bigelow, *The Writings and Speeches of Samuel J. Tilden,* 2 vols. (New York, 1885); Thomas M. Cook and Thomas W. Knox, comp., *Public Record . . . of Horatio Seymour* (New York, 1868); Samuel S. Cox, *Three Decades of Federal Legislation, 1855–1885* (Providence, 1855), and his *Eight Years in Congress, 1857–1865: Memoirs and Speeches* (New York, 1865); *Letters, Speeches and Addresses of August Belmont* (n.p., 1890); August Belmont, *A Few Letters and Speeches of the Late Civil War* (New York, 1870); John Bassett Moore, ed., *The Works of James Buchanan,* 11 vols. (Philadelphia, 1910); and two collections by and about Vallandigham, *The Record of Hon. C. L. Vallandigham on Abolition, the Union, and the Civil War* (Columbus, Ohio, 1863); and the more comprehensive *Speeches, Arguments and Addresses of Clement L. Vallandigham* (New York, 1864). Among the War Democrats, a very useful collection is John R. Dicksinson, ed., *Speeches, Correspondence, Etc. of the Late Daniel S. Dickinson of New York,* 2 vols. (New York, 1867). There are many published small collections of similar letters in historical journals and in separate publications.

There are extensive published collections of non-Democrats. The most valuable were Howard K. Beale, ed., *Diary of Gideon Welles* (New York, 1960); James G. Blaine, *Twenty Years of Congress, Lincoln to Garfield,* 2 vols. (Norwich, Conn., 1893); Joseph Schafer, ed., *Intimate Letters of Carl Schurz, 1841–1861* (Madison, Wis., 1928); Rachel Sherman Thorndike, *The Sherman Letters* (New York, 1894); and Charles Williams, *Diary and Letters of Rutherford B. Hayes,* 3 vols. (Columbus, Ohio, 1924).

Many Democratic newspapers have survived, with some readily available on microfilm. The New York *World,* edited by Manton

Marble, dominates the field after September 1862, when it became a party organ and the national spokesman for the Legitimist faith. No one paper dominated the Purist side, but four provocative and prominent ones were the *Chicago Times,* the *Cincinnati Daily Enquirer,* the Columbus (Ohio) *Crisis* (which ended publication in early 1865), and the *New York Daily News* (edited by Fernando Wood's brother).

Other Democratic newspapers were selected to reflect different regions and states. Among the most useful were the *Boston Post,* Concord *New Hampshire Patriot; Detroit Daily Free Press;* Indianapolis *Daily State Sentinel;* Springfield *Daily Illinois State Register* and the *Louisville Daily Democrat.* Many others are available and are similarly useful. The *New York Herald* was in a class by itself. It was independent (and formerly Democratic) and often quite hostile to the Democracy. It contained a great deal of inside news of party meetings, etc., supplied by its political correspondents in Washington and Albany. The *New York Tribune,* the *Chicago Tribune,* and the New York *Nation* were consulted for various aspects of the Republican viewpoint. The *New York Times* was particularly helpful during the 1865–1867 period since its editor, Henry Raymond, allied himself with Andrew Johnson for a while.

The nineteenth century was an age of political pamphleteering. In every election, and in between as well, short and long and highly partisan pamphlets were issued in floods by local, state, and national party organizations and such groups as the Society for the Diffusion of Political Knowledge (for the Democrats) and the Loyal Publication Society (for the Republicans). The pamphlets include reprints of individual speeches by prominent men, formal addresses to the people by state and local party conventions, and details of the records of themselves and of their opponents. It is a vast literature buried in rare book rooms and archives. Frank Freidel, *Union Pamphlets of the Civil War,* 2 vols. (Cambridge, Mass., 1967), provides a good sample of some of them. Andrew D. White, then a New York state senator, collected many of them and his collections are bound in more than one hundred volumes in the Cornell University Library. Others were found in the Library of Congress, New York Public Library, University of Chicago Library, and the British Museum. Among the many consulted, the following give the flavor of what is available: "The Abolition Conspiracy To Destroy The Union" (New York, 1863); "Address to the Soldiers of Ohio by the Democratic State Central Committee" (Columbus, Ohio, 1863); "Puritanism in Politics, Speech of Hon. S. S. Cox, of Ohio, Before the Democratic Union Association, January 13, 1863" (New York, 1863); William B. Reed, "A Paper Containing a Statement and A Vindication of Certain Political Opinions" (Philadelphia, 1862); "Speeches of Hon. S. S. Cox in Maine, Pennsylvania and New York During the Campaign of 1868" (New York, 1868).

The national platforms of both parties are in Kirk H. Porter and Donald Bruce Johnson, *National Party Platforms, 1840–1972*, 5th ed. (Urbana, Ill., 1973). The proceedings of the national conventions themselves were issued as pamphlets by the respective parties. See *Official Proceedings of the Democratic National Convention Held in 1864 at Chicago* (Chicago, 1864); and *Official Proceedings of the National Democratic Convention 1868* (Boston, 1868). Similar official proceedings of state conventions were also published, as were proceedings of subgroupings within the parties. *The American Annual Cyclopaedia and Register of Important Events of the Year 1862* (and other years) (New York, 1862–1869) is a storehouse of such proceedings, their resolutions, etc., usually listed under individual state headings.

The *Congressional Globe* contains the debates of both House of Congress during the 1860s, and *The Biographical Directory of the American Congress, 1774–1971* (Washington, D.C., 1971) contains state lists of members by each Congress and individual biographies of every congressman as well. There are petitions and other materials from involved political groups to Congress in the published *Miscellaneous Documents* of each session of Congress.

Voting returns by nation, the states, and congressional districts for presidential, congressional, and gubernatorial elections are easily accessible in *Congressional Quarterly's Guide to U.S. Elections* (Washington, D.C., 1975). I supplemented this with the New York *Tribune Almanac* which contains off-year elections, usually listed by counties within states, in its annual editions. Voting returns were also available in newspapers, particularly those published in the state capitals. As mentioned in the text, the Inter-University Consortium for Political and Social Research at Ann Arbor, Michigan, has collected and processed into computer-readable form county-level election data on presidential, congressional, and gubernatorial contests throughout American history.

Index